THE ESSENTIAL GUIDE TO
Decorating

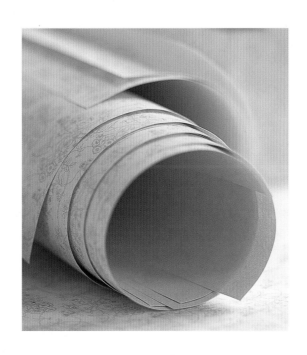

THE ESSENTIAL GUIDE TO
Decorating

Vinny Lee

bay books

Contents

Introduction

This book is an informative and illustrated guide to all aspects of decorating your home, introducing the basics such as planning your decorative scheme, explaining the main techniques that you may need and providing you with ideas and inspiration for every room. Armed with this book and a little imagination you can create the interior that you have always longed for.

Above: It is important to think about how functional and decorative objects will work together in a room's overall scheme as you plan it.

Opposite: This contemporary interior has white walls but set against them are strong accent colours used in the sofa and accessories such as cushions and even paintings. The wooden floor also adds a touch of warmth.

A changing world

Interest in decorating has become increasingly popular recently due to changes in both the approach to our home lives and in our response to personal environments. Where colours were once dictated by what was available in the local shops or by a limited palette of standard shades produced by a few commercial paint manufacturers, it seems now that the sky is the limit. For example, paint colours can be blended to match fabrics exactly and created a la carte to suit your whims and wishes.

Available to all

The increasing DIY market, inspired by numerous TV programmes and magazine features, has brought the once secretive world of the professional decorator, painter, carpenter and other specialists out into the open. Large supermarket style stores offer everything, from light fittings to kitchen sinks and from wallpaper borders to bed throws, direct to the public. Items that were once bought through trade shops or had to be specially made to measure are now available instantly.

As decorating has become such a readily accessible activity there is a growing need for good, basic information about how to create a decorating scheme, on elementary techniques and also tips of the trade, so that the enthusiastic lay person can get to grips with the terminology and practical aspects of decorating. Because technology and advancements in paints and other finishes means that there is an increasingly wide range of products to choose from, it can be difficult to know where to start, so a little guidance is useful when making your selection.

Using this book

It is important to get the basics right, to do the groundwork and to accumulate some knowledge about what is involved and how to go about a project. In this book, we look at the basics of decorating the home before moving on to the dressing and styling of each room. This is accompanied by a variety of inspiring projects to recreate. These vary in difficulty and size so that there is something for everyone to tackle, from the cautious starter to the more confident, advanced decorator. Written in an easy-to-follow manner, they incorporate clear, step-by-step photographs. We also look at where to find inspiration and how to build up sample boards. Building up a scheme should be an exciting and creative experience and an opportunity to learn how to focus your taste and what suits your lifestyle.

Essential Decorator is aimed at all enthusiasts, for those in permanent or temporary accommodation, in large or small homes and in urban or rural settings. It is a practical and informative guide to making the most of your own space as well as an inspirational book that will show you how to create your own style.

Creating your own environment

Tailoring your surroundings to suit the layout, style and shape of the building, as well as your personal tastes, is what makes a house into a home. Home is a fixed residence, a place where you return to; it is familiar and should be designed to accommodate your needs and requirements.

The home itself has become an important part of our daily life – it is no longer just a place to wash, eat and sleep. Although these functions are important, the home is also a place where you can express yourself, your taste, interests and personal style. It can be a gallery or showcase for things you admire and enjoy, such as artefacts and objects that you have picked up on local walks, on holiday or on extended travels. Home is a place to unwind and relax as well as to party and entertain friends. It may also be a place where you work or exercise, which means that many different functions have to be incorporated around the basic domestic agenda.

Finding your own style

Because of the increasing choice of materials available to us it is now easier to tailor our environment to our own individual taste. As such, your home and the way it is decorated says a lot about you. Some may decorate in an aspirational classic period style, some may opt for a look that is practical and easy to live with while others may choose to follow a fashion or trend.

The most important thing is to create a space that you are comfortable living in. There are strong, fashionable trends that hit the headlines and make the pages of leading interior magazines, which may have an influence on the interiors market for a time, but they may not be right for you. Although a particular look may appeal, you may have to dilute or adapt it to suit your space and lifestyle.

For example, the minimalist style of the work of the architect Claudio Silvestrin, a master of the spiritually clean environment, is a purist's dream. His interiors are almost monastic, made up mainly of white and linear spaces but Silvestrin happily admits that his look is not for everyone – you have to be disciplined to live with it and appreciate the thought that goes in to achieving the balance of space and light.

Below: Your home should be an expression of your own style. Here dark colours are twinned with bold accessories to create a dramatic look.

But you can admire the perfection of Silvestrin's work without having to follow it slavishly. Start with the principal features – the clean lines and beautiful shapes – and then make use of ample storage space, editing down your possessions. In time, you may find you are throwing out more and buying less, slowly becoming a follower of the minimalist regime.

You might find yourself inspired by a photograph of the inside of a fantastic house in a glossy book or magazine. The room shown would have cost a great deal of money and taken many months or even years of dedicated work to achieve – that may all be way beyond your means and inclination. The key here is to think practically, analyze the pictures or photographs and extract the elements that really appeal to you.

Ask yourself what it is that draws you to that particular room. Is it the colour of the walls? The style and arrangement of the furniture? The floor covering or the aspect of the room? Once you have worked out exactly what it is, then think through whether it is a practical style for you and how it can be recreated. Will it work in your room and suit your lifestyle? Most importantly, is it just a fad that you will tire of?

Personalizing your space

French designer extraordinaire Philippe Starck once said: 'It is important to inject love into the place where you live. It is not healthy to rent an interior designer to create a home for you because it is not good to live in another person's fantasy. People should select for themselves and stamp their own identity on a place. They should mix and match everything to make their own cocktail.'

When embarking on decorating your home think about your lifestyle and how and where you live. Do you have a room in a shared house? Are there communal living areas shared by others? You might be a student with a room in a rented house, a teenage child in a family home or own your own flat within a block of apartments.

The degree of personalization of a space may vary. For example, your own room may be the place where you can truly express yourself, but a shared area such as a sitting room or dining area may need to be a compromise scheme that works around the likes and dislikes of others who are using the space too.

In a shared room, a neutral décor may suit best with a background of simple wall and floor coverings that can be enlivened by accessories. In shared utility areas such as a kitchen or bathroom, the priority is most likely to be practicality – surfaces that are hardwearing and can be easily, regularly and thoroughly cleaned will be the best option.

You may also choose to keep 'public' rooms, such as living and dining areas where people beyond the family circle are admitted, in a looser style of decoration so that there are some personal elements but you haven't created an overpowering or over intimate space that visitors will find it uncomfortable to be in.

Changing tastes

Your own tastes generally change over time. Your childhood likes and dislikes will probably not have been the same as those you had in adolescence. Similarly, after you left home (an environment that was influenced by your parents and their choice of décor) you will have started to experiment with

your own schemes. The compromise will have started again when you met a partner and set up home together. Then, if you have a family, your ideas and style will have had to be modified to accommodate their needs too. Time and circumstances, as well as fashions, trends and the very location of your home will all have an effect on the way you live and decorate your space.

Above: Glass can be used to create the illusion of space, as it is here in this stunning contemporary stairwell.

Colour and texture

Colour and texture are important ingredients in the overall appearance of a room. Colour helps to define the mood and ambience and can be used to disguise or accentuate features. Texture will add highlights and interest, not just to wall surfaces but also to furniture and accessories.

Finding inspiration

Bringing together a colour palette for a room's overall scheme will depend on the style or type of decoration that you opt for, and the key to deciding this is inspiration. You may start by finding a curtain fabric that you like and the colours in the pattern will lead you into a scheme, or it might be a painting, a piece of furniture or a handmade piece of craftwork that triggers your ideas.

Inspiration now comes from all over the globe. Film, television and increased accessibility to world travel mean that the look of the sun-washed walls of an Italian villa can be recreated in a kitchen in London, the subtle grey blues and greens of a traditional Scandinavian home can be found in a New York apartment and the tribal art of a remote African village may be displayed in all its glory in a chic studio flat in Paris.

Themes, such as a collection of Oriental china or African masks, can be the basis and inspiration for a whole decorating scheme. If artworks aren't your thing then explore the wealth of materials and finishes available. Be brave and experiment with unusual materials to create a unique look.

Colour theory

When it comes to planning a colour scheme there are various options – including choosing colours that are part of the same family (have a similar base colour), colours that are opposites or tonal colours. The easiest way to see these choices is to look at a colour wheel. The colour wheel is like the rainbow but the colours are laid round in a circle, rather than laterally in an arc. The primary colours, red, yellow and blue, are the main spokes, and between them you get colours

that are made up from a mix of them. This means that between red and yellow you will find a red with a hint of yellow, then a true orange followed by yellow with a hint of red. Between yellow and blue the colours are yellow with a hint of blue, true green and blue with a hint of yellow.

Colours that belong to the same family are these mixed ones, so red, yellow and orange are of the same family as red, purple and blue. Opposite or contrasting colours are those diametrically facing on the wheel so red and green, orange and blue, yellow and violet are opposites. Tonal schemes select a single colour such as red and use darker and lighter shades of it rather than mixing with other colours.

Choosing your colours

Choosing colour is very personal and people react differently to various shades. You should, above all, choose colours that you and your family feel comfortable with. For example, one person may find red a warming colour but to another it can be overpowering.

Neutral colours have long been popular – the universally favoured painter's finish, magnolia, is a standard as are beige, soft yellows and off-whites because they are all easy to live with and make a room look light and bright.

Below: This yellow vase is shown against an orange wall. Yellow and orange are compatible colours within the same 'family'.

There is a standard decorating guideline that says that dark colours make surfaces advance and that light colours make them recede but there are exceptions to the rule. Dark colours can be effective in making a ceiling seem further away, for example a well lit, shiny deep blue or black will make the ceiling seem infinite, like a sky at night. Like texture, dark colours can also be used to disguise or camouflage uneven surfaces and architectural imbalances.

For impact and drama, bold colours are the best. Many people are wary of using them and of making such a definite statement when decorating their home, but if you take the plunge the effect can be rewarding. It may take time for your eyes to get accustomed to rich, dark shades so you can always take it step by step, building up gradually to a really deep shade. Paint one wall in a strong shade and live with it for a few weeks until you get used to it or start with an undercoat of a paler shade and add a top layer of the darker colour later, so that you have time to adapt and become familiar with the change.

Also remember that when you first see the bare walls painted in a dark colour they may appear strong, even overwhelming, but as soon as you have added carpets, furniture, pictures, lights and soft furnishings to the room, the effect will be dramatically reduced.

Tone on tone schemes

You could use the interior designers' trick of tone on tone schemes – this involves using a variety of different shades of the same colour. For example, if you paint your walls in a mid-coffee brown and put a paler, light brown carpet on the floor, you can use a patterned upholstery fabric that contains both those shades and perhaps add a deeper tone of

furniture to make a stronger statement. The accessories can then consist of lighter and darker tones of the same base colour so that all the shades have the same harmonious ground note. However, you should take care to ensure the scheme does not look dull. To avoid this, add glass, brass, gold or silver and plenty of patterns and textures.

Texture

The type of finish that you choose for the walls will also influence the overall effect. A matt, chalky surface will make a dark tone seem duskier and softer, or even silky. It will absorb light making the effect a little darker. A shiny gloss surface will emphasize the depth of colour and, because the surface is light reflective, can double the impact of natural or artificial lighting.

Texture is important not only for your wall finish but also in the mix of materials, throws and covers that you use – a room full of soft, smooth surfaces will look flat to the eye, but introduce a few cushions covers in a rich, knobbly chenille and you will add variety.

Top: *A tone on tone scheme of pale yellow and white creates a subtle effect.*

Above: *This heavily textured rug provides contrast in a room that has lots of smooth surfaces.*

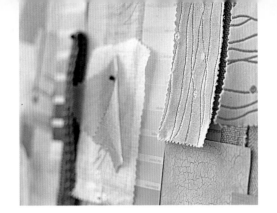

Mood boards

Mood boards are put together by professional decorators to show their clients a selection of materials, paint colours, wallpapers, trimmings and floor coverings, so that the textures and colours can be seen together. Mood boards are a way of showing all the ingredients of the recipe before it is prepared.

Opposite: A mood board encapsulates your ideas for a decorative scheme, including your chosen colours, textures, patterns and fabrics.

Below: When you have created your mood board, you can recreate the ideas for real in your home.

A mood board is a way of gathering together elements of decorating materials so that you can see and touch them, and mix and match until you find your perfect scheme. Trying to explain to someone verbally, or imagine in your mind's eye, how colours and textures work together is almost impossible. One person will say that they are looking at a cream colour while someone else may describe it as yellow or golden. The word 'fringe' can be used to describe a million different trimmings and finishes, but only one will be the right one for your lampshade or pelmet, so to see an actual sample is important.

The mood board also gives you the chance to play around with various samples and see how they relate. For example, if you like a warm cream paint and have found a fabric with a similar colour, then you can try them with different highlighting colours such as red or green, to see which works best for an overall palette.

Making a mood board

To construct a mood board, you need a large sheet of thick white card. Start by pinning small swatches and samples to it. As you update or modify the board remove and discard the older or replaced pieces. Eventually, when you have arrived at a final selection, glue them in place so that that there is no fear of pieces falling off or being lost.

Although the board is primarily a visual guide, make sure that you keep the references of items that you attach to it, so that you have a record of the manufacturers' details.

The board is also a useful way of seeing how the colours and fabrics react in different lights. You can take it to a window and see if the colours look good together in daylight, then at night try them under an electric light to see if they are still compatible and if any tonal alterations occur.

You should make a separate board for each room in the house – don't try and cram two or three schemes onto one board or it will become a confusing muddle. It can also be helpful to take the board with you when you go to choose furnishing, floor covering or other finishes, as it will give both you and the supplier or shopkeeper a point of reference.

Items for mood boards

Some items on the board can just be temporary – for example, you may find a leaf or a sweet paper that is just the right colour for a paint or fabric you want. Keep the paper or leaf and pin it to the board until you can find the paint colour to match. You may also come across inspirational pictures or postcards that show a room, setting or piece of furniture that has the right features or is an interesting shape – you can pin any of these to your boards to remind you of what you are looking for. Remember, inspiration is all around you.

Style and period

You can create your own unique style by mixing antique and modern schemes or old and new furniture. You may choose a period design that is appropriate to the age of your home or one that you admire. Whatever elements you decide on, try to use a cohesive colour and fabric scheme to tie them together.

Finding your style

The past, future or current trends can influence your decorating scheme. The building you live in may be of a certain period or style that relates to a range of colours and a certain type of furniture and this may inspire you to echo those elements in your décor. For example, a 1950s or 1960s built block of flats would be the perfect setting for the collectable retro-style furniture with geometric print fabrics. An early 20th century house may still have original features such as cornicing, plaster details and marble or plaster fireplaces – these may take you in the direction of a more classic collection of furniture and fabrics.

Even if the building in which your home is located doesn't have a tangible style, there may be periods of history or eras that you have a nostalgic feeling for or enjoy. For example, you may favour Art Deco and the Jazz Age, with its angular boxy furniture, champagne tinted mirrors and feeling of opulence and decadence. Or perhaps the American Shaker style is more to your taste – restrained and wholesome with an emphasis on craftsmanship and utility.

Oriental influences in interior style tend to be cyclical – the black and red lacquer furnishings and Zen-style simplicity are both currently fashionable but during the early 1900s the more ornate Oriental style was in vogue. The fashion was for Chinoiserie and richly embroidered silks, ornately painted and inlaid furniture and large vases and painted bowls. So although the inspiration was derived from the same source, the Orient, this influence was interpreted in different ways.

Recreating period style

Tastes in style and period living vary widely too. There are those who choose to ignore totally the style of the building or apartment in which they live and cover over cornicing details and block out door panels so that they are left with a blank canvas on which they can create their own individual look. Others spend a great deal of time and money trying to put back elements of the original décor of their home, searching through markets and specialist clearance warehouses to find just the right period fireplace and employ master craftsmen to copy back old plaster details.

Whichever path you choose to follow it is important to be 100 per cent behind it. If you are going to restore a place to its original period style, then do your research into the colours and fabrics that were available. For example, there is no point in using obviously synthetic fabrics such as shiny nylon curtains in a turn of the century room because nylon was not invented until the 1930s. Large pictorial printed fabrics featuring Chinese urns and cranes will look equally odd in a 1960s-inspired flat.

All decorative elements, from the curtains to the carpets, wall colours and furnishings should be

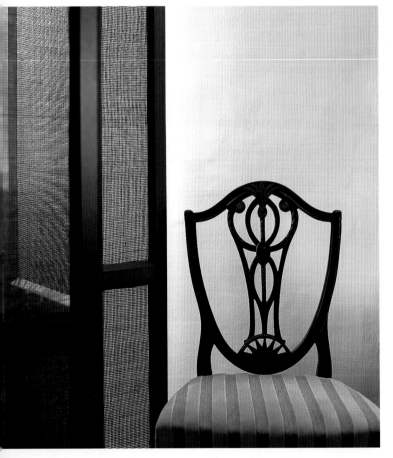

Below: This shieldback chair is a classic period feature, which would also look effective in a modern setting.

harmonious – they don't have to be from exactly the same year but should have a common theme.

When recreating a certain period, start with the basics, such as paint. There are now many paint companies that specialize in historically accurate paint colours and finishes so it should be easy to find a period paint colour. Some companies even emulate the old matt and chalk effects within their paints.

With the revival of interest in wallpaper it is also easier to find the geometric 1950s and 1960s style prints, many of which have had a 21st century adaptation in colouring. Designers such as Todhunter Earle have used 1960s-style shapes in their collection of wallpapers but in subtle rather than garish tones. For the more fun cartoon-style prints Cath Kidston has created a delightful range of nostalgic floral prints and cowboy designs.

An eclectic mix

For those who opt for a more eclectic and easy going style, it is, however, simple enough to mix the old and the new together. You do not have to stick rigidly to every decorating rule in order to create a successful interior so feel free to experiment with what you already have.

Many people inherit pieces of furniture from family and friends or build up a collection over the years from different homes. Not all the pieces will necessarily be of the same period or style so, if you have an eclectic selection, you have to find a way to link them by some other means. In this case the background elements play an important role in bringing all the pieces together. For example, the walls, floor covering and curtains should be of a similar or contrasting but compatible palette.

The larger pieces of furniture such as sofas and armchairs can be linked by using the same upholstery fabric on them. Another option is to cover some pieces of furniture in a patterned fabric and then to pick out plain colours from the pattern for the seats and covers on the other pieces. Scatter cushions and throws can also be used to create a conformity among diverse styles and shapes of furniture.

There are many timeless pieces of furniture that fit into almost any scheme or design of room – they stand alone like pieces of sculpture or art. For example, the Eames Model 670 rosewood faced seat with leather covered cushions and matching footstool first went into production in 1956 and it is still being manufactured today. This chair can be seen in many contemporary homes from the bare white minimalist surrounding and retro 1950s devotee to the eclectic mix of the average home.

Other classics include the Corbusier recliner, Sori Yanagi Butterfly footstool, Thonet bentwood chairs and original Lloyd Loom chairs, all of which will sit comfortably in any home, if a fairly classic or neutral style of décor has been adopted.

Above: Timeless pieces, such as this chrome and wood table, fit into any scheme.

Seasonal living

Seasons and cycles of time bring different needs and requirements. For example, we often long to be cool in the height of summer and warm in the depths of winter – our surroundings should be arranged so that they are adaptable enough to cope and make us comfortable with these extremes.

After the long dark days of winter spring is a welcome change, bringing buds, brightness and a feeling of freshness and renewal. This is a good time to fling open windows and blow away the hibernal cobwebs. As spring turns into summer and the weather warms, flowers are abundant and succulent fruits come into season, which can add zesty freshness and colour to your rooms.

The autumn is a rich time of harvest and changing colours. Russet reds, bronze and copper colours abound. As winter comes round again we settle down to rest in our cosy homes and await the arrival of the next burst of spring.

Seasonal fabrics

In recent times the trend for replacing the summer surface dressings of a room with winter ones has become popular. This may be because soft furnishings have become less expensive and easier to buy so there is huge choice and availability. Also, having two sets of covers spreads the wear and tear on the materials and leaves one change free for repairs, cleaning or washing.

If you want to change the appearance of a room significantly, start with the windows. Take down dark coloured, heavyweight winter curtains and replace them with fine pale or white cotton voiles or sheers for spring and summer. Then swap the covers on scatter cushions from richly textured, jewel tones and ornate patterns to crisp cotton, linen and slub silk in pastel shades and light checks or prints. Finally, replace woollen throws and blankets with waffle or textured cotton. You aren't changing the furnishings, just the dressings, but you will feel a really noticeable difference in your surroundings inside as the seasons change outside.

Tabard covers for bedheads and high back dining chairs are simple ways of ringing seasonal changes. Purchase rich warm coloured covers for the winter and autumn and fresh zesty ones for the spring and summer. Tabards also help to preserve the fitted covers underneath and are easily removed for washing if they become stained or marked.

Seasonal changes can also give a cosmetic lift to your surroundings, creating a welcome change that echoes the cycles of

Below and right: Yellow is an adaptable colour. It can be strong, warm and sunny or pale and refreshing.

Natural seasonal features

Colours can be highlighted with the addition of seasonal blooms and what better way to emphasize the periodic changes than with plants and flowers.

In winter, glossy green pot plants such as holly and ivy can be used to pad out arrangements when flowers are scarce or expensive. You may also add scented bowls of wood chips or pine cones, and orange pommanders decorated with cloves. Springtime is a season for vivid yellow, bright green and fresh flowers – these can be bought cut but will last much longer if grown from bulbs. Summer is a time when flowers are abundant in gardens and meadows. Indoors you can echo the feeling of heat and sun with an arrangement of small cacti or exotic flowers such as orchids. Autumn sees the leaves falling and a rich mellowness of orange, red and rust in parks and pathways. Collect some beautiful leaves, dry them and arrange in a bowl under a pile of hazelnuts.

Left: *These deep purple flowers are enhanced by being placed in polished silver or glass containers.*

Above: *Bright green and white flowers are ideal to bring a breath of spring air to a room.*

Below: *Roses complement any interior throughout the spring and summer.*

nature and the landscape outside. It can also be beneficial to your health and outlook. For example, you probably change your bedding from a winter weight feather or down duvet to a light, waffle cotton blanket between winter and summer, so why not change to a linen sheet or cover during the hot months.

Reversible fabrics are useful for seasonal changes. For example, curtains with a dark side and a light side could be used with the pale side to the front in the summer and the more colourful side to the fore in the winter.

Seasonal mood changes

Removable covers also give you the opportunity to change the pace or style of your home – for example, one set of covers and soft furnishings could be classic or neutral and the other modern or bright so that it is not only a seasonal change but also a mood or style change as well.

Variety is the spice of life, so changing the emphasis of colour and/or pattern in your home will alleviate any staleness or

boredom with your surroundings. The changes don't have to be radical to have an effect.

By linking colour and pattern subtle but impressive changes can be made. Take, for example, a room with pale to mid-blue walls. For the winter, use accessories from the darker end of the spectrum such as navy and midnight blue. Then inject warmth with mulberry and burgundy, which have a blue base note but also a warm red element that heats up an otherwise cool colour. In the spring and summer, the blue could be made cooler with the addition of silver grey, white and icy blue accessories, to enhance the colour's coldish trait.

A neutral room with white, pale cream or beige walls offers a whole range of opportunities when it comes to seasonal accessorizing. For example, spring and summer could be a time for vivid, zesty colours such as orange, green and lemon, but in the winter you could add the mellow tones of mink, mouse, toffee and coffee for a snug, relaxing and cosy environment.

Fabrics

Fabrics are either made up of natural or synthetic fibres and come in plain, self-patterned, textured, printed or woven designs in a wide variety of weights and finishes. When choosing material for a scheme try to visualize the overall effect it will have. If the room is otherwise plain you can afford to indulge in a pattern at the window or on the sofa and armchairs, but if the room is full of pattern then keep it simple and plain. Some fabrics are better for upholstery than others, so make sure that you choose a fabric of a specific upholstery weight. Cost will be another factor in your choice of fabrics. If you have large windows and you want to dress them from floor to ceiling with generously gathered curtains then you will need to buy a large amount of fabric. This may mean that you opt for a cheaper fabric. If you fall in love with an expensive fabric, limit its use to smaller areas. A little can be made to go a long way if it is used well. For example, you could place the fabric on a couple of scatter cushions that are strategically placed on a sofa.

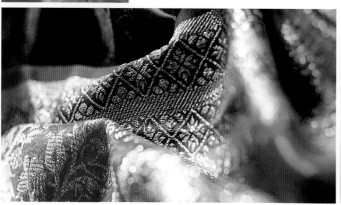

CLOCKWISE FROM TOP LEFT:

Long pile fabrics are more suitable for cushions and small areas rather than larger upholstery requirements.

Trimmings and braids can lift and embellish a plain cushion or curtain – these small glass beads add to the opulence of the shiny cushion cover.

The fabrics that you choose will have a lasting effect on the overall feel of a room. This sheer devoré velvet will add a sense of romance wherever it is placed.

Sheer voile is an effective window dressing because it lets in plenty of light.

A blanket does not need to be monochrome – here the blanket is rich mix of blue, brown and cream colours.

For curtains and blinds choose materials that are soft and drape well. A stiff or rigid fabric will hang awkwardly in lumps and ridges rather than soft furls and pleats.

Try using rich velvets and chenilles on throws and cushions to add a feeling of luxury to a room.

Vivid colours and geometric patterns can be used on rugs to create a dramatic floor area.

Thick chenille like this is well-suited to all general upholstery needs.

Fun fur is often made from synthetic fibres and should carry a flame retardant label to ensure its safe use.

Loose weave fabrics, like this open configuration in mohair, is decorative rather than practical and may be used as a throw over the back of a chair or sofa or as a wall hanging.

Intricately woven patterned fabrics with no surface pile or loops are good for upholstery and curtains.

Light colourful materials with fresh summery prints can help to lift a dark or basement room where natural light is restricted.

Classic patterns, such as this cheerful check, never seem to decline in their popularity.

Planning your home

Before you start work on a new property or alterations to an existing home, take time to plan and discuss your aims. Ask yourself what it is you want and how best this can be achieved. It is easier and less costly to spend more time and effort on planning, than to rush in and make errors that will need to be fixed later.

Opposite: Plan the link between rooms and ensure that adjacent areas are decorated in a complementary fashion.

Below: Before you decorate, draw a detailed plan featuring fixed items, such as fireplaces and alcoves, and furniture, such as tables and chairs.

Drawing out your plan

The first thing to do when tackling decorating is to look at the overall layout of your home. Write down a list of functions that take place in each room. If it is a studio flat or includes a home office-cum-spare room you will need to combine several functions in one place and devise a scheme that will work around the various activities. If you have a larger home then there will be rooms that have only a single purpose, and the decoration can be focused on that single activity.

Once you have made a list of functions, work out the allocation of space. Even within a sole purpose room you will need to define areas for storage and larger pieces of furniture. Draw a room plan to scale on squared paper with a pencil and put in the features and immovable objects such as windows, doors, fireplaces and chimney breasts.

When you are happy with the plan, ink in the outline with a permanent marker or pen.

Once the room plan is finished, make small, scaled cut-outs of the larger moveable pieces of furniture, such as bookcases, sofas and beds. Place these on the floor plan of the room and move them around until you think you have the right configuration. It is much easier to move small pieces of paper around than to lift and shift heavy furniture in situ.

Planning each room

There is a logical procedure for laying out furniture. Think of the way the room is used – imagine walking into it and carrying out the activity appropriate to the space such as working, bathing or cooking. For example, in a study area the desk should be near the phone and light sockets and by a window to use natural light.

In a bedroom, try to keep electrical appliances to a minimum, and avoid keeping computers and work items here. If you have a studio flat, place a screen or mobile wall in front of the work area to create a barrier between the sleeping and working parts of the room.

Kitchens and bathrooms are usually located according to the layout of waste and water pipes, which will be placed so that they connect with main sewers and drains. In some homes, these rooms become dual purpose due to their size. For example, if you have a small kitchen and a large bathroom consider putting the washing machine in the bathroom. If the bathroom is small but drying space is needed place a retractable drying line over the bath.

In a large bathroom, you may want to keep a yoga or exercise mat and light weights or a tape and player so that you can do keep fit or exercise routines.

If so, storage for these items will also have to be allotted in your plan.

The kitchen is increasingly becoming the main living area of the home, with open plan dining and seating areas joining up with the cooking space. When planning an area like this, keep certain constraints in mind. The kitchen sink or main section of worktop is best placed by a window so that most of the natural light will be focused on one of the primary working areas.

Include a barrier between the kitchen and dining areas – this is especially useful in households where there are young children. A breakfast bar or similar mid-height divide will enable someone in the kitchen to keep an eye on small children playing nearby but also form a protective barrier that will

make it easier to confine children to a safe distance away from the heat and dangers of the kitchen (see box, page 214).

Decorating the utility areas such as bathrooms and kitchens usually centres on the need for durable and waterproof materials. Both rooms require good ventilation but the surfaces and materials used within the space should also be easy to wipe down and clean. Ceramic tiles have long been the favoured surface behind sinks and handbasins but now reinforced glass, stainless steel and cement are often used.

Bathrooms, shower and wet rooms and separate lavatories are sometimes windowless, dark and boxy so a decorative scheme should counteract this by making the place appear light, colourful and spacious.

Making the most of natural light

According to Oriental traditions, you should wake facing the sunrise and go to sleep in the direction of the sunset. Orientating your home on this axis has many practical elements in that you start the day and spend the morning in rooms that make the most of the natural daylight, but as the light fades, your activities move to other rooms where light is not as readily available but may not be as necessary. You may find that by removing or opening up internal walls, you get a better and more effective flow of light from one side of the building to the other.

Basic techniques

Getting started

Before you start decorating, take time out for research and preparation. Do some research into the materials so that you can choose the right finish for the right area. Next, do any preparatory work. The more preparation you put in, the better the end result will be. All that filling and sanding, washing and stripping will seem worthwhile when you see the final, smooth painted ceiling or papered wall. Once this is done, you can start decorating – this chapter explores the basic techniques, from painting to wallpapering, tiling to flooring, and also looks at ways of using architectural features to their best advantage.

This chapter will provide you with a thorough grounding in all the basic decorating techniques. After a brief introduction to each method of decorating, the book focuses on the range of materials available and tools and applicators that are recommended. The practical step-by-step sections take you through all the essential groundwork (such as filling holes or stripping wallpaper), as well as covering more complex techniques (such as laying tongue and groove wood floor or making a fire surround).

For competent DIY enthusiasts this information is a good way of refreshing the memory, whereas for the beginner it is aimed to be instructive as well as helpful. Even if you are not going to be tackling the decorations yourself this will help you in planning a timescale and enable you to check on the progress of the work.

Preparing a room

To prepare a room for decoration, you should empty it as much as possible. Take out all the furniture, pictures, fabrics and fittings that you can. Anything that has to stay

Above: *Preparation is the key to a successful finish – here a wooden floor is being sanded before a finish is applied.*

Right: *Any cracks and holes in walls will need filling in before you can decorate.*

behind and is not being decorated should be protected against any splashes or spills. Good wooden floors should be protected with a copious amount of old newspaper or a large, heavy-duty plastic sheet – such sheeting can be bought at most good DIY stores.

Very large pieces of furniture may need to be moved to the centre of the room and protected with dust covers or old bed sheets. You can buy roller bases – extendible metal brackets with rollers at each end – which make it easier to manoeuvre large cupboards and chests around.

Be very careful when moving furniture – don't do it single-handed; get a couple of friends round to help.

Order of work

Unsightly features may need to be camouflaged and this is the time to plan how and where it will be done. Water pipes, telephone cables and other domestic wiring are best boxed in or hidden behind a window seat or some other piece of built-in furniture. In some cases, wiring can be laid under floorboards or put under the edge of a fitted carpet.

If you are going for a radical redecoration, this is the time to have wiring chased into the walls. If you have contemplated underfloor heating this is also the time to install it, when carpets and furniture are out of the way and you have easy access to the uncovered floor covering or boards. Try to think from the underneath out, so that all the work is carried out in logical stages before the paint or paper is put in place.

Stripping varnish or paint finishes off a wooden floor should be done well before any paint pot is opened. The micro-fine dust generated by an electric sander and even handheld abrasive

paper will take time to settle and will only be thoroughly removed after a couple of wipe overs with a damp cloth. Even lifting a carpet will cause dust to rise, so mats, rugs and carpets should be removed before walls and paintwork are wiped down.

Don't be tempted to start jobs in the wrong order. For example, sanding down the window frames while the wall paint is drying elsewhere in the room is not a good idea because the dust from the frames will stick to the wet wall paint and damage the surface and finish of the wall. Always think through the order of your jobs before starting them.

Preparing the surfaces

Unless you are moving into a recently completed conversion or a newly built home you will have to prepare the walls and ceiling before any decoration takes place. Even in newly built homes you may need to rake out and fill in cracks. Fresh plaster will shrink as it dries and if it dries quickly in a room where central heating is in use then fine hair line cracks will

appear where the plaster has been used over joins in plasterboard or in corners. There is also a certain amount of what is known in the trade as 'settling', as bricks and boards adjust to their resting places.

In an older building or room that has been previously decorated you will most likely need to strip off the existing paper. This is a laborious task but you can hire industrial steamers from commercial hire shops, which will make the job much easier.

It is well worth spending time on preparation, even filling in small holes where picture pins have been, because the effort put into the groundwork will ensure that the final finish is good. It is pointless slapping up sheets of expensive wallpaper over a badly prepared surface because they won't adhere properly and when the paper dries the surface will be lumpy and uneven. Plain painted surfaces also need to be well prepared because any blemish or mark will be all the more noticeable as there is no pattern to distract the eye.

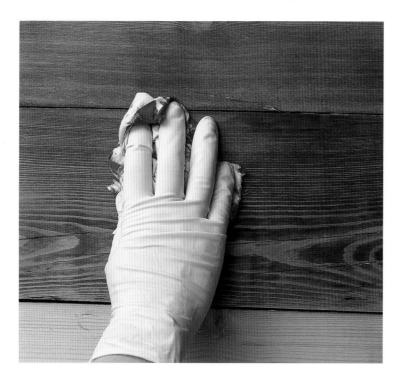

Left: Before you start decorating your home, make sure that you have all the necessary protective clothing such as these gloves, which protect your hands when you are applying woodstain.

Wearing suitable clothing

When tackling any DIY project, make sure that you are properly dressed for it. Even for furniture moving you should wear good stout shoes or boots that will protect your feet, ankles and toes. If you are doing a messy job such as sanding, rubbing down or using a caustic paint remover or similar chemical-based product you should leave windows and doors open for good ventilation. It is also vital that you wear a mask over your mouth as well as protective glasses.

Choosing your paint

Paint is one of the most versatile and easy finishes to apply – it can look plain, smooth and matt or rough and textured. Patterns can be painted over a base coat, block printed or stencilled. Paints can also be used to create a faux or trompe l'oeil effect that makes the wall look like marble or wood.

Early paint sources

In early times pigments came from natural sources such as earth – for example, the colour Sienna is named after the red Tuscan earth from which it was made. Plants, leaves and mosses were frequently used to obtain green colourings and red was often made using animal blood or crushed insects. Blue used to be extracted from the woad plant, which is a member of the mustard family, and indigo, most commonly known as the colour of denim jeans, came from the *Indigofera* plant and was introduced into Europe from the East in the 16th century.

History of paint

Paint is usually a liquid, made up of a pigment that is dissolved in water or oil. Many centuries ago, pigments used to come from natural sources (see box, left). These early paints were expensive because they took time and trouble to prepare and the basic ingredients had to be imported from far away. Therefore wall paints tended to be confined to the homes of wealthy city dwellers and would be mixed on site by master craftsmen.

The Industrial Revolution had an effect on paint – carbon or gas black was a by-product of the incomplete combustion of natural gas. Some discoveries are relatively recent – the earliest synthetic dye, mauve, was obtained at the end of the 19th century, while the vivid greens like forest and emerald were not developed until 1938.

Even though the dyes and pigments themselves have advanced there are many who look to the past for inspiration. There is an increasing interest not only in traditional colours but also in old techniques, such as limewashing and distemper, which, with some modifications, can be a more stable and long lasting finish than it was when originally in use.

Right: Consider applying bands of different colours to a single wall to create a striking look.

Choosing a colour

The best way to get an idea of the range of colours available is to get hold of some sample cards. These are strips of a whole range of shades of one colour and they are available from most paint and DIY stores. Take some strips home and see how they look next to furniture and fabrics. Isolate one or two of the tones that you feel comfortable with and then buy sample pots. These are small tester quantities of paint, which give you the scope to try out the colours in situ without buying a lot

of paint. You can either paint the colour directly onto a patch of wall or use a piece of lining paper or card that can be pinned or temporarily stuck up on the wall.

This trial patch will give you a chance to see a volume of colour and to study it in different lights. Look at the paint patch during the day in natural light and then again in the evening in artificial illumination, as colours can vary. What appears to be a muted ochre yellow in daylight may look sad and sludgy by electric light.

When building up a wall colour from a pale base you may well be advised by the paint manufacturer to choose a coloured base coat that complements the final paint colour. A coloured base coat will

help build up the depth of colour. Conversely if you are going to use a lighter colour over a dark base, put down a base coat of white or beige first to block out the strong tones as completely as possible, before applying the top coat.

There are now a number of 'one-coat' paints on the market too, which claim that they will cover walls in one, single application, on a prepared wall without undercoat. This does work well if you are applying a colour with a similar strength of tone as the colour already on the wall. However, when it comes to painting a much lighter colour over a dark base colour then you may still have to use two coats of this paint.

There is a huge range of paint effects available (see pages 38–9) and these can look good in moderation, if skillfully carried out. In a period setting, they can be used to create panels of interest in a long corridor or to mimic the effect of expensive wallpapers or woods. But the fashion for paint effects has also spread to wallpapers and you can now buy papers printed with rag-rolled effects, for example, which may be a simpler alternative for you.

The paint finish that you choose will also affect lighting. Dark matt surfaces absorb light whereas light and shiny paint surfaces reflect it more. Textured surfaces are also more light absorbent than smooth finishes.

Above: *Dark matt paint colours, such as this deep blue decorative scheme, tend to absorb light and so they work well in rooms that have ample natural lighting.*

Lettering and numbers

Lettering is a popular form of decoration and can be achieved in a number of ways. Lines of poetry or quotations work particularly well in bathrooms – try recipes in kitchens and numerals in home offices. Experiment with different sizes and typefaces to achieve different styles.

Using plastic lettering

Tools and materials

Spirit level

Pencil

Plastic letters

Emulsion (acrylic) and small paintbrush

1 Use a spirit level to draw a faint horizontal pencil line in the place where you want the lettering. Use large plastic letters to draw around.

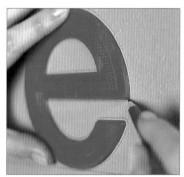

Hold your chosen letters up to the wall and draw around each one.

2 Fill in with paint. If needed, make a brush rest using a cane with some wadding wrapped in cotton.

Use a small paintbrush to paint the inside of the letters on the wall.

Using a projector

Hire or borrow an overhead projector. Write freehand or photocopy the writing of your choice onto acetate then project the writing onto the wall where you want to paint the letters. Draw around the letters with soft pencil then fill in with paint (see recipe wall project pages 220–21).

Using stencils

Tools and materials

Spirit level

Pencil

Stencil

Masking tape

Paint and large stencil brush

Varnish (optional)

1 Use lettering stencils to spell out your chosen words along a straight pencil line on the wall. Apply the paint by dabbing sparingly through the stencils using a large, blunt stencil brush.

Dab the paint through the stencils to colour in your chosen words.

2 Remove the stencil carefully by peeling it away and then varnish over the whole surface if necessary to finish.

Once the paint has dried, peel off the stencil from the wall.

Left: If you don't want to use letters, then experiment with other shapes, such as this natural vine leaf design.

45

Choosing your wallpaper

Wallpaper adds softness to a wall and can help reduce echoes and the emptiness of a large room. Papers can be very decorative with a large all-over print, simply striped or even printed to look like a paint effect such as marbling, so that you get the effect without ever having to dip your brush in a pot.

History of wallpapering

Wallpaper was developed for the middle and upper classes as an inexpensive alternative to wood panelling, tapestry and cloth hangings, which were favoured up until the 17th century. But even as a less expensive alternative it was still a luxury item printed with hand-applied blocks and intricately carved and colour-separated rollers. There are still a few exclusive wallpaper manufacturers who produce luxurious, often hand-coloured tableaux panels and papers that are close to the original quality and craftsmanship of the earlier varieties.

Wallpaper grew in popularity in the 19th century when mechanized engraved cylinders and continuous rolls of paper were produced. The Arts and Crafts period saw it reach new heights with the artist William Morris producing many highly coloured designs that are still in production today.

Other older styles of paper, such as anaglypta and lincrusta, have also seen something of a revival with people restoring period homes. These papers first became popular in Victorian times and have a stamped pattern that stands out in relief against the background. They were commonly used on ceilings and below dado rails, for example, between the skirting and waist height. They are sometimes painted today with gloss paints for a high shine, wipeable finish and even matt finishes in order to create a chalky appearance.

During the 1950s and 1960s further advances in the production of wallpaper took place. Coatings, such as a fine layer of plastic, saw the introduction of vinyl papers, which were better able to cope with the extremes of temperature

Right: Floral patterns work well in a traditional bedroom. If you are using an elaborate pattern, then consider papering just half the wall, above the dado rail.

Left: *A simple repeated motif can look elegant and effective as a wallpaper pattern.*

and moisture in bathrooms. Metallic-backed papers with silvery backgrounds and iridescent finishes were also produced at this time.

Other wallcovering options include textured woodchip papers, which were popular in the 1950s and 1960s but have been in decline for some time now. They do have some advantages though. These thick, textural papers cover over and disguise a multitude of sins such as cracks and bumps on uneven wall surfaces.

During the 1980s and early 1990s the popularity of wallpaper began to wane with paint becoming the primary wallcovering, but in the late 1990s a new vogue for papers began to arise once more.

Choosing wallpaper

The wallpaper that you choose will depend on the shape, size and function of the room being decorated. If the walls are uneven, you may want to choose a thicker paper. In rooms with a lot of pictures, a simple, quiet design will probably be the best option to take.

The next step is to look through as many books of papers available as possible. Some of the sample books have visuals of sets using the various designs, which can be very helpful.

The current trend for paper is to use it as a panel or on one wall rather than on all four walls. This is mixed with painted surfaces and becomes a highlight or feature of a room rather than a complete covering.

Lining paper that is left unpainted is another slightly obscure but attractive finish that has been in vogue for a number of years. The paper, which is off-white when applied, 'ages' in sunlight and takes on a yellow, almost parchment-coloured hue. Plain brown wrapping paper has also been used to great effect, especially in small rooms such as studies or cloakrooms. Good quality brown paper has a slight stripe in it, and so needs to be hung carefully to ensure that all the lines run in the same direction. The paper itself can be bought in large commercial quantities.

Hessian, silk and grass have all been applied to paper backings and are still popular in parts of northern Europe and France.

types of

wallpaper

Before you choose your wallpaper, you must decide what type of paper to use. There is a wide variety of different types of paper available on the market today. They are manufactured in a number of ways and produce different effects on your wall. As such, it is important to bear in mind the decorative style that you are trying to achieve when choosing your paper – for example, a heavily embossed paper will look fine in a period setting but may be at odds with a minimal contemporary design.

Wallpaper

Standard wallpaper

Standard printed rolls are 52cm (20¾in) wide. They come in an enormous variety of colours and designs, usually with a matt finish.

Hand blocked/printed wallpaper

These have standard dimensions but the designs have been printed by hand, making them much more expensive than standard varieties.

Vinyl wallpaper

These designs consist of a paper backing with a printed vinyl top coat. They are easy to hang and strip, and are also very hardwearing and resistant to scuffing. They can look shiny.

Textured/embossed papers

These papers are ideal for using on walls that are slightly uneven as their raised surface pattern disguises minor imperfections. They are hung in the same way as standard wallpapers but often require longer soaking, so always follow manufacturer's instructions.

Anaglypta and lincrusta

Anaglypta is an embossed paper, which was first used by the Victorians and is made from a combination of cotton and paper pulp. This is passed through patterned rollers when wet, which press out the design onto the paper. It is particularly popular for heavy-wear areas such as hallways as it is resilient to knocks and bumps. It comes uncoloured so you can paint it to match your colour scheme – it can also be used as a base for creating a number of broken colour paint effects as the glaze sits in the recesses and highlights the pattern. Lincrusta is an embossed wallcovering like anaglypta but is made from a linoleum mixture – it is super durable.

Textured vinyl paper

Printed paper

Standard vinyl paper

Printed paper

Printed paper

Woodchip wallpaper

This is a favourite in the refurbishment trade as the small 'chips' of wood can hide a multitude of sins, giving walls a porridge-like texture. Take great care when removing woodchip as it may well be holding the plaster behind it together – by removing it you run the risk of exposing a wall that may need replastering professionally.

Blown vinyl wallpaper

This is a vinyl paper with a raised pattern created by a special printing process: on heating, the printed area expands giving a three-dimensional effect. Designs used to be fairly old fashioned but recently ranges have expanded to include mosaic tiles, metal treadplate and natural fibres.

Tools

Pasting table

These light, folding tables are cheap to buy and make wallpapering much easier as they are just wider than a roll of paper and long enough to spread paste without creasing the paper.

Paperhanger's brush

This is a wide slim brush used for smoothing down paper once it has been hung.

Pasting brush

This large, synthetic bristled brush is used for spreading paste over paper. It is worth getting one that includes a plastic hook to stop it falling into the paste and making a mess.

Plumb lines

The simplest form is a weight that hangs from a string, enabling you to mark a perfectly vertical line. It is also possible to buy versions that include a chalk reservoir. This chalks the string, enabling you to 'snap' it against a surface to produce a chalk line.

Seam roller

This small tool has a revolving roller, which is used to roll over the seams of wallpapers and borders for a flat join.

Steam stripper

These electric machines can be bought or hired by the day and are useful when you are stripping large areas of wallpaper. They are filled with water, which is heated to boiling point. The steam then travels up a rubber or plastic tube to a plate, which is held against the wall – the steam gets under the paper and loosens the adhesive.

Decorator's scissors

These scissors have long blades for cutting wallpaper in a straight line. They also have shaped blunt ends for use when creasing the wallpaper as a guide to cutting.

Adhesive

This includes all types of wallpaper paste and comes in ready mixed or powder form. There is also a border adhesive, which comes in a squeezy tube and is useful for sticking down paper edges.

Pasting brush

Pasting table

Seam roller

Paperhanger's brush

Decorator's scissors

Printed paper

Printed paper

Standard vinyl paper

Standard vinyl paper

Anaglypta

wallpapering techniques

Many people are wary of using wallpaper because there is a persistent belief (mainly among those who have never tried) that it is incredibly difficult to put up. In fact, hanging wallpaper is not only quite straightforward if approached in a methodical manner, but also immensely satisfying and fun to do. The next few pages will take you through the basic wallpapering techniques and help you with the tricky jobs, such as papering around corners and obstacles.

Preparation

Strip the walls of any existing paper and patch up any cracks or holes in the plaster (see page 32–4). Before painting or wallpapering the walls, size them with diluted wallpaper paste, which gives them 'good slip' and allows the paper to be moved about. Then line the walls with lining paper. This is available in different weights – the heaviest gives the best coverage and the smoothest surface to work on. If you are painting the walls, hang the lining paper vertically: fill and sand any small gaps between the joints first and follow the instructions for normal wallpapering (see opposite).

Cross lining walls with lining paper

If you are wallpapering you should 'cross line' the walls – this means hanging the paper horizontally. The reason for doing this is to avoid the joins of the lining paper and wallpaper lining up. If you don't feel confident about cross lining, hang the lining paper vertically but take care when positioning the wallpaper on top of it, making sure that the joins don't line up.

Tools and materials

Tape measure
Spirit level
Soft pencil
Scissors
Wallpaper paste
Old paintbrush
Lining paper
Pasting brush
Decorator's brush
Filling knife
Craft knife

1 Measure the width of the lining paper and, using a tape measure, mark this measurement at intervals starting at the top of the wall. Use a spirit level to draw horizontal lines across the room with a soft pencil. Measure the length of each wall and work out the number of lengths of lining paper that you need to cut (allow several centimetres or inches excess at each end).

Fold the paper into a concertina shape, ready to hang on the wall.

3 Start hanging the paper in the top right-hand corner of the room, smoothing it into the corner with a decorator's brush. When you reach the other end of the room, trim the paper to fit.

Draw a horizontal line around the room, using a spirit level and pencil.

2 Measure and cut the lengths of lining paper. Paste the first length, taking care to cover the edges. Once pasted, fold the paper into a concertina shape (paste against paste) and allow to soak for the recommended time. Paste the second length while the first is soaking.

Hang the concertina of lining paper, gradually smoothing it across the wall.

4 Hang the second length of paper, butting it up to the first piece. Continue around the room, one wall at a time. When you reach the skirting board use a filling knife to push the paper into the angle between the skirting and the wall. Hold firmly in place and trim using a sharp craft knife.

Starting points

Traditional advice recommends starting the run of wallpaper by centring it at a focal point such as a fireplace. This makes sense if you are using a paper with an obvious pattern because it will make the design look balanced. However, if it is your first attempt at wallpapering, there is no harm in starting with the longest wall, which does not have any obstacles. This will give you confidence to handle other obstacles as you work your way clockwise around the room.

Butt the top edge of the second piece up to the bottom edge of the first.

Hanging wallpaper

Tools and materials

Tape measure

Spirit level

Wallpaper

Scissors or craft knife

Pasting table and brush

Wallpaper paste

Plumb line

Metal straightedge

Decorator's brush

1 Measure the drop from the ceiling to the skirting and add a couple of centimetres (about an inch) top and bottom to provide an overlap. If you are working with patterned wallpaper, take the repeat into account. Cut the first few lengths and lay them on the pasting table. Paste carefully, from the centre of the paper outwards, with the edge overlapping the table slightly to avoid getting paste on the face of the paper.

Apply paste from the centre outwards towards the edges.

2 Making sure that the first drop of wallpaper is hung straight is vital and, as most walls are not completely square, you will need a plumb line. Choose a point in the room that is close to the darkest corner and measure just under a width of the wallpaper away from the corner. Hold the string at the top of the wall, let the plumb fall to the skirting and wait until it has completely stopped moving. Then mark with a pencil at intervals along the string. Join up the line with a metal straightedge.

Use a plumb line to ensure that you hang your paper perfectly straight.

3 Starting at the top, smooth the paper onto the wall, allowing an overlap of a couple of centimetres (about an inch). Work down the length using the decorator's brush to smooth the paper from the centre outwards, squeezing out any air bubbles. The paper should be worked well into the corner and overlap the adjacent wall by about 1cm (½in).

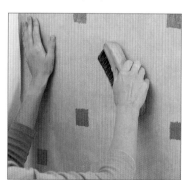

Use a decorator's brush to squeeze out any air bubbles.

4 Use the rounded tip of the decorator's scissors in order to crease the paper carefully at the point where it meets the ceiling. Slowly pull the wallpaper away from the wall at the top and use the scissors to trim away the excess. Then carefully smooth the paper back down the wall using the decorator's brush. Repeat the process at the point where the wall meets the skirting board.

Make a crease in the paper where the wall meets the skirting board.

5 Hang the second drop of paper by carefully aligning it with the edge of the first drop and sliding it up against it to achieve a 'butt' joint (the two edges should meet without any trace of a gap at all). If you are using a patterned wallpaper, then you will need to slide the paper along the wall until the two halves of the pattern meet up at the correct position.

6 Trim the top and bottom of the paper as shown in step 4. Repeat the process around the whole room. Make sure that the last drop of paper overlaps the corner by approximately 1cm (½in) and is pushed well into the corner using the decorator's brush. Finally, finish off by wiping away any wallpaper paste that may have been left on the ceiling or cornice and skirting board using a clean, damp sponge.

Buying wallpaper

When buying wallpaper, take along a note of the dimensions of your room and the height of the ceilings – the shop should be able to advise you of the number of rolls to buy. Always buy a couple more than you will need because these can be stored in case you need to make any repairs. Check that all the rolls of wallpaper are from the same 'batch' or print run – this should be marked clearly as a batch number on the side of the packaging. If you run out of paper and need to buy more, make sure that you get the same batch because colours on different batches always vary slightly because of the printing process.

Papering around corners

Once you have mastered a straight run of wallpapering, turning corners shouldn't be a problem. The key is to allow 1–2cm (½–1in) overlap.

Internal corners

Tools and materials

As for Hanging wallpaper (see page 51)

1 When you have hung the last drop of paper before reaching the corner, stop and measure the width of the next drop. Do not assume that the wall is completely true – measure the gap at the top, bottom and middle and add a couple of centimetres (about an inch) to the largest measurement.

Measure the width of the drop you need to reach the corner.

2 Lay the paper on the floor or pasting table and, using a straightedge, mark the paper and cut with scissors. Make sure that the cut edge is the one nearest the corner that will be covered. Paste and allow to soak. Reserve the offcut if it is a decent size.

3 Hang the paper as above, ensuring that it is pushed well into the corner with the papering brush. If the paper creases where it turns the corner, make a few snips along the edge with scissors and smooth into place.

If the paper creases at the corner, snip into the edge with scissors.

4 If the cut lengths before the corner left you with a decent-sized offcut use this piece to continue – if not begin with a fresh length. Measure the width of the offcut and hang a plumb line at this distance from the corner on the new wall. Paste, soak then hang in position over the overlap, flush with the corner with the cut side nearest the corner. Continue the process around the room.

Hang the next piece so that the cut side is nearest the corner.

External corners

External corners are usually found in rooms with fireplaces. If you have started papering in the middle of a chimney breast cut the length of paper before the corner so that it is wide enough to wrap around the corner with a couple of centimetres (about an inch) spare as an overlap. If you are approaching an external corner from an alcove, however, then use the following steps to hang the wallpaper.

Tools and materials

As for Hanging wallpaper (see page 51)

1 Measure the depth of the chimney breast at three points then cut a length of paper that width plus 2.5cm (1in), which will be wrapped around the corner. Paste, soak then hang as described above using the brush to smooth the cut edge gently around the external corner.

Use the decorator's brush to smooth the paper round the corner.

2 Measure the offcut and plumb a line as described above on the new wall. Paste, soak then smooth in place, covering the overlap. Trim on the top and bottom.

Put the offcut in place on the new wall, covering the overlap.

Papering around obstacles

The same principles apply to papering around most obstacles. The key is to crease the paper carefully around the object, which will indicate where to cut.

Papering around a fireplace

Tools and materials

As for Hanging wallpaper
(see page 51)

1 Smooth the length of wallpaper down towards the top of the fireplace stopping about 30cm (1ft) above it. Use the brush to smooth the paper carefully into the corner where the edge of the fireplace meets the wall.

Use the decorator's brush to smooth the paper into the corner.

2 Use a sharp craft knife or pair of scissors to make a horizontal slit along the centre of the mantle shelf from the point where the fireplace meets the wall.

Use scissors to cut a series of slits in the wallpaper.

3 Smooth the wallpaper down above the mantle shelf, and trim as described above. Use your fingertips to press the paper gently around any mouldings below the mantle shelf and trim using a sharp craft knife.

Smooth the paper, trimming around any mouldings on the fireplace.

Papering around a recessed window

Tools and materials

As for Hanging wallpaper
(see page 51)

1 Make sure that the final drop of wallpaper is wide enough to cover the depth of the recess when cut. Smooth down the paper over the window then carefully cut horizontal slits across the top and bottom of the window to the corners of the recess. Fold the resulting flap over into the recess and trim but do not smooth down.

2 Cut a small length of paper 2.5cm (1in) deeper and wider than the area left at the top of the recess and smooth it in place under the long drop. Cut a small triangle off the corner of the paper to fold it neatly over the edge of the recess. Smooth the long drop of wallpaper in place over the smaller piece.

Papering around a door (or window without a recess)

1 Cut a length of wallpaper, which will hang over the door, and apply paste to it avoiding the area that will be cut away. Hang it loosely over the door and cut away the area over the door leaving around a 5cm (2in) overlap. Use the wallpapering brush to push the paper into the recess between the door frame and the wall.

Make a small diagonal slit in the wallpaper to the corner of the door frame.

2 Use the papering brush to smooth the paper around the frame and trim using a craft knife.

Papering around light switches and power points

Tools and materials

As for Hanging wallpaper
(see page 51)

1 Hang the paper loosely over the switch and use the brush to locate the switch position through the paper. Using a craft knife cut two diagonal slits from corner to corner.

Locate the switch plate and then cut diagonal slits in the paper.

2 Fold back the paper triangles and smooth the paper around the switch plate with the brush. Use a craft knife to trim the triangles as close to the switch as possible.

Fold the triangles back and then trim them as neatly as possible.

Alternative method

There is an alternative method for papering around light switches and power points. Turn off the power at the fuse box and unscrew the front of the switch plate just far enough to allow you to push the excess paper underneath.

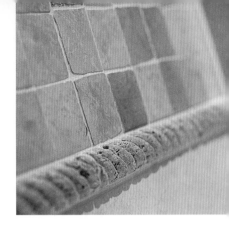

Choosing your tiles

Tiles have long been a standard wall covering for bathrooms and cloakrooms, as well as splashbacks and other surfaces in the kitchen. The advantage of these glazed or fired ceramic squares is that they are waterproof, hardwearing, easy to wipe clean and dry and they come in a huge range of colours.

History of tiling

Although these days tiles are machine-made in many materials, originally they would have all been ceramic, handcrafted from local clay and baked in a fire or, later, a kiln. Ceramic tiles are made in virtually every country in the world and the ceramic tradition dates back thousands of years. Among the most widely found base for tiles is terracotta, a low-fired red clay. In its basic form this tile can be simply glazed or waxed to cover the porous surface, but in more sophisticated realms it can be highly decorated. The Greeks and Romans both used this type of decorated tile in the interiors of their homes and examples of fine mosaic patterns, made from hundreds of tiny coloured tiles, can be seen in ancient sites throughout the world.

Other tiles were made with an earthenware base. During the 16th century this type was favoured by the craftsmen in the town of Delft, in southern Holland, where the tiles were glazed with a white background and decorated with patterns in various depths of blue. For over 400 years this blue and white configuration has been popular, and tiles are still made to this scheme.

Choosing your style

There is a wide variety of tiles to choose from and you should select yours to suit the size of the room you are decorating as well as to complement your scheme.

In a large bathroom walls of tiny mosaic tiles may look bitty and lost and conversely in a small room large ceramic panels may make the room feel smaller.

Right: Small mosaic tiles are very popular in bathrooms today. Mix and match colours to create a pattern.

Far right: These matt tiles are made in very subtle, neutral colouring, which provides a sense of calm.

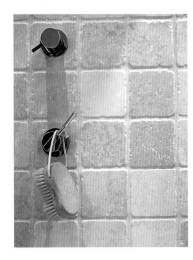

Therefore, you should ensure that you choose the right size of tile to be in proportion to the setting. In most bathrooms it is usual to panel the area above the bath and handbasin with tiles in order to protect the immediate surrounding wall from water splashes and dampness. The walls, and even the ceiling and floor, of a shower enclosure may also be covered in tiles for the very same reason.

Tiles can be chosen to be plain and innocuous so that they are simply a background or you can select them to enhance and endorse a particular design. For example, in a Moorish bathroom tiles will be a feature – they are not only popular in the indigenous decoration of the country and are therefore appropriate when recreating such a style, but they are also colourful, incorporating dramatic, geometric patterns.

Small mosaics tiles can be used to form patterns or create pictures. Some of the popular patterns made using these small tiles include the ombre or shadow effect, which is a graduation of a single colour that starts with dark toned tiles near the floor and gradually fades to the palest shade near the ceiling. If you are using blues you can create an underwater effect so that, when lying in the bath, it is as if you are at the bottom of a lagoon looking up to the sky above.

Larger, traditional tiles, (10 x 10cm/4 x 4in) can be laid in regular lines parallel to the surface or floor, or set on their points to form a diamond pattern. You may also mix two or three shades of the same colour, or contrasting shades such as black and white or blue and orange, to form a chequerboard effect.

Another way of dividing up a large expanse of tiles is to create a frieze or border. This can be

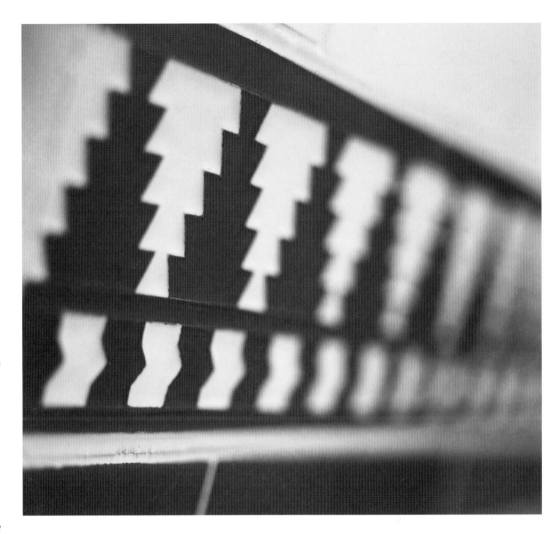

done by introducing a narrow band of smaller tiles such as mosaics, a contrasting line of narrow, linear tiles or a slightly raised feature tile that will form a divide between the upper and lower levels on the wall. The lower level may be in one colour or size of tile while above there may be a deeper shade, different pattern or even paint or paper.

Most ceramic tiles are machine-made so that they are exactly the same size, thickness and colour, which makes them easy to lay and provides a uniform finish. But, for more rustic or bohemian settings, there are also hand-made tiles and those that are manufactured so that they appear handmade. The surface of these tiles is uneven, slightly undulating and the colours vary a little too.

Matt finished tiles are extremely popular today. These tiles date back to Victorian times when they were manufactured as encaustic tiles. They were especially favoured by architects such as Pugin, who used them in grand civil buildings such as the The Palace of Westminster, in London, England.

The pattern on these original, and now reproduction, Victorian tiles is made by inlaying contrasting colours of clay into the surface of the tile. This is fired and the colours fused and set. Some of the matt finish tiles have a sandstone appearance, and can be used in conjunction with other natural tiling material such as stone, slate and even cement in more contemporary style settings.

Above: Here is an example of a strong, colourful Moorish bathroom tile design. Why not try incorporating such tiles in your own bathroom scheme and make a feature of them?

types of
tiles

Tiling is the most popular choice for protecting the walls in kitchens, bathrooms and other areas where water is in use. When tiles are properly applied to a wall they provide a water-resistant barrier, which is easy to clean and maintain. Tiles of different sizes, made from many different materials, are now widely available. Tiling a small, regular shaped area is a fairly easy DIY task, although you should be aware before beginning that you will need to leave sufficient drying time between tiling and grouting.

Types of tiles

Handmade tiles

These ceramic tiles are made by hand from slabs of clay, which gives them their characteristic individual appearance. Slight differences in thickness and size will be noticeable and, as they are glazed and fired in small batches, colours will vary from batch to batch. They are more expensive than mass-produced equivalents because they are labour intensive.

Machine-made ceramic tiles

These tiles are made in large batches, often using liquid clay poured into a mould to ensure the right consistency. Many have a printed surface decoration, which mimics expensive materials such as marble and stone.

They come in a large variety of different shapes and sizes from conventional squares to large rectangular slabs. Some manufactured tiles have a raised surface decoration, which is applied before firing. Some have an undulating surface and uneven edges to mimic handmade tiles.

Mosaic tiles

Mosaic tiles or 'tesserae' come in a wide variety of materials including glass, ceramic and stone. The most expensive tesserae are made from a thin layer of gold leaf sandwiched between two pieces of glass. Most often associated with swimming pools, their versatility has made them increasingly popular in private homes over the last few years. Although mosaics appear in ultra contemporary interiors, they have been used since Roman times in elaborate floor designs. Tesserae are much smaller than conventional tiles and are often supplied on a paper or woven-fibre backing sheet. Mosaic tiles can also be purchased in loose form.

Mesh-backed mosaics

Machine-made ceramic tiles

Paper-backed mosaics

New materials

Designers are constantly exploring new materials, which can be made into tiles. Metal tiles or tiles with a metallic glaze have become a popular choice to complement stainless steel and industrial style kitchens. Resin tiles are available in a wide range of colours and have an opaque quality, which suits contemporary interiors. Glass artists have developed a range of tiles, which fuse clear glass with other decorative materials. Printing techniques can also be used to apply a photographic image to your tiles.

Profile gauge

Tile nippers

Tile-cutting tool

Tools and equipment

Tile-cutting tools

A variety of methods can be used for cutting tiles. The cheapest and simplest is a handheld tool that scores through the glaze of the tile, which will then snap along the line when pressure is applied. A sturdy version of the same tool incorporates a measuring gauge for accurate cutting and has a lever-operated snapping tool, which grips the tile. For thicker tiles, including quarry tiles, it is worth buying or hiring an electric tile cutter, which incorporates a water reservoir, making cutting easier. Tile nibblers and tile saws can be used for cutting irregular shapes from tiles, but both methods require practice.

Tile spacers

These small plastic crosses act as spacers, ensuring that each tile is an equal distance from the next. Different sizes are made to suit wall and floor tiles. They are pressed into the tile adhesive, making sure that they are below the surface of the tile so that when grout is applied they are hidden.

Grout and adhesive

Adhesive is spread directly onto the wall surface with a notched spreader, which is often supplied with the adhesive. Tiles are pressed into the adhesive, which is allowed to dry before grout is applied. Grout is applied over the tiles with a smooth edged tool, which forces it into the spaces between the tiles. It is important to choose the correct adhesive and grout for the situation. Areas that will get very wet, like shower cubicles, should be tiled using waterproof adhesive and grout, which will prevent water seeping through the grout lines into the wall. Areas like kitchen splash backs, which will occasionally be splashed with water, do not require a waterproof grout and adhesive. Grout is available in a variety of colours – you can also buy touch-up pens to refresh worn or dirty looking grout.

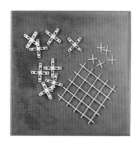

Tile saw

Tile spacers

Metallic tile

Handmade rustic tiles

Machine-made rustic-style tile

Handmade rustic tile

tiling techniques

To achieve a perfectly tiled surface plan your tiling scheme carefully to avoid awkward cuts and joins in obvious places. Make sure that you have ordered sufficient tiles for the job – always order around ten per cent extra to allow for any breakages. It is also a good idea to keep some spare tiles anyway, for future repairs, safely stored and labelled. Another vital tip is to always use a sheet of graph paper to plan complicated tile designs before you begin.

Cutting tiles

To cut tiles into regular shapes, score and cut with a tile cutter. To cut away irregular shapes, follow the instructions below.

Tools and materials

Tile cutter

Tile nibbler

1 Score the glaze with a series of cross-hatched lines.

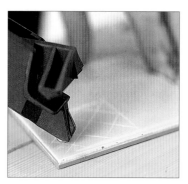

Score the glaze with the scorer part of the tile cutting tool.

2 Use a tile nibbler in order to 'bite' away the pieces of unwanted tile.

Use a tile nibbler to break away the unwanted pieces of the tile.

Tiling difficult areas

If you are tiling difficult-to-reach areas such as the wall above a bath, sink or kitchen worktop, it is important to check the level with a spirit level before you begin tiling. Also, make sure that you take time to plan the spacing before you begin, so that you can avoid awkward tile cuts.

Tiling a wall

Tools and materials

Spirit level

Timber batten (optional)

Nails

Hammer

Notched trowel or spreader

Tiles and spacers

Adhesive

Grout

Flexible spreader

Cloth

1 If you are tiling onto a blank wall you should first establish a level by nailing a batten onto the wall, which will provide your starting point.

Nail a batten to a wall in a straight line to provide a starting point.

2 Use a notched trowel or spreader to apply an even layer of tile adhesive to the wall. It is best to work on an area measuring 1 m sq (1 yd sq) at a time – any larger and the adhesive will dry before you can apply all the tiles.

Use a notched trowel to apply adhesive to the wall.

3 Apply the first row of tiles so that they butt up against the baton. Then remove one prong from each spacer to form a 't' shape and push into position. If you need to use any half tiles or cut tiles, make sure that you position these in the darkest corner of the room where they are least likely to be seen. Before positioning the second row of tiles push whole spacers in place to ensure that they are evenly spaced. Allow the adhesive to dry thoroughly overnight before you begin to grout.

Cut spacers into a 't' shape and position them between each tile.

4 Use a flexible spreader to apply the grout, pushing it well into the gaps between the tiles. Remove any excess with a damp cloth and allow to dry. Polish to remove any remaining film.

Use a flexible spreader to apply grout between the tiles.

Tiling a kitchen worktop

If you are tiling an awkwardly shaped object, such as a kitchen worktop, ensure that the top is level with a spirit level before you begin. If it is not perfectly flat, you may have to fit a piece of plyboard to the top before you begin tiling.

Tools and materials

PVA solution

Paintbrush

Tiles

Notched trowel or spreader

Adhesive

Spacers

Grout

Tile cutter

Cloth

1 To ensure the best finish, it is worth laying the tiles out dry before applying any adhesive. By doing this you can plan the design and work out the ideal places to use cut tiles. It is best to begin with full tiles along the front edge of the work surface, so that any cuts can be planned to appear along the back junction with the wall. Likewise, if the work surface includes a corner,

it is best to start with a full tile in the corner, and build up the rest of the design from this point.

2 To make the tiling easier, apply a coat of pva solution (1 part PVA to 5 parts water) to the ply surface. This helps to seal the ply, making it much easier to spread adhesive. Allow the ply to dry before proceeding to tile.

3 Use a notched trowel or spreader, ideally a large one, to spread adhesive across the ply surface. Do not spread more than about 1 metre square (1 yd sq) at a time. Use the notches to maintain a consistent depth of adhesive, which helps to ensure a consistent tile level.

Apply adhesive to the surface using a notched spreader.

4 Apply the tiles, pressing them down into the adhesive with a slight twisting motion. Since the tiles are applied to a horizontal surface there is no risk of them slipping down but it still pays to be vigilant. If rows of tiles are allowed to go out of 'square', this will affect the finish and lead to some unsightly tile cutting. So take time to position the tiles correctly, and use spacers to keep all gaps consistent. Spacers will also be required, albeit temporarily, along the junction between the edge tiles and the wooden edge strip, to ensure the lines of tiles are kept consistent.

Use spacers to ensure that the gap between tiles is even.

5 Once the adhesive has dried completely, grout the tiled surface with an epoxy grout. This type of grout is more hardwearing than standard grout, and more hygienic for surfaces upon which food will almost certainly be prepared. It is best to concentrate on small areas at a time, since epoxy grout can be difficult to work with and also tends to dry extremely quickly. Make sure that you force the grout firmly into every joint, removing any excess as quickly as possible with a damp sponge, before it has had a chance to dry.

Spread the grout, taking care to force it into the joints.

6 Wait until the grout has completely dried out, then give the tiled surface a final wipe over before polishing with a cotton cloth. This will help to remove any remaining grout residue and will leave a clean and bright finished surface.

Choosing your flooring

Flooring comes in a wide range of finishes, from natural wood and stone to the woven fibres of coconut husks and jute stems that form coir and sisal. These surfaces can be plain or decorative, rough or smooth – whichever you choose ensure that it has the durability required for your room.

History of flooring

The earliest homes had beaten mud floors covered with hunks of grass or rushes, but as time went by flagstones were hewn and laid and mats woven of rush became more commonplace. Clay tiles were used in Egypt and the Romans developed concrete for their decorative mosaic tile floors.

Wood has also been popular for centuries, from the simple timbered plank arrangements to the more ornate herringbone, parquet and even inlaid floors dating back to the Tudor and Stuart periods. In the early 18th century woven carpets were popular in grand homes. Less expensive painted canvas floorcloths were also popular in Britain and America at this time.

Animal skins and hides have also been used as floor coverings through the ages and, like a woollen mat or rug, can be used to bring warmth and softness to an area of hard stone or tile covering. Although pile carpets were developed in India before the 12th century most floor coverings in the West were flat-woven until the 19th century.

In the 1840s a revolution started that brought the luxury of carpets and rugs to a far wider audience, when a steam engine was used to power a loom. By the 1950s the high-speed tufting machine was developed and the rug and carpet industry took on the mass market. With the ability to manufacture carpet by the mile new, cheaper synthetic fibres were also introduced. These fibres, such as nylon and acrylic, brought the prices down even further.

Choosing your style

When choosing flooring, make sure that you incorporate the floor coverings into the overall decorative scheme. As a general rule, it is best to have a mix of pattern and plain in a room: for example, plain walls look good with a patterned floor as does a plain floor with patterned walls. Avoid using pattern on all surfaces because it can be overwhelming. It may also be appropriate to consider the style and period of your home and the furniture that is to be used in the room where the floor covering is to be fitted.

Choosing the right floor for each room

Different areas of the home will require different types of flooring to suit the demands of the room. For example, kitchen and bathroom floors have to be easy to wipe clean and capable of putting up with water splashes and drips. In a bedroom the floor covering should be warm and comfortable under bare feet. Hallways may be carpeted but if you want to protect the main track or pathway, you could lay a runner or rug over the wall to wall floor covering.

Right: Neutral coloured natural fibre floor coverings can tie in with any colour scheme.

Natural floor coverings have become increasingly fashionable and include wood, cork, coir, various stones and terracotta and brick tiles. Wood generally has a warm colouring, is pleasant to walk on and when polished reflects light back into the room. When installed in large rooms or areas it softens sounds and is less likely to cause echoing than harder surfaces such as stone. As a rule, wood improves with age as the colour mellows and becomes richer. Dents and marks only add to its character and in fact some contemporary floor suppliers 'distress' their new wood floors to give them a worn and vintage appearance. Wood is also a good canvas – it can be stripped, sanded and stained. Paint decorative borders around the edge or opt for an all-over pattern.

Another natural floor covering is natural matting, which is made from coir sisal and jute. Some have patterns woven or printed onto the edges, creating a traditional carpet effect, and coloured bindings of leather or woven wool can be used to link in to the colour theme of the whole room.

Marble, granite, limestone and slate have natural decoration in the veins and striations of their formation. Stone floors tend to be expensive but withstand hard treatment and are easy to clean. To soften hardness and reduce echoing use kelims and mats to break up large areas.

The rich red colouring of brick and terracotta tiles adds warmth to any room. Brick comes in a variety of shades from yellow through to browns and red, and these various shades can be used to create patterns. Or single-coloured bricks can be laid to form an attractive herringbone design. These surfaces are ideal for halls, kitchens, cloakrooms and conservatories.

Above: *Limestone floors look stylish and are also easy to look after.*

Left: *The expanse of these large white tiles has been broken up by using small black tiles.*

types of
flooring

When deciding on the flooring for each room of your home, it is important to consider the amount of wear and tear that each area will receive and choose a floor type accordingly. Flooring falls into several categories ranging from soft flooring, which includes carpets and rugs, to hard flooring, which includes wood, stone and tile at the other extreme. Semi-hard flooring is the in-between category, which includes materials such as vinyl, linoleum and rubber.

Soft flooring
Carpet

Carpet is one of the most comfortable and luxurious floor coverings. The best quality carpets have a high wool content – wool fibre repels dirt naturally, is soft underfoot and has a long lifespan. Synthetic fibres take colour well and can be treated to make them resistant to stains. They are often combined with wool to produce hardwearing carpets for areas of heavy wear. Common types of carpet pile are twist and velvet: twist pile is denser and more suitable for heavy-wear areas, while velvet pile is longer and softer making it the ideal choice for bedrooms.

Coir, sisal and jute

Natural floor coverings have become increasingly popular in recent years. Natural matting made from coir, sisal and jute can be fitted like a carpet or used in bound squares or runners for halls, stairways or as a central panel over a wood or stone floor.

Most natural fibre floor coverings have a latex rubber backing and require specialist fitting. Some combine the toughness of natural fibres with the softness of wool carpeting on a hessian backing. There are also unusual woven paper floor coverings available, which are tough and durable due to the tightness of the weave. These come from renewable sources so are environmentally sound, but, because it is a dried material, it is not advisable to use natural fibre

Wood veneer tongue and groove flooring

Terracotta quarry tile

Marble floor tile

Slate floor tile

Ceramic floor tile

directly in front of a fireplace where sparks may tumble out and burn it, or by a sink where water will splash and cause damage.

Hard flooring

Wood

There are various types of wood used for floors. The more expensive are the hardwoods such as oak, ash, walnut, Iroko, elm and maple. The cheaper softwoods such as pine are often stained or decorated because they lack the rich colour of hardwoods. Left in its natural state, wood flooring can be laid in herringbone patterns, in parquet-style designs or as planks in a staggered configuration so that a pattern is formed by the wood.

Wood is a 'living' material and so should be properly treated and dried before being laid. Central heating can cause the boards to dry out and shrink whereas a spillage of water, such as a regular leak from a pipe, will make the boards swell. New wood floors should be left for at least 48 hours to acclimatize to a room's environment before being laid.

As an everyday surface, wood is comparatively easy to clean – you can simply brush it or wipe over the top with a damp cloth or mop. Depending on the finish of the wood it may need to be wax polished every month or so or, if it is varnished, stripped and recoated about every ten years, depending on its location and the wear that it takes.

A cheap alternative to wood is laminate flooring. The laminating process involves taking a photographic image of woodgrain, printing it onto paper that is then sandwiched between chipboard and a plastic-coated surface to make a realistic-looking plank of flooring.

Stone

One of the advantages of stone is that it is virtually indestructible, making it an ideal choice for the kitchen. On the negative side it is unforgiving to items accidentally dropped onto it. Also, stone can feel cold underfoot, although this can be easily remedied with underfloor heating elements, which make it pleasant to walk on

with bare feet. Because of the cost of stone, it is advisable to have it fitted by a professional.

Tiles

Tiles come in a huge variety of designs, many of which mimic stone and marble. Glazed ceramic floor tiles can be fitted by the competent DIY enthusiast and are less costly than other hard floor coverings. The tiles should be made specifically for floor use, as tiles destined for wall or work surfaces (see pages 56–7) will not be as thick or heavy and will, in time, crack and break if used underfoot. The shiny surface of ceramic tiles makes them very easy to clean but they are prone to breaking and chipping if a heavy object is dropped on them or if they are laid on anything other than a perfectly flat surface.

Industrial style floors

Industrial style floor coverings have also crossed over into the home and include hard materials such as concrete, stone, metal and rubber. Concrete can be coloured and polished to a high

Alternative flooring

New technology is bringing exciting advances in floor coverings. Cork floor tiles that combine natural material with photographic images of subjects such as pebbles, grass and leaves are available. Vinyl floor tiles that mimic materials such as mosaic exotic woods and metal give the appearance of the materials they imitate without the hardness underfoot. Floor coverings that utilize the large amount of waste plastic we produce are also being pioneered.

Natural sisal (front example has coloured weft)

Mosaic-style vinyl

Ribbed wool carpets with a sisal weft

Wool twist carpet

Self-adhesive vinyl tile

Handsaw

sheen, when it will take on a highly decorative appearance and can therefore work well in homes.

Metal 'treadplate' tiles have become increasingly popular in kitchens – they complement stainless steel accessories and add to the professional appearance of a kitchen. Rubber flooring, which has long been associated with schools and hospitals, is now valued in the home for its warmth underfoot and non-slip qualities, making it an ideal choice for the bathroom.

Semi-hard floorings
Manmade floor coverings

These include linoleum, rubber and vinyl tiles. They can be laid in many patterns, the most common being the black and white chequerboard design. Linoleum, vinyl and cushioned vinyl floor coverings also come by the roll and can be cut and fitted like a carpet. Most are hardwearing and low on

maintenance but the surface may be harmed by a sharp or hot object. Linoleum was developed in the late 19th century but went out of fashion until recently – it is now definitely back in vogue. This type of flooring is regarded as being utilitarian so is most appropriate for bathrooms, kitchens and hallways.

Cork

Cork, which is also returning to popularity, is usually treated with a rubber backing and a surface sealant (especially if in tile form) to prevent it from becoming damaged by water or moisture.

Cork comes from the outer bark of the cork oak tree, which regrows so is a renewable resource. It is also a soft surface to walk on and it has good insulating properties.

Essential tools

When fitting carpet, in addition to a craft knife for cutting the carpet,

you will require a knee kicker to stretch the carpet as well as a bolster chisel and mallet to anchor it over the gripper rods.

Installation kits for tongue and groove wood and laminate flooring include plastic spacers, cork expansion strips as well as a metal edging device used with a hammer to fit the plank nearest the wall. You will also need a handsaw to cut the final planks in a row to the correct size.

Use a large notched spreader to apply the correct depth of adhesive when laying a tiled floor. When working with thicker tiles it is worth hiring a professional tile cutter or angle grinder.

Paint, stain or varnish can be applied to floors with brushes or small rollers. When applying a clear finish, such as a varnish, it is worth investing in a good quality woodcare brush. Use a smaller brush if you are painting a detailed pattern – the fitch is ideal for applying thin lines.

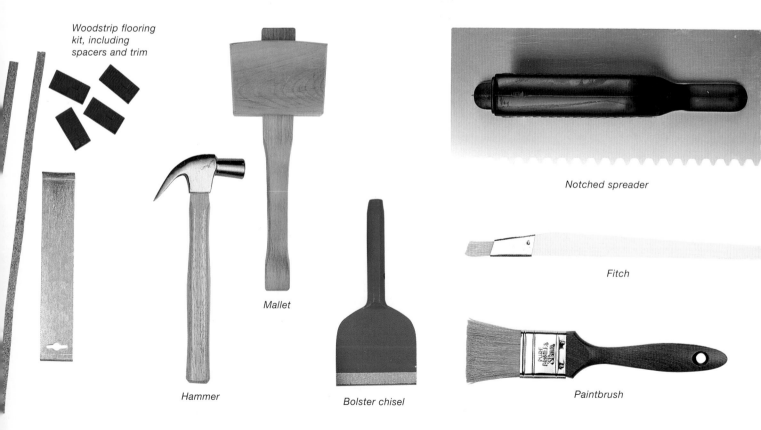

Woodstrip flooring kit, including spacers and trim

Hammer

Mallet

Bolster chisel

Notched spreader

Fitch

Paintbrush

flooring techniques

Before installing a new floor or refurbishing an old one, you must first consider the length of time that the room will be out of use, as this may affect the technique that you choose to use. You also need to remove all furniture and fittings and make sure that the room is thoroughly cleared before beginning to lay anything. It is also a good idea to draw a floor plan on a piece of graph paper to enable you to work out the quantities needed with accuracy.

Wooden floorboards

Wooden flooring is a practical option for every room. Most older houses have floorboards throughout, which, if you are lucky, will be in good enough condition to restore. There are a number of different ways in which you can finish floorboards that have a build up of years of old finishes. Sanding them back to bare wood is quite a labour intensive job but it gives you the option of applying a natural finish or tinting with a translucent varnish in a variety of shades. Or, if you do not want the disruption of sanding the floor there are specialist floor paints available in a wide range of colours. They can be painted directly onto unstripped floorboards. This is a quick option but it is an opaque finish, so will not show the grain. On the plus side it gives you the option of applying a decorative pattern or motif to the floor.

Preparation and repair of floorboards

Tools and materials

Hammer

Blunt chisel and pliers

Nail punch

Clout nails

1 If the room is carpeted, roll up the carpet and remove. Hessian-backed carpet will have been tacked in place with carpet tacks or gripper strips – work your way around the edges of the room with a hammer, blunt chisel and a pair of pliers pulling up the gripper strips or tacks that held the carpet in place.

2 Use the hammer and nail punch to drive down any nails that are sticking proud of the surface (this is very important if you are going to be using an electric sander as rogue nails can tear the sanding belt and damage the machine).

Drive down any nails that are sticking proud of the surface.

3 Check for loose floorboards and secure them to the joists with clout nails.

Applying a painted finish over old floorboards

Tools and materials

Floor cleaner

Sanding block and coarse-grade abrasive paper

Flexible wood filler and knife

Masking tape

Paintbrush or roller and extension pole and paint

1 Vacuum to remove dust then clean the floor thoroughly with a proprietary floor cleaner that will remove traces of old wax or polish. Allow to dry. Use a sanding block and coarse-grade abrasive paper to remove any stubborn marks and areas of raised grain that might show through the paint. Use flexible wood filler to fill in any gouges or holes that will spoil the finish.

2 Mask off the skirting boards with masking tape and begin to apply the paint starting from the corner of the room furthest away from the door. You can use a large paintbrush or, if you prefer, a roller attached to an extension pole. Work quickly in the direction of the grain. Allow the paint to dry and recoat if necessary.

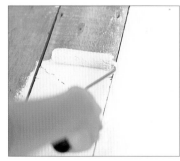

Use a roller to paint the floorboards in the direction of the woodgrain.

Electric sanders

Make sure that you hire sanders from a reputable firm who will explain the safety drill and controls before you start. Most hire firms hire floor sanders and edging sanders as a package that you pay for by the day or the weekend – you will pay extra for the sanding disks and belts. It is essential to wear ear plugs, a dust mask and goggles while operating the machines. Also, tape a plastic dust sheet over the door to the room in which you are working, to prevent the sawdust from spreading to other rooms.

Stripping and finishing floorboards

Large electric sanders can look a bit off-putting, but make stripping floorboards a much less arduous task (see box, left).

Tools and materials

Electric floor sander

Abrasive paper – from coarse-grade through to fine

Wire wool, cloth and white spirit

Floor finish

Paintbrush

1 Fit the floor sander with coarse-grade abrasive paper. Position it in the corner of the room so that you will be able to work your way across the room in diagonal strips. Holding the machine by the handle, tilt it back so that the sanding belt is off the floor. Turn the machine on and lower the machine so that the sanding belt makes contact with the floor. Begin pushing the machine forward immediately because if you leave it stationary in one place, it will sand a deep gouge in the floorboards. When you reach the end of the room tilt the machine back and reposition it to sand the next strip. Work your way diagonally across the room. Change to medium-grade abrasive paper and work your way back across the room at right angles to the first direction.

Use the sander in a diagonal direction across the floor.

2 Use the edging sander around the edges of the room, working your way through the grades of abrasive paper. Finish tricky internal corners by hand with wire wool and a little white spirit, or with the pointed end of a shaped electric sander. Complete this task before finishing off with the drum (step 3) so that you will avoid walking across the finished boards unnecessarily.

Work around the edges of the room using the edging sander.

3 Finish off with fine-grade abrasive paper fitted to the drum sander and work your way backwards and forwards along the floorboards in the direction of the grain for a really smooth finish. Allow the dust to settle, vacuum thoroughly then wipe away any residue of sawdust with a cloth dampened with white spirit.

Finish the sanding by fitting the drum with fine-grade abrasive paper.

4 Seal with the finish of your choice. There are a large number of different varieties of floor finish available: the most hardwearing types are oil-based with a gloss finish; acrylic-based finishes dry more quickly making it easier to complete the job in a single weekend. Some finishes are completely clear while others are tinted, stained or dyed, which will subtly change the final colour of the floorboards. Apply the floor finish with a large, good quality paintbrush working from the corner of the room towards the door. Leave the finish to dry completely and then reapply if necessary.

Apply your chosen floor finish with a good quality paintbrush.

Tongue and groove wood and laminate flooring

Tongue and groove flooring is available in many different varieties. The most expensive is solid wood, which is both attractive and hardwearing, and can be sanded and refinished if necessary. Most manufacturers recommend tongue and groove flooring for every room except the bathroom where water could cause warping. Wood veneer varieties are mid-priced and have a surface of real wood on a composite base. Laminated designs vary enormously in price – the really good quality ones are virtually indistinguishable from real wood and they are also almost indestructible.

When laying laminate, some systems require the tongue and groove joints to be glued and left overnight to dry. The newest varieties on the market simply click together and can be walked on immediately.

Tools and materials

Laminate and underlay
Handsaw or jigsaw
Plastic spacers and tool
Hammer
Metal S-shaped tool
Quadrant beading
Mitre saw
Panel pins

1 Unpack the flooring and leave it in the room in which it is to be fitted for 24 hours – this allows it to acclimatize to the temperature. If possible the skirting boards should be removed. This will allow the expansion strip to be fitted underneath. If it is not possible to remove the skirting boards, a quadrant beading will be needed to hide the expansion strip. Lay the manufacturer's recommended underlay – this usually consists of a polythene damp-proof layer followed by a cushioning foam layer.

Lay down the foam underlay before you begin.

2 Cut the first board using a sharp handsaw or jigsaw, following the instructions on the packet. Place the cut end in the corner of the room with the cut end against the wall. Use the recommended wood glue applied sparingly into the groove of the floorboards.

3 Continue adding planks of flooring following the pattern set out in the instructions. Use plastic spacers around the outside edge of the floor in between the boards and the wall (or skirting if it has remained in place). This will become an expansion gap. Use the plastic tool provided to join the planks by tapping gently with a hammer.

Join the planks together by tapping on the plastic tool with a hammer.

4 When you get to the end of a row of planks, hook the metal S-shaped tool over the edge of the last plank and gently hammer against the other end of the tool to fix the plank in place.

Use the S-shaped tool to fix the last piece of floor into place.

5 Repeat the whole process for the next row of planks and continue until the floor has been laid using the same method. Then remove the plastic spacers and push the cork expansion strips between the last plank and the wall (or skirting).

Lay down the cork expansion strips between the last plank and the wall.

6 Replace the skirting board, or fit quadrant beading against the skirting, using panel pins, to cover the expansion gap. Cut the quadrant with a mitre saw to fit internal and external corners.

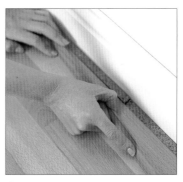

Fit quadrant beading between the flooring edge and skirting boards.

Laying laminate flooring

Do not attempt to lay one of the more expensive tongue and groove floors yourself as you may actually invalidate the manufacturers' guarantee if you make a mistake. The cheaper, laminate varieties are relatively easy to fit yourself with a bit of planning (see steps, left).

Below: Tongue and groove flooring creates a clean and contemporary look.

Curtain poles

Curtain poles are available in wood or metal and in a multitude of finishes. They are often used in conjunction with curtain rings, which fit onto the pole. The hooks on the curtain heading are then suspended from a small metal loop at the bottom of the ring. Curtain poles are held on brackets, which are attached to the wall or a wooden batten about 15cm (6in) above the window. Special poles with flexible or angled sections are available to fit angular bay windows. Generally curtains on poles are simply drawn by hand, although some more expensive tracks are 'corded' – opened and closed with a cord system.

Fitting a curtain pole with concealed fixings

Tools and materials

Tape measure

Spirit level

Curtain pole

Fixing plates and brackets

Masonry bit and drill

Screwdriver

Curtain rings

1 Use a tape measure and spirit level to mark the positions of the brackets in pencil. The brackets should be at equal distances from the corners of the window. Poles over 2m (6½ft) long should also

Use a screwdriver to fix the plates securely in place.

have a central support bracket to prevent bowing. Use a masonry bit to drill the holes, then plug with suitable wall plugs. Screw fixing plates firmly in position.

2 Slot the wooden bracket over the fixing plate then tighten the screw, which anchors it in place.

Fix the wooden bracket in place over the fixing plate.

3 Fit the pole in position with the curtain rings in place. Remember to leave a ring on the bracket side of the pole to hold the curtains in position. Tighten the small screw on the underside of the bracket, which holds the pole in position.

Secure the bracket and curtain pole with a screw.

Curtain tracks

Curtain tracks are an alternative to poles and are available in plastic or heavy-duty metal. Tracks are suitable for awkward rounded bay windows. Curtain tracks have hooks, which are looped through the curtain heading tape and slide along the tracks. Corded tracks, which work on a pulley system,

are available. Most tracks simply slot onto brackets screwed into the wall or onto a batten.

Tools and materials

Tape measure

Spirit level

Drill

Wall bracket

Screwdriver

Hack saw

Curtain track

Curtain hooks

1 Use a tape measure, spirit level and pencil to mark the position of the brackets at equal intervals. Drill, plug and screw into place.

Screw the wall brackets to the wall at equal intervals.

2 If necessary use a hacksaw to cut the track to the correct length, then fix the end stop in place by tightening the small screw.

After cutting the track to length, fix the end stop in place.

3 Finally, slot the track into place on the brackets following manufacturer's instructions.

Measuring curtain lengths

Decide on the length of the curtains: either to the floor, sill or above a radiator. (It is a good idea to buy or make curtains slightly too long to allow for any shrinkage during washing.)

For sill and radiator length curtains, measure from the track or ring mark to 5mm (¼in) above the sill or heater and add a hem allowance. For floor length curtains, measure to 1cm (½in) above the ground, to allow for carpet clearance, and add a hem allowance. For floor draped curtains that have a generous overflow and break over the carpet or floor, measure to the floor and add 5–10cm (2–4in) plus the hem allowance.

4 To hang the curtains, simply hook the metal or plastic curtain hook over the sliding runners.

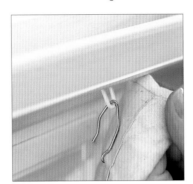

Slot the curtain hooks onto the integral sliding runners.

Fitting tension wire

This is a recent invention, which gives lightweight curtains a modern look. Steel wire is stretched on a tension system between walls, or on brackets. The curtains are held on small rings with pincer-style clips, which grip the fabric and slide along the wire.

Tools and materials

Tension wire

Wire cutters

Alan key

Drill

Screwdriver

Wall brackets and cover pieces

Curtain rings and pincer clips

1 Cut the tension wire to length with a pair of wire cutters and use the Alan key provided to fix the end piece in place at each end.

Once you have cut the tension wire to length, fix the end pieces in place.

2 Drill, plug and screw the two wall brackets in place on opposite walls.

Use a screwdriver to fix the wall brackets in place on opposite walls.

3 Screw the cover piece in place over the wall bracket. Feed the curtain rings onto the wire and then fix the other end to the opposite wall. (If you are using tab-top curtains, thread them onto the wire first.) Pull the wire tight.

Fix the torpedo-shaped cover pieces over the top of the wall brackets.

4 Use the pincer clips attached to the rings to secure your curtain panel in place.

Attach the curtains to the rings using the pincer clips.

Alternative window treatments

Curtains and blinds are not the only methods that you can use to screen or dress your windows – the only limit is your imagination. New, exciting materials to treat glass are available allowing you to create your own etched or stained glass effects. If you prefer something more substantial shutters are a good solution and give your windows a bit of additional security.

Shutters

Although most traditional shutters are made from wood, they can be made from a variety of materials including perspex, MDF and metal.

Tools and materials

Tape measure

Shutters

Screwdriver

Hinges

Bradawl

Spirit level

1 Measure your window carefully and order the correct size shutters – the supplier will advise on the best way of fixing them to your window. Screw hinges in equidistant positions from the top and the bottom of the shutters.

Fix hinges halfway between the top and bottom of the shutter.

2 Use a bradawl to make pilot holes then screw the hinges in place at the top and bottom of the window.

Screw the hinges to the side of the window.

3 Fit battens to the sides of the windows if required. Check with a spirit level to ensure that they are straight.

Creating a frosted window panel

Frosted windows can give bathrooms a more contemporary look than old-fashioned textured glass. Using spray-on frosting gives a temporary finish that will stand up to cleaning but can be removed with a sharp blade if you feel like a change. If you want a more permanent type of frosting, you can commission a personalized sandblasted design from a glazing merchant or get a signwriting company to custom make a design on frosted sticky film.

Temporary frosted finish

Tools and materials

Glass cleaner

Cloth

Glass etch spray

Clean the window thoroughly with glass cleaner to remove grease and grime. Spray the glass etch evenly all over the window. Use two thin coats rather than one heavy coat to avoid runs.

Spray glass etch onto the window, ensuring an even coverage.

Semi permanent frosted finish

Tools and materials

Glazier's frost film

Straightedge

Sharp craft knife

Cloth

Squeegee

1 Cut the frost film to size with a straightedge and craft knife. Wet the window with a damp cloth.

Use a damp cloth to wet the entire surface of the window.

2 Peel off a corner of the backing film and position the frosted film in position in one corner of the window. Gently peel away the remainder of the backing.

3 Use a good quality squeegee to smooth the film gently in place – the water will act as a lubricant. Use the squeegee gradually to force all bubbles away to the sides of the film, leaving it smooth and wrinkle free.

Use a squeegee to remove all the air bubbles from beneath the film.

Below: Shutters are not only an attractive window dressing, they can also increase security.

Fires and fireplaces

Fireplaces were once the sole source of heat in a room. Now they are mainly decorative as central or underfloor heating provide warmth. There are ornate period fireplaces, the classic architrave style surrounds and modern versions using gas flames and ceramic shapes to create the effect of a real fire.

Types of fireplaces

Although there have been many innovations in the world of heating, with hot air and central heating and the revival of underfloor heating, there is something special about the glow of an open fire that still holds universal appeal. The flicker and appearance of the flame may still look to us as it did to prehistoric man, but there have been many developments in how the fire is fuelled and laid. Coal and wood are traditional fuels whereas in most cities gas and electricity now supply the power. The modern 'fake' fire is often chosen over the traditional variety because it provides all the colour, glow, flicker and warmth without the soot, ashes and effort of having to light the fire and refuel it.

Early log fires consisted of chunks of wood laid on an earthen hearth but sometimes the wood was raised up from the floor by resting it on fire irons or fire dogs. This allowed the air to circulate through the wood. Later fire dogs were replaced with a basket then a grate. The latter comes with a façade that forms a panel inside the surround. Fire baskets are now placed on a non-combustible base made of marble, stone or granite.

Structure of a fireplace

Fireplaces usually come in two main sections: the surround and the jambs. The surround is made from stone such as limestone and marble or wood such as pine. The jambs are the two upright sides of the fireplace, which often have foot blocks at the base. The jambs line up on either side of the opening to support the shelf, which runs across the top.

The details found on large fireplaces include a mantel, a fire front and the grate (the cast iron

Below: The jamb (the upright part of a fireplace) can be engraved to match other architectural features in the room such as a dado or cornice.

Below right: An open fire makes a dramatic feature in a contemporary 'hole in the wall' fireplace.

Left: *This elaborate carved fireplace is a focal point of this dining room.*

Below: *When choosing a fireplace, ensure that it will suit the décor of the rest of your room. This impressive example would look good in a large period-style room, but might look out of place in a small, minimalist setting.*

part), which holds the coal or wood. The hearth is the area inset into the floorboards and is often made of stone, marble or tiled, which protects the flooring from falling coals. In bedrooms you usually find smaller fireplaces, cast in one piece out of molten iron and called 'registers'.

In recent years the fireplace has been reinvented so you will find that a basic 'hole in the wall' look is becoming popular.

Fireplace style

Fireplaces vary widely in style from the roughly hewn oak or timber beam with a brick or stone interior in a rustic home or farmhouse to ornately carved marble in a period house. Surrounds can be simple with little detailing or highly ornate with swags, cameos, mythical scenes, recesses, foliage and urns carved into the jambs and shelf. The most important thing when buying a fireplace is to choose a style, size and shape that sits comfortably within the

Right: *In the summer months, you can create a display in your fireplace, such as these logs.*

room it is to be positioned in. If the room is small then opt for a neat, simple design that will be a focal point but not overwhelm the space. If the room is large with period features then try to match the decoration of the fire surround to the other features in the room and choose a material that is also in keeping.

The classic style of fireplace with jambs, columns and pilasters is still popular and found in many homes today. The salvaged originals command high prices and even modern reproductions are far from cheap. Marble fire surrounds are among the most expensive, but a cheaper pine or more inexpensive carved wood surround can be painted to look like marble. Pine can also be stained and waxed in order to give it the appearance of a richer wood such as mahogany.

Some modern fires use geometric ceramic shapes called 'geologs' that sit in a stainless steel or black geometric grate.

Gas flames flicker around the 'geologs', which come in matt black, orange, blue, green and yellow. Or you can choose to have flames coming from a hearth of pebbles.

Restoring or replacing your old fireplace

Putting a new fireplace into your home has its own set of complications whereas reviving one that has been boxed in or painted over by a previous owner provides a different agenda. If an old fireplace has been boxed in you may be lucky and find that it is in good condition and needs nothing more than a thorough clean. However, if it has been painted over then it will require some work to restore it.

First of all you need to establish what sort of material the fireplace is made from. In an area near the wall on the base of the footblock, take a sharp knife and scratch away the upper layers until you come to the original surface.

Once you have established what it is made from you should be able to find a proprietary paint stripper or peeler that will remove the layers of paint (see pages 90–1 for further details on how to do this).

Modern gas fires can run off mains or bottled gas, will have automatic ignition and a flame failure device as well as oxygen depletion sensor.

Looking after your fire

With real coal and log fires the chimneys should be regularly swept by a professional who works to an authorized code of practice – otherwise soot will build up and may lead to a chimney fire. Smoky fires can be caused by the material you burn, such as damp logs, or perhaps through poor ventilation. Another reason can be the incorrect ratio of distances between the hearth, the chimney opening and the chimney top. This latter problem can only be remedied by a professional who may raise the hearth, add extra height to the chimney or put a baffle or shield on the front of the hearth.

Dressing your fireplace

There are a number of dressings and accessories associated with the fireplace, including the fender. This is a metal frame that prevents coals that spill out of the fire from falling onto the carpet. In Victorian times the small border fender grew into a surround with leather padded ends that doubled as a stool.

Fire dogs may no longer be required for their original purpose of supporting burning logs off the earth floor, but they can be a decorative feature and may now be used to prop up a fire poker, tongs and shovel.

Even when the fireplace is not being used, you can employ the mantelpiece or shelf as a focal point and decorate it accordingly. In the summer months the 'black hole' can be camouflaged with a screen, decorative tray or panel. Or, place a wicker basket of logs in front or an arrangement of branches or wild grasses. You could also make a decorative feature of the space by placing church candles or a display of fossils and pebbles in it or, in an unused grate, by storing books or magazines in it.

Safety tips

For safety, always have a secure firescreen or guard that can be placed in front of a fire when children are in the room or if a real fire is to be left unattended because lumps of lit coal or logs may tumble out onto the floor in front of the fireplace. You may consider installing a fire alarm to give you ample warning should a fire start. Carbon monoxide alarms are also available and can be a useful check on air level.

You should also ensure that there is good ventilation around your fireplace. Most companies working with modern fittings will insist on there being an air brick in the wall of the room where a gas log fire is installed to ensure a through flow of fresh air.

Left: *Marble is a particularly attractive material to use for fireplaces.*

Fireplace techniques

Restoring an existing fireplace or installing a new one will require the services of a professional, if you want it to function as a fire. However, there is nothing to prevent you from preparing a reclaimed fireplace ready for its installation. Make sure that the grate you have chosen will fit your chimney breast. If there is no breast then you could always construct a simple surround yourself, which will be used for show purposes only.

Safety tips

Ensure that you wear thick household gloves when applying paint stripper, and take care not to splash any on your skin.

If you are painting a working fireplace do not paint the parts that will come into direct contact with the fire. You must also ensure that you choose paint that has been specially formulated for heat resistance for the surround.

Restoring fireplaces

Original fireplaces that have been overpainted for many years lose the sharpness of their details. If you have a chimney breast that is missing a fireplace, then it is often cheaper to buy an unrestored one from an architectural salvage company rather than installing a reproduction. In either situation it is well worth spending the time and effort to strip the surround and restore it carefully in a sympathetic manner.

Before starting the restoration, identify the material from which the fire surround is made. The most common materials are wood, cast iron, marble, stone and brick while in houses built in the 1920s and 1930s decorative fireplaces were stepped tiled designs often holding electric fires. Each material needs to be treated differently during restoration. Wood surrounds can be stripped using chemical paint stripper in a gel or paste form. Stripping with a heat gun is less advisable because of the danger of singeing. Cast iron can be stripped using a heat gun but beware of scraping the surface, which is prone to scratching – the best option is to use a paste stripper, which peels off gently.

Marble, stone and brick are porous materials that are therefore prone to staining so check the recommendations of any chemical stripper before you use it on your fireplace.

Wooden fire surrounds

Tools and materials

Chemical paint stripper in gel or paste form
Heavy-duty rubber gloves
Paint scraper
Fine-grade steel wool
Neutral wax polish and soft cloth

1 Apply the paint stripper according to manufacturer's instructions – use a paint scraper to push the stripper into any crevices and mouldings. Leave for the manufacturer's recommended time when the paint will bubble.

Use a paint scraper to push the stripper into the crevices.

2 Remove the paint carefully with the paint scraper and reapply stripper if necessary. Remove any stubborn traces of paint using liquid stripper dipped in fine-grade steel wool. Neutralize the wooden surface by wiping with a rag moistened with white spirit.

Use the paint scraper to take off the stripper and paint layers.

3 If you want to achieve a natural finish sand the surface lightly with fine-grade abrasive paper then simply apply a neutral wax polish with fine-grade steel wool. Allow this to dry then polish with a soft cloth.

Apply a neutral wax polish and, once this is dry, polish with a soft cloth.

4 If you prefer a painted to a wooden finish, apply a quick-drying primer/undercoat and gently sand with wet and dry paper. Finish with a satinwood paint of your choice. Apply two coats and sand with wet and dry paper between coats.

Cast iron registers and grates

Tools and materials

Liquid or gel chemical stripper

Old paintbrush

Heavy-duty rubber gloves

Paint scraper

Fine-grade wire wool

Stiff wire brush

Rust-inhibiting solution

Grate polish

Soft cloths

1 Apply the paint stripper thickly, following manufacturer's instructions, using an old paintbrush to work it well into any crevices.

Apply the paste stripper to your fireplace using an old paintbrush.

2 Wait for the recommended time to elapse. When the paint begins to blister and bubble remove the stripper and old paint carefully with a paint scraper, taking care not to gouge or scratch the surface.

Use a paint scraper to take off the layers of stripper and paint.

3 Re-apply where necessary – remove any stubborn paint residue with fine-grade steel wool dipped in stripper.

If there are some stubborn areas, use steel wool and liquid stripper.

4 Before re-finishing the fireplace remove any rust. First brush away any flaky rust and corrosion with a stiff wire brush.

Remove any rust and corrosion with a wire brush.

5 Paint on a rust-inhibiting solution – choose one that also inhibits new rust forming. Leave for the recommended time, then clean with fine-grade wire wool.

Use the old paintbrush to apply a rust-inhibiting primer.

6 To retain a cast iron finish, apply black grate polish with a shoe brush or cloth.

Apply black grate polish with a soft cloth.

7 When the polish is completely dry, use a clean soft cloth to buff to a graphite sheen.

When the polish is dry, polish to a graphite sheen with a soft cloth.

Above: A cast iron fireplace restored to its former beauty is a magnificent addition to any room.

Painted finish

For a painted finish on a cast-iron grate, first apply a rust-inhibiting undercoat/ primer, which is formulated for ferrous metals and allow to dry. Apply two coats of your chosen paint colour.

Changing fireplaces

If you wish to restore a working fireplace to a chimney breast that has been boarded up or is inactive, then it is important to get professional advice. You will need to have the flue checked for obstacles and ensure that the fireproof lining is intact. A chimney that has been unused for several years will almost certainly need to be swept. A simple test to see if a chimney is 'drawing' properly (removing smoke) is to hold a lit spill in the opening – the flame should be noticeably drawn upwards. If the flame splutters or dies completely it clearly indicates a lack of oxygen, often caused by blockages further up the chimney.

Once your chimney and flue are in working order you can then consider the type of fireplace you wish to install. A gas fire is a popular choice for many people. Many cities also have a smoke ban, meaning the only coal that can be burnt on an open fire is an expensive smokeless variety. However, real fires are appealing if you live in an area without a smoke ban as nothing can beat the evocative smell and sound.

Period fireplaces are not to everyone's taste – heavily tiled, dark marble and overly ornate fireplaces can dominate a room and make it difficult to create a contemporary look. However, many people consider removing a period fireplace as sacrilege and before taking this drastic step you should consider carefully how it could affect the value of your home. Period features are a highly sought after selling point and, although it may not appeal to you, your period fireplace could be highly appreciated by the next owners. If you find a fireplace too overpowering to live with consider less drastic ways of disguising it.

Painting over a tiled fireplace

Victorian and Edwardian fireplaces often have tiled 'slips' set into a cast iron insert. If the colours of these tiles are not to your taste they can be painted over in a more neutral shade. 1920s- and 1930s-style fireplaces, which are often tiled in murky colours, can be painted in the same way to make them less obtrusive.

Tools and materials

Tile cleaner/detergent and cloth

Tile primer

Specialized tile paint or gloss/satinwood paint

Two small foam rollers and trays

Low-tack masking tape

Wet and dry paper

1 Clean the tiles thoroughly to remove any traces of dirt or grease. Mask off the tiles that are to be painted.

2 Apply the tile primer sparingly to avoid drips using a foam roller. Allow to dry. If the pattern or colour has not been covered apply a second coat.

3 Sand lightly with wet and dry paper. Apply the top coat using a foam roller and allow to dry. Sand again lightly with wet and dry paper before applying a second coat.

Making a simple MDF surround

This plain surround will not dominate a room but provides a focal point to display a few carefully chosen items. It can be used to dress up a bare chimney breast where there is no working fireplace or be made to fit over an existing fireplace that you do not like. This type of surround is purely decorative and should not be used in conjunction with a working fire.

Tools and materials

Paper and pencil

One sheet of 18mm (¾in) MDF

Several lengths of square planed timber

Electric jigsaw

Electric screwdriver with countersink bit

Screws with countersink heads

Mirror plates

Rawlplugs

Masonry drill bit

Wood filler

Paint of your choice

Straightedge

1 Sketch out a plan for your fireplace, taking into account any existing fireplace you wish to cover. The dimensions will vary according to the width of your chimney breast. If there is no existing fireplace the new version should sit comfortably in the available space, allowing about 30cm (1ft) of space each side. Draw out the components of the new fireplace on the sheets of MDF. You will need a front piece, two side pieces, three inside pieces and a top piece cut from the 18mm (¾in) MDF. Use a straightedge clamped to the MDF to make accurate cuts – alternatively ask your local timber merchant to cut the pieces for you. Cut lengths of timber to frame the opening and outside of the fireplace.

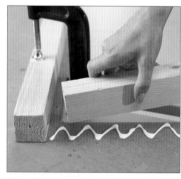

Glue the frames to the fireplace and fix in place with a clamp.

2 Apply wood glue and clamp the timber frames to the outside and inside of the front piece of the fireplace.

3 Make pilot holes and use a countersink bit to screw the pieces together. Screw the outside and inside panels in place in the same way.

Screw the panels in place using a screwdriver.

4 Fill all the screwholes with wood filler, allow to dry then sand until smooth.

Fill all the screw holes that you have made with wood filler.

5 Prime and then paint in a colour of your choice using a paintbrush or roller. Leave it until it is completely dry. Sit the new fireplace on the hearth that has been cut from a piece of thick MDF, then attach to the wall using mirror plates screwed to the inside of the fireplace. Once the fireplace is securely fixed in place on the wall, touch up any areas that need additional paint.

Prime and paint the fireplace in a colour of your choice.

Fitting a salvaged fireplace

When shopping for a salvaged fireplace, take the dimensions of the existing hole with you so that you can ensure the new fireplace will fit. Try to choose a style appropriate to the age of house that you live in if you want it to look original. Consult period-style books for advice on what to look out for (if you have neighbours living in houses built at the same time who have original fireplaces, take photographs for reference). If you want the fireplace to be a working one, consult a builder or gas fitter before purchasing a fireplace. Make sure that a salvaged fireplace is complete – it can be tricky finding items such as grates to fit your particular fireplace if they are missing when you buy it. Decide on a material for the hearth, which should be sympathetic to your chosen surround. If you are choosing a wooden surround your salvage merchant should be able to recommend a cast iron insert to fit.

Tools and materials

Brick bolster

Mallet

Mortar

Electric drill with masonry bit

Suitable wall plugs and screws

Screwdriver/electric drill bit

One-coat plaster

Plasterer's trowel

Stiff brush

Spirit level

Abrasive paper

Emulsion (acrylic) and paintbrush

1 Remove the existing hearth material. If it is concrete, chip it out with a brick bolster but, if tiled, use a blunt chisel to lever them up. Mix up a dryish mortar and apply it to the hearth, using a piece of timber notched to the thickness of the new hearth material as a depth gauge.

2 Lay the new hearth material in place and tamp down firmly with a rubber mallet, using a spirit level for accuracy. Allow the mortar to harden. Mark the position of the new fireplace in the centre of the chimney breast. Note the height of the fixing plates and use a brick bolster to remove some plaster from around the fixing. Make a hole with a masonry bit, fit a Rawlplug and screw in place.

3 Use a plasterer's trowel to apply a one-coat plaster mix over the fixing; allow it to harden slightly before levelling off with a dampened trowel. Sand and then paint.

Below: You can paint your fireplace or retain the original stone finish.

Architectural features

Many architectural features started life as purely practical fixtures – an architrave around a window helped to hold it in place and reduce drafts, picture rails were used to hang pictures and protect the soft plaster walls while dado rails would prevent furniture from chipping or cracking paintwork.

Ancient influences

It is said that the level of the dado and picture rails, as well as the cornice and skirting, echoes the various levels and elements of a classic Greek or Roman column. This reference to classic style shows how many of the traditional elements of interior design are based on ancient logic, form and scale.

Decorative mouldings

Mouldings have always played a fundamental role in the quality period house. On a practical level they were usually applied to conceal the join between the wall and ceiling, and on a decorative level they added relief and embellishment to plain areas.

There are various types of moulding, which are generally applied in three main areas. Firstly, the cornice, which is positioned over the join between the walls and ceiling. Secondly, the skirting, which runs between the wall and floor. Thirdly, the architrave, which is found between the door surround and the wall.

As well as their practical purpose, mouldings were also used to add to the grandeur and status of a room. This can be clearly seen in the panel work and ceilings in grand period homes and important civic buildings.

Skirting boards

Although decorative moulding is rarely found in modern homes, skirting and skirting boards have survived the test of time because they are still practical. They not only provide a neat join between wall and floor, but also protect the plaster and paintwork from knocks from feet and furniture. They can also be used to hide wiring or even a safety deposit box.

Above right: Well positioned lighting may be used to highlight ornate mouldings.

Restoring or adding mouldings

To restore existing ornate plasterwork, it is best to employ a professional. For smaller cracks and touching up, you may be able to do it yourself with a thick mix of filler. If your mouldings suffer from years of overpainting, take the time to strip them back.

If you have a room without any such features, then you can add simple detailing with coving.

Coving is a straightforward plaster curve that arcs between the wall and ceiling – simple and cheap versions of these are easily glued in place and then painted over. Ceiling roses and cornicing at the upper levels of a room are not subjected to close scrutiny, so cheap imitation products can work well. Fine wooden beading can also be used to create panelling on doors and walls.

Dado and picture rails

In some classic or period style homes you will find that walls are divided and decorated with dado and picture rails. Originating in the 18th and 19th centuries, these rails had a practical purpose too. The dado rail, which is roughly at hip height, protected the fragile wall finish of the time (which was made from horse hair, lath and plaster) from being damaged by people or furniture banging or bumping against it.

These days dado rails are often employed for purely cosmetic or decorative purposes, to divide up a large expanse of wall or to create a two-tone or bi-coloured scheme for a hall or staircase. You can also create interest by using different textured wallpaper above and below the rail. A dado rail can easily be applied to a wall using both glue and screws.

The picture rail was also a functional feature in such homes, providing a hanging point for pictures. Today, pictures are hung from deep brass clamps that clip over the thickness of the rail, which is now often metal. Modern picture rails tend to stand proud of the wall rather than being an integral part of it.

Staircases

In many period houses the main staircase was often a show piece with decorative carved wood or iron balustrades (the vertical supports for the handrail).

In modern homes, the staircase is not just a means of getting from one level to another, it is a way of making the most of available light. Light from a skylight above can filter down through many levels if the staircase is of an open construction. As such, high tension steel wire, like yachting rigging, and reinforced glass panelling is popular for the sides of staircases.

Restoration and decoration

If you are restoring or repairing an existing staircase you may need to replace some of the balustrades or change them completely. Wood is the most common and cheapest material used for these supports and it can be fashioned either into simple, four-sided pillars or more ornately carved and turned spindles. When it comes to decorating, the wood can be left plain, painted or stained.

Iron is also a common feature of period houses – staircases used to be edged with ornate balustrades. Iron balustrades can be found through salvage specialists or new ones can be made by a blacksmith. The last balustrade on a flight of stairs is usually finished with a thicker post, which is often decorated with a knob or carving.

Left: Splitting colour above and below a picture or dado rail will help you to break up a large expanse of wall.

Below: Staircases need not just be a practical feature – be bold and make a feature of them.

Fitting stair carpets

When it comes to decorating a staircase safety must be foremost in your mind. Whichever floor covering you choose, it should be well fitted so that there is no overhang or surplus on the nose or edge of the step. This is the surface that is most prone to wear as it receives the brunt of the weight and frequent rubbing from the soles of shoes. If it is ill-fitting it may also cause someone to slip.

Architectural features techniques

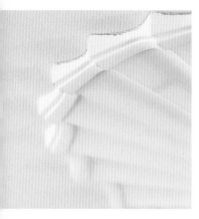

Many people are put off by the prospect of adding architectural features to a room because they think that this may entail major structural work. In fact the opposite is true – it is relatively easy to fit mouldings and wall panelling. Make sure that you opt for an architectural feature that is in keeping with your style of house. For example, while a traditional wall panelling may look stunning in a period house, it may look out of place in a contemporary style interior.

Fitting decorative mouldings

Most decorative mouldings are fitted using the same methods. In period houses these mouldings were simply nailed into wooden plugs, which were fixed into the masonry. Recent advances in adhesives mean that nails can be replaced with adhesive applied with a mastic gun. Alternatively you can countersink small screws into the mouldings and fill with wood filler. The most important device to master is using the mitre block, which allows you to cut perfect internal and external corners.

Putting up a dado rail

Tools and materials

Tape measure

Mitre box

Hand or tenon saw

Mastic adhesive

Panel pins and hammer

Drill with countersink wood and masonry bits

Screws with countersunk heads

Rawlplugs

Chalk snap line

Pencil

Wooden mouldings

Pliers

Filler

1 Use a tape measure to measure the length required and cut using the mitre box to achieve an internal or external corner.

Use a mitre box and saw to cut the corners.

2 Use a spirit level and tape measure to mark a straight line to indicate the position of the bottom of the moulding. If this moulding is a dado rail like that shown here, then it should be positioned about a third of the way up the wall from the floor. Use a pin hammer to tap a line of small panel pins gently along the length of the line.

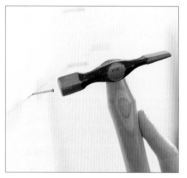

Tap a line of panel pins along the line marking the bottom of the moulding.

3 Apply the adhesive with a mastic gun along the entire length of the wooden moulding.

Use a mastic gun to apply adhesive to the moulding.

4 Press the wooden moulding firmly into position against the wall. The panel pins will support it and hold it firmly in place while it dries. Leave the moulding until it is completely dry.

5 When the moulding is dry, remove the panel pins from below the moulding carefully using either a pair of pliers or the end of a claw hammer.

Use pliers to remove the panel pins when the adhesive is dry.

6 Fill the holes that are left behind with a quick drying ready-mixed filler.

Putting up skirting boards

Tools and materials

Tape measure

Mitre box

Hand or tenon saw

Drill with countersink wood and masonry bits

Nails and screws

Rawlplug

1 Measure and cut the boards as above. Pre-drill holes near the ends and the centre of the boards.

Drill holes near the ends and centre of the skirting boards.

2 Use a nail to mark the corresponding position on the wall.

With a nail, mark the corresponding position onto the wall.

3 Drill holes with a masonry bit and tap a plastic Rawlplug in place. Glue as shown above but use screws to ensure a firm fixing, fill and sand screw holes before painting or staining with a colour of your choice.

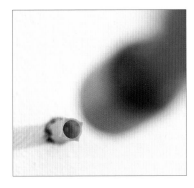

Tap a Rawlplug into place before fixing the skirting board in position.

Wall panelling

Wall panelling is a common period feature in older houses. It reached the height of popularity in Georgian times when the main reception rooms of a house were often panelled up to dado height. By Victorian times panelling had become rarer and was made of softwood, which was then painted to mimic more expensive hardwoods.

Putting up tongue and groove cladding

This common wall panelling is made up of thin planks of wood, which slot together with the tongue of one plank fitting into the groove of the next. It is an excellent way of covering up a less than perfect wall surface and is commonly used to update kitchens and bathrooms as it can be treated with a water-repellent varnish. It can be painted to suit any colour scheme or given a clear finish, which allows the grain to show through. There are various types of tongue and groove cladding: some incorporate a rounded bead between each plank. Most types of tongue and groove can be fitted vertically or horizontally, and it can be used on ceilings as well as walls.

It pays to buy quality tongue and groove cladding as the cheaper, thinner varieties tend to warp and bow. It can be fitted using a variety of methods including secret nailing into the tongue of the boards. Some varieties have special 'clad clips', which are metal fixings holding each board in place. For quick results you can also use panel adhesive to stick the boards directly onto the wall. Vertical tongue and groove cladding is usually finished off with a skirting board at the base and a rounded or hockey stick moulding on top.

Tools and materials

Spirit level

Timber battening

Jigsaw

Tongue and groove cladding

Wood screws

Rawlplugs

Nail punch

Long panel pins or panel adhesive

Pin hammer

Neutral colour wood filler

Hockey stick or right-angled moulding

1 Decide on the height of your tongue and grooving – it is available pre-cut to dado height – and cut it to size if necessary. Use a spirit level to mark two lines on the wall, one towards the top and the other towards the bottom of where the cladding will sit. Cut the battening to size then drill, plug and screw it in place along the marked lines.

Screw the battening, checking that it is straight with a spirit level.

2 If your room has external corners, use one as your starting point so that any cut boards will be hidden in the corner of the room. Start with the groove of the board lined up with the external corner. Use the pin hammer to knock the panel pins in place and a nail punch to make sure that the heads of the panel pins are knocked below the surface of the wood. Fill with a neutral colour wood filler.

Use a nail punch to knock the head of the pin below the surface.

3 Continue along the wall and when you reach the corner cut the tongue off the final board to ensure a good fit. To turn the corner butt the groove of the next board against the previous board and pin in place.

4 To turn an external corner, cut the tongue of the first board and butt it up to the groove of the previous board to form a neat corner. Cover the corner with a piece of right-angled moulding.

Use a right-angled moulding to cover external corners.

5 When the cladding is complete cap with lengths of hockey stick or right-angled moulding mitred at the corners and held in place with panel adhesive or panel pins.

To finish the cladding, apply lengths of moulding to the top.

Plaster mouldings

This term encompasses all the different types of decorative details in the home that are made from plaster and plaster composites, including coving, cornice, ceiling roses, corbels, pediments and niches. They are commonly found in period houses. If you have damaged mouldings it is possible to have them copied by specialist firms who will make a mould from a cast of the existing moulding and reproduce it. This can be a costly process, but there is a wide range of standard mass-produced reproductions available.

Putting up plaster coving

This will help to soften the gap between wall and ceiling. There are lightweight varieties available made from a number of different materials. It is advisable to choose the most authentic looking design for the style of your house – an ornate period style coving will look out of place in a contemporary interior. If you do not feel confident about mitring corners, some manufacturers make internal and external corner pieces, which fit snugly over the gap.

Tools and materials

Paint scraper

Straightedge

Spirit level

Adhesive

Plaster coving

Filling knife

Small nails or panel pins

Decorator's caulk

Mastic gun

1 Remove any loose or flaky areas of plaster or paint and use a straightedge and spirit level to mark the position of the coving on the wall and ceiling to provide you with guidelines.

2 Mix up the adhesive following manufacturer's instructions and butter it onto the back of the coving using a filling knife.

3 Press the coving firmly into position on the wall and gently tap small nails or panel pins above and below it to support it while the adhesive dries.

4 Remove the nails and fill the resulting holes. Use excess adhesive or flexible decorator's caulk applied with a mastic gun to fill any gaps between the coving and the wall/ceiling.

Fitting a decorative ceiling rose

Ceiling roses were traditionally positioned above the light fittings in period houses. When fitting or replacing a ceiling rose it is important to identify the position of the joists to make a firm fixing. You can do this by lifting up the floorboards in the room above, or by using a bradawl to pierce the ceiling until you find one. There are also various electronic gadgets available that locate the presence of metal in walls or ceilings, which may help you in this task. Make sure that if there is a working light fitting in the position where you want to fit the ceiling rose that you turn off the mains electricity supply and disconnect the fitting before you start drilling in the area.

Tools and materials

Ceiling rose

Pencil

Drill with countersunk drill bits

Specialist plastic coving adhesive

Screws with countersunk heads

Screwdriver

All-purpose white filler

1 Hold the ceiling rose in position and draw around it using a soft pencil.

Hold the rose in place on the ceiling and draw around the shape.

2 Drill holes to accommodate the wiring for the light fitting (if required) and also make a hole on one of the flat areas on each side of the rose.

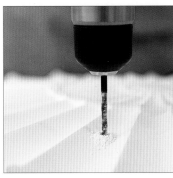

Drill a hole on a flat area on each side of the ceiling rose.

3 Mix the adhesive following the manufacturer's instructions and then press the rose firmly into position on the ceiling.

Mix up the adhesive and spread it to the back of the rose.

4 Use two long countersunk screws to support the rose. Screw them directly into the joist. Fill over the screw head with white filler.

Use countersunk screws to fix the rose securely in place.

Left: An elegant cornice such as this can add the finishing touch to your wall.

Living
rooms

Planning your living room

A living room is a relaxing space where family and friends meet but it is also a public room where the interior decoration should make a statement. As such, planning is essential – for example, furniture should be arranged in sociable groups yet without obstacles blocking any pathways through the room.

Planning your space

Unless you are fortunate enough to have a den or private space where you alone can closet yourself away, the main focus for daytime relaxation in the home tends to be the living room. But the living room is a hybrid space, often a public venue where, at certain times, guests and friends are entertained. It is also a family room where group, as well as individual, rest and leisure time is spent.

Because the living room is a shared space, it is usually the focus of communal family gatherings and a place where a number of activities take place at the same time. Children may play games or watch TV while adults read or listen to music.

As well as being adaptable for day-to-day family life the living room should also be able to cope with the changes that are brought about between

Below: It important that the main pathway through the living space is free of clutter and obstacles so that a person entering can reach their destination easily.

being a night and daytime venue as well as a summer and winter location.

During the day the room should be a bright and enjoyable place to be, lit by natural light. In the evening, with curtains or blinds closed, the emphasis is on a more cosy and secure environment. During this time, different levels of lighting that are focused on the various recreational tasks and activities that take place in the room are important.

In the summer, the room should be appealing because it is cool and fresh and in the winter, a comforting place into which you can retreat, leaving the cold and dark outside.

As such the planning and furnishing of the space needs to be thought out carefully so that the room can cope with these various requirements and levels of wear and tear.

History of the living room

In centuries gone by, the furniture in the living room was arranged around the walls. This, the main entertaining room, was a formal place for people to gather and talk, so the centre of the room was left empty to enable people to walk around or stand still and converse.

Later, in Georgian and Victorian times, the living room was a drawing room or salon in the homes of the wealthy and the middle classes. This room was used only for special entertaining or for adult family gatherings. The drawing room, or more properly with-drawing room, was the place that the ladies withdrew to as the men smoked cigars and drank port after a meal. In more humble homes this room was known as the parlour, but nevertheless it still had the formal, rather straight-laced approach to relaxation time.

Above: *This traditional room has chairs and sofas arranged near a natural light source.*

Left: *You can make the most of period features in your living room, such as this elaborate fireplace, and draw attention to them by arranging seating nearby.*

Creating play areas

It is useful for children to have their own play space. In an ideal allocation of rooms the play area should be separate from the bedroom so that it is not associated with play or entertainment at all.

If children can have their own play area this will give them freedom to make noise and play without restrictions. It will also leave the main living area for mostly adult use. In turn, this allows the living space to be clearer and the decoration more orientated towards relaxation.

However, you can create a play area within a living room by using a screen or mobile divider to partition off an appropriate space.

In grand houses the drawing room was often on the first floor and in some modern homes this layout has been adopted in order to make the most of a view or to raise the room above street level and car noise.

Instead of the nursery, play room, morning room, study and parlour being separate spaces and in different parts of the house, some or all of these functions are now housed in the living room. A lot more is expected of the contemporary space and, in turn, the general decorative style has become more simple and streamlined. Beneath the layout, however, storage and planning has become more complex.

An effective layout

Current interior design thinking advocates making rooms within rooms, and this can work well in a large living area. Furniture and rugs can be used to delineate different areas. For example, if there is a fireplace then that will probably be the focal point of the room around which people gather. The fireplace area can be defined by a large rug on which a U or semi-circle arrangement of sofas or armchairs are placed around a central coffee table. The U shape may have to be broken to allow access, but its outline marks the sociable area, where people will sit.

Arranging seating

Make an effort to avoid long or continuous lines of seats – this is visually uninviting but also makes it difficult for a group of people to communicate. Arrange chairs and sofas so that they form a unit enabling people to talk to those opposite them or at an angle to them. Also, avoid placing small tables between every chair or setting a chair in a space on its own because this creates a barrier between those sitting in the main seats and a feeling of isolation for those on their own. The backs of the chairs and sofas form a visual barrier, making suggested walls enclosing the space in front.

Elsewhere in the room, perhaps by a window or French doors, there could be a chaise or recliner that is specifically placed on its own, denoting another 'room' reserved for private reading or contemplation. In a different area there could be a TV and bean bags or a small two seater sofa for children to sit on and watch TV or play with games.

By dividing the room into sections you can accommodate various requirements. The only problem that will occur is in volume control when all three divisions of the room need to be used at the same time – this is when headphones can be useful.

Another configuration that works well is the extendible seating unit: this can be L-shaped with a short side in front of the window (so as not to block out too much light) or near a wall and the long back of the seats placed across the open room. The open end of the sofa, without an arm, makes it accessible and open to those arriving in the room. This configuration does not create such an enclosed space as the U shape, but the long back of the sofa or the backs of a similar arrangement of chairs still

provides a delineation between one part of the room and another. The corner of the L also creates a small, more intimate space where people can sit side by side to talk.

Another option is the parallel line configuration. This lines up a matching pair of sofas or a sofa and two armchairs on either side of a fireplace or central room feature. This provides two equally sized and spaced seating areas that connect face to face.

Heavier pieces of furniture such as sofas and armchairs can be supplemented by lighter, easier to manoeuvre chairs that can be kept against a wall or in an arrangement by a table or light and brought into the main space when guests arrive. In a small apartment or living area these chairs could be foldaway. Chairs without arms look less bulky.

If your setting is contemporary or you want a feature chair, then opt for a work of a classic, modern designer – such as Arne Jacobsen's series 7 chair or the Tom Dixon's S chair.

Adjustable and adaptable furniture is important in a living room. There may be times when you need to clear the centre of the room for a drinks party or social function. Some chairs and smaller sofas can be moved more easily if put on castors or wheels, which enable them to be pushed without much effort. The wheels or castors may need to be placed in cups – solid plastic dishes that fit under the wheels – to protect a deep pile carpet or valuable rug.

Positioning tables

Smaller pieces of furniture, such as tables, should serve as useful accessories rather than clutter the limited space or become obstacles to easy movement.

Opposite far left: This U-shaped configuration of built-in seating maximizes a small space and forms an intimate salon away from the main living room.

Opposite left: A raised area in a bay window creates a private sitting place with a 180-degree view.

Above: The sofas in this room are arranged in an inviting manner so that people can talk to each other easily while relaxing in a comfortable seat.

buy a table that incorporates laminated or reinforced glass, which are both tough and resilient and can withstand most knocks and bumps.

Another style of table that is useful in a living room is a console table, which has a narrow format. Traditional styles are supported by brackets fixed to the wall while modern console tables are usually free-standing.

Subconsciously many people prefer to sit with their backs to a wall and to have a clear view of anyone entering the room, but in a circular or group arrangement of chairs and sofas this is not usually practical. To create a barrier between the back of a sofa and an open space behind, a console table can be placed so that it butts up to the back of the seat. This creates a screen or small wall-like feature, which makes the sitter feel less vulnerable and the room less open. The console table is also an area where small displays of photographs or treasures can be displayed, but the number of artefacts should be limited so as to avoid it becoming cluttered and a hazard for people walking past.

Above: This period-style room has a large ottoman for books and a small console table against one wall for ornaments.

Right: This coffee table is positioned within easy reach of the daybed, so that the person seated there can reach it without getting up.

Opposite: In a split-level space like this it is important to have schemes that work together because you can see both areas at the same time. Here the spot decorated cushions act as a link between the upper and lower levels.

The positioning of side tables is particularly important. To encourage and promote relaxation, a table should be within easy reach of the person in an armchair or on a sofa. For example, a good reading light should be to hand on a table in order to avoid eye strain. There should also be space where a drink can be placed or where a book, newspaper, pen or pencil can be laid. To meet these requirements you may need a series of small tables, which are more formally known as occasional tables. Or, you could use a nest of tables – tables of graduated sizes that fit one on top of another. When selecting or buying this type of table, ensure that it is at the right height for the chair. In a family room the tables should also be robust with good solid legs to make them resilient to the occasional knock or bump.

Glass-topped coffee tables are extremely popular because the material is attractive to look at and can make a pleasant feature in a room. However, it may be dangerous so make sure that you

Above: *A radiator cover can be used as a display surface instead of a side table.*

Below: *The layout is arranged so that there is room to move between the tables and chairs.*

It is worth thinking carefully about where you place your tables, and how many of them you use. If you have a long wall with a doorway in the centre, or a fireplace with space on either side, then you can position a table on either side of the feature and use it to support a pair of table lamps or a pair of artefacts such as marble columns or large glass vases. The pleasing nature of matching items appeals to our sense of symmetry and proportion, which alludes to Classical style.

Traffic paths

One of the most important factors in arranging a busy area such as a living room is to work out the traffic paths. People will need access from one side of the room to another as well as to bookcases, TV and other elements within the space. Your priority should be to avoid arranging the main seating area so that it has a path of through traffic, entering and exiting, as this will be disruptive for those sitting there and awkward for those passing through.

Try to map out the areas where a clear pathway is necessary and arrange the placement of the furniture to accommodate this. If the room is small then there may be only one main thoroughfare, but in a large room there may be several routes. The journey around a room should be simple and easy to execute, not an assault course of low stools, haphazardly arranged side and coffee tables and baskets of newspapers, magazines or logs for the fire. Try to place small objects adjacent to the large one they are meant to be used with. For example, slot a foot stool under a seat or coffee table so that it is out of the way when it is not in use. A log basket should be set right beside the fireplace. Baskets of magazines and newspapers should be regularly edited so that only a few relevant issues are kept.

Focal points

In a living room a focal point, such as a fire or a particular painting, can be attractive as well as reassuring. There should be at least one object that draws the eye and on which the mind can focus. This helps in the calming procedure and the process of unwinding, as well as providing a centre of attraction for the space.

If the fireplace is the focal point of the room, the area around it should be well planned. The space directly in front of the fire may be a hearth or stone block

Left: *The fireplace is the focal point in this room and the side table and pictures have been arranged symmetrically on either side to bring the eye back to the centre point.*

Above: *This small, modern niche fireplace breaks up an expanse of wall and, although there is no traditional fire surround, a single painting hung above the fire alludes to a more conventional setting.*

that protects the floor from sparks. To either side you could build seats under which you could have cupboards. These seats would allow the sitter to use the wall as a back support and should have a padded cushion on the base to make it comfortable. Scatter cushions or a covered pad suspended from hooks or a pole attached to the wall would also work well. In a contemporary setting this could be a low, wide wooden shelf that doubles as an occasional sitting area as well as a place for display.

In a traditional style of sitting or living room there are often deep recesses on either side of the chimney breast. These areas are commonly filled with bookcases or cupboards at the lower levels and with shelves above. In a classic setting the top shelf may be finished off with a decorative feature such as a pediment or broken pediment. This is a triangular or pyramid-shaped feature originally used to crown the top point or level of an important Grecian or Roman building. The arrangement of shelving can vary in width to accommodate differing heights of books and artefacts but the shelves should be equally spaced on either side of the chimney breast so that they form a continuous line. Having them staggered or at irregular distances will upset the harmony and balance of the layout.

If the fireplace is opposite a window, an appropriately framed mirror can be a useful feature to reflect and increase the effect of the daylight. The space opposite a fireplace could alternatively be used to display a painting or print. As this wall space is usually quite substantial in size the picture could be large. Although elsewhere in the room groups of pictures may be arranged to create a feature, the area above the fireplace is generally reserved for one single, impressive image.

Incorporating sounds and scents

Scents and sounds can be used, like colour, to create the perfect atmosphere. Scents are very personal – some people love a room richly scented with perfumed room candles and the oriental aromas of sandalwood and musk, while others opt for the fresh smells of pine, lemon, lime and orange peel.

Sounds can be therapeutic and relaxing too. The soft tinkle of a water feature outside a window or the gentle movement of wind in the branches of trees serve as a reminder of nature and open spaces. A favourite piece of music played at a gentle volume can be all that is required after a busy day of ringing phones and traffic noises.

When framing an overmantel mirror or picture, take a reference for the frame from the fire surround itself. If the surround is simple with geometric or linear detail then the frame of the picture should complement that. On the other hand, if the fire surround is ornate (such as carved with swags and cherubs), then the picture frame you choose can also afford to be a lot more decorative.

If your living room doesn't have a fireplace, there are other ways to create a focal point. Firstly, the arrangement of furniture will draw the eye to a certain point in the room. For example, if the majority of chairs and sofas are arranged around a coffee table, then that will become a focus. A piece of sculpture or art that is well framed and highlighted by a picture or task light will also draw the eye.

A room that has no focus will feel unsettling and vacant, but if you want to opt for a minimalist style of decoration then use colour to create interest. In a room that is all white or decorated in neutral colours, a bowl of bright red flowers on a table or a group of vivid blue cushions on the end of a sofa will catch the attention of the person entering the room.

It is best to keep the focal point at standing eye level. If you use a mat or rug then too much attention will be drawn to the floor. Or, a wildly coloured central lightshade will cause people to look up, rather than at your feature.

Communal living areas

The living area of a home may also be linked to another room. It is increasingly common in contemporary homes for an open-plan living area to incorporate the dining and/or kitchen space too. The barriers and walls that once divided these different rooms are being knocked down to provide large, through spaces. These large, all-in-one living areas need to be linked by decoration because it looks odd if the kitchen is a cool, minimal contemporary scheme while the sitting area is decked out in full-blown Victorian drapes and rich colours. The key is to find a base colour that works in all areas and then use accessories to vary the tempo and mood in each space.

Opposite top: *This contemporary radiator has a sculptural quality and sits low on the floor so does not interrupt or impinge on the wall space.*

Opposite bottom: *This centrally positioned contemporary fireplace brings the focal point of the room away from the walls and in to the centre. It is a useful way of dividing up a large room and creating a cosier sitting area in a corner, rather than in the middle of the space.*

Left: *This vibrantly coloured scheme works well because of the natural light that pours in through the wall of sliding glass panels.*

The simplest way is to choose a neutral base scheme, for example, a beige or pale grey for floors and wall, throughout, with white woodwork and detailing.

Using colour

To create a truly relaxing environment you need to think about colour. Depending on the size of the room, your character and your likes and dislikes, you may find that rich warm colours help to create a calm atmosphere. Deep reds or dark blues can be enveloping and give a sense of security, but conversely these colours may also make some people feel boxed in and uneasy, especially in a small space. Those who prefer lighter colours may find a mousy, mid-brown or a muted shade of green much more comforting and relaxing.

You may, however, choose to paint your living room white. There are actually many shades of white available today that have a hint of another tone – for example stone-white, which is slightly muted with grey, and sand white, which has a soft brown tinge. These off-whites prevent the walls from becoming too stark and clinical, while still providing a minimal background.

At-a-glance colour guide

Traditional colours that suit sitting rooms are red, against which gilt-framed pictures and mirrors work well, blue, which is attractive with silver accessories and bottle green, which is often associated with Victorian private clubs and gentleman's studies.

Mid-shades such as yellow and magnolia are classic and help to bring a subtle form of light and colour to a room while still providing a presence in the background.

Contemporary sitting rooms often have white or off-white walls.

stencilled

autumn leaves floorboards

Use this simple idea to create the illusion of colourful autumn leaves that have been blown in by the wind. You will need to start off with new or unfinished floorboards that can be washed white. Then simply gather fallen leaves and flatten them for a few days inside a heavy book before using them as templates.

Materials

Pressed leaves of various shapes and sizes

Piece of glass

Acetate sheet

Wood filler

Wood wash in white, terracotta, amber and driftwood grey – buy ready-made or use a diluted emulsion (acrylic)

Spray adhesive

Satin floor varnish

Tools

Chinagraph pencil

Stencil cutter

Filling knife

Fine-grade abrasive paper with sanding block or an electric sander

Large brush

Stencil brushes

Fine paintbrush

Positioning the leaves

1 Space the flattened leaves out and place a piece of glass over the top of them.

Tracing the leaves

2 Place the acetate sheet over the leaves then use a chinagraph pencil to draw around each of them.

3 When the stencil cutter has heated up, use it to trace along the pencil lines. Then carefully remove the waste pieces of acetate and throw them away.

Smoothing the floor surface

4 Fill any holes or dents in the floorboards with wood filler and sand until smooth.

Applying the wood wash

5 Apply white wood wash in the direction of the woodgrain over the floorboards.

Fixing the stencil to the floor

6 Use spray adhesive to stick the stencils to the floor.

Colouring in the leaves

7 Dab the coloured wood washes with a dry stencil brush and apply, working away from the edges of the stencils.

8 Use pale grey wood wash to paint shadows. Allow to dry then varnish with satin floor varnish.

Space out your chosen leaves in a row so that you can place a piece of glass over them.

Put a piece of acetate over the top and draw around the leaves with a chinagraph pencil.

Once you have filled any holes or dents with wood filler, sand the surface until smooth.

Using a large brush, apply white wood wash over the whole surface of the floor.

For a realistic effect, paint shadows on the leaves, ensuring that they fall in one direction.

creating
your own wall art

Finding the perfect piece of artwork to complement your interior can be difficult, so why not create your own? You don't have to be a talented artist, just choose colours that inspire you and work well together. You can buy ready-made canvases but it is much more economical to stretch your own canvas before you begin to decorate it. And don't be afraid to experiment with colour and texture. You can create impact by hanging several similar-sized canvases side by size, or create one giant canvas that will give dramatic impact to your room.

Materials

4 x 2.5cm (1½ x 1in) timber

Hardboard offcuts

Panel pins

Fine-gauge artist's canvas

Gesso primer

A selection of emulsion or artist's acrylic colours

Low-tack tape

Texturizing medium

Coarse sand

Gilt transfer leaf

Tools

Mitre saw

Jigsaw

Hammer

Scissors

Staple gun

Spray gun and water

Paintbrushes

Palette knife

Establishing frame dimensions

1 Decide on the dimensions of your frame and then cut the four pieces of timber to length with a mitre saw to ensure snug mitre joints.

Making the frame

2 Cut the hardboard into triangular pieces using a

jigsaw. Then butt the corners of the frame together and place the pieces of triangular hardboard over the top of the joints. Use panel pins in order to secure the hardboard in position.

Stapling the canvas

3 Cut a piece of canvas that is large enough to fit over the

whole frame. Then secure the canvas on the reverse of the frame using a staple gun (see picture bottom left, page 116). You should work systematically around the frame, pulling the canvas taut to ensure that it is evenly stretched. You should also make sure that the corners of the canvas are neatly folded under.

Use a mitre saw to cut the four pieces of timber, ensuring the joins are tight.

Position the triangular pieces of hardboard over the timber joints and use panel pins to fix.

Know your materials

• Gesso is a white, plaster-like substance, used to seal the absorbent surface of the canvas before painting. It gives a smooth, fine surface to work upon.

• Texturizing medium is similar in appearance to Gesso but is thicker. When mixed with paint or pigment it enables you to build up a thick 'impasto' or textured relief, giving the work a three-dimensional quality.

• Gilt transfer leaf is a thick layer of metal backed with greaseproof paper that allows you to position the leaf accurately before peeling away the backing.

Preparing the canvas

4 Spray the canvas with a fine mist of water to make the cotton fibres shrink slightly. This will improve the overall tension of the canvas. Once dry, prime it with two coats of Gesso primer and then allow this to dry for approximately one hour.

5 Paint the entire canvas, including the edges, with a base coat, which will be the dominant colour. Allow to dry.

Applying colour

6 To add a block or stripe of texture mask off an area with low-tack tape. Then mix your second chosen paint colour with texturizing medium and apply this to the canvas with a flat palette knife. Before the medium has set, pull away the tape so that you avoid pulling away dried paint.

Adding texture

7 When the second colour is dry, mask off different areas of the canvas. Choose another paint colour and mix coarse sand into it. Apply this to the masked off areas and allow to touch dry.

8 Add the finishing touches with gilt highlights. To do this, press squares of gilt transfer leaf onto areas of paint while they are still tacky. Smooth the squares down with your fingers then peel off the backing paper.

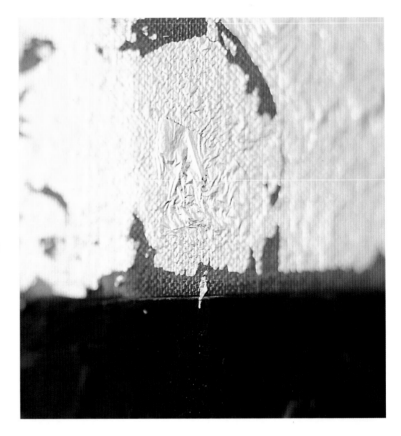

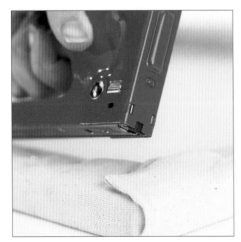

Staple the canvas into place on the back of the frame using a staple gun.

Paint the whole surface of the canvas with Gesso primer and allow it to dry.

Choose your dominant colour and cover the whole canvas with it.

Alternative

A single, large-scale painting can look just as effective as a group of smaller paintings. Creating a canvas of simple stripes in colours that compliment your interior is an ideal way of using up leftover household paint.

A quick alternative to stretching your own canvas is to use a piece of lightweight MDF instead. This can be fixed to the wall using screw eyes or mirror plates.

Lightly sand then seal the MDF with a base coat of multi-purpose primer or a slightly diluted coat of standard emulsion (acrylic) before you begin. Choose the colour that you wish to dominate the painting and apply it with a brush or small roller to the MDF surface and allow it to dry. Decide where you would like to position your stripes, then draw them in lightly with a soft pencil using a set square. Mark out the stripes using low-tack masking tape, then apply the different colours. Finally, you should pull off the masking tape before the paint dries completely.

Mix your second colour with texturizing medium and apply it using a flat palette knife.

Mask off various areas of the canvas and apply paint mixed with coarse sand into them.

Use gilt transfer leaf as a highlight over the design and then peel off the backing paper.

decorative

screen with coloured panels

This practical screen has many uses in the living room. It is both light and easy to move and the semi-translucent panels make it suitable for positioning in front of a window if you require extra privacy during the day but do not want to lose any light. It is also excellent as a room divider, so can be used to screen off a dining or home office area. We have constructed the screen using simple butt joints and used a natural beech woodstain to colour the frame though you may prefer to paint or stain it in a darker shade. Feel free to experiment...

Materials

12 lengths of 1.8m (6ft) planed 5 x 5cm (2 x 2in) softwood timber

Wood glue

Wood screws

Wood filler

Square beading to form the rebates

Panel pins

White spirit

Beech varnish

8 sheets of polypropylene in various colours

9 flush hinges

Tools

Paper and pencil

Handsaw or electric jigsaw

Set/combination square

D cramp

Drill

Screwdriver

Palette knife

Pin hammer

Medium- and fine-grade abrasive paper with sanding block

Cloth

Paintbrush

Sharp craft knife

Staple gun

Planning the screen

1 Start by drawing a plan of your screen. To work out the spacing of the horizontal battens multiply the thickness of the timber by six. Take the resulting number away from the height of vertical uprights. Now divide this number by five to find out the internal height of each square. (If you are using the suggested timber this measurement should be 30cm/1ft). Use a sharp handsaw or electric jigsaw to cut out each of the 16 horizontal battens. The vertical lengths should also be 30cm (1ft) long. Cut these out in the same way.

2 Mark the final positions of the horizontal battens on the vertical timber lengths using a set square.

Fixing the joints

3 Clamp the joints together using a D cramp, then drill a pilot hole in the centre of each

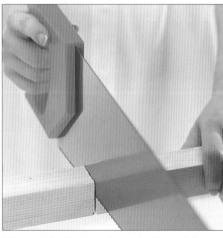

Work out the lengths of each batten and then, using a handsaw, cut them to size.

With a pencil, mark the positions of the horizontal battens on the vertical lengths.

Know your materials

Polypropylene is a type of plastic sheet, thin enough to cut with scissors or a craft knife but stiff enough for use in this screen project. It comes in a variety of translucent and opaque colours and textures. Because light filters through it, it is also suitable for making modern lamp shades, window hangings and mobiles. It is readily available from all good art materials suppliers.

joint using a small wood bit. Make sure you use a countersink bit to ensure that the screw head sits beneath the surface of the wood. This is important because you don't want the screw heads to be visible on the finished screen. Spread a thin layer of wood glue over the joint then make sure the screw is firmly in place. Continue this process at each joint until all the panels are complete.

4 Fill the countersunk screw holes with a neutral coloured filler. Allow the filler to dry (following manufacturer's instructions), then sand the surface smooth.

Fixing the rebate battening

5 Cut the rebate battening to the required lengths. (You will need eight pieces per screen square.) Use a pin hammer and

panel pins to fix the battening in place, slightly inset, around each square in order to form a rebate on the front of each panel. (Blunt each panel pin by tapping the point with the hammer as this will help to prevent splits in the wood.) The second set of rebates will be fitted later to hold the polypropylene in place.

Varnishing the screen

6 Sand the whole surface of the panel frames thoroughly using medium- then fine-grade abrasive paper wrapped around a sanding block. Once you have finished, remove any remaining sawdust with a cloth that has been dampened in white spirit. Next, apply beech varnish to the panel frames using a 2.5cm (1in) paintbrush. Allow the varnish to dry and then lightly sand over the areas as before. You should

now apply a second coat of the varnish in exactly the same way.

Stapling the sheets

7 Carefully cut the sheets of polypropylene so that they will fit neatly over each square. Use a sharp craft knife to do this. Then fix the sheets in place against the rebate using a staple gun. For a tidy finish you should now fit the second set of rebates in place on the back of the screen using the pin hammer as before.

Assembling the panels

8 Fix each screen panel together to create the large screen. This should be done using three flush hinges screwed at equidistant points along the length of each panel. Hold the hinges in place and mark the positions of the screw holes. Drill holes and screw the hinges firmly in place.

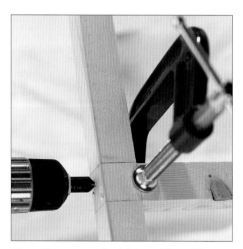
Use a D cramp on the joints and then drill a pilot hole to fit a screw to hold them together.

Fill the countersunk screw holes with a neutral coloured filler and leave it to dry.

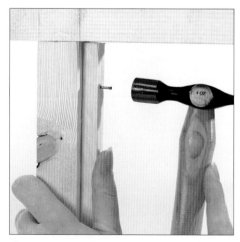
Cut the rebate battening to the correct lengths and then hammer them into place.

Alternative

Decorative screens can make ideal display panels for photographs – you can make a simple display screen using MDF.

Get your timber merchant to cut one 2.4 x 1.2m (8 x 4ft) sheet of 12mm (½in) MDF lengthways into three equal pieces. Mark out the five photo apertures, and the feet at the bottom of each panel using a pencil and set square. Drill a pilot hole in the inside corner of each square then use a jigsaw with a sharp blade to cut out the apertures and around the feet. Sand lightly then apply several coats of black eggshell paint with a small paintbrush or mini gloss roller and allow to dry. Get a glazier to cut sheets of clear perspex or safety glass about two centimetres (just under an inch) larger than each of the apertures. Enlarge all your photographs so that they are the same size as the glass or perspex. Cut stiff cardboard to fit to the back of each and use metal mirror corner plates to fix the glass, photograph and cardboard in place on the back of the screen.

Sand the panel frames, apply two coats of beech varnish and allow to dry.

Cut the polypropylene sheets to size and then staple them to the rebate battening.

Use three flush hinges on each panel and screw them into place to complete the screen.

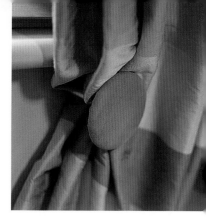

Furnishings and textiles

Furnishings and textiles are like the make-up, shoes and belt that go with a dress – they are the finishing touches that create individual style and appearance. Furniture should be selected for comfort, quality and shape, while textiles can introduce fashionable or seasonal colours and patterns.

Choosing your furniture

The type of furniture you choose for your living area should be conducive to relaxation. When trying to imagine a place for unwinding, the first thing that comes to mind is a huge, squashy, enveloping sofa, but this type of seat can be uncomfortable and detrimental to your relaxation.

Finding the right sofa

You should take your time and try out plenty of sofas before buying one. You may want to rush out and buy the inviting-looking squashy sofa mentioned before, but there is often no proper lumbar support on this type of seating, unless of course you lie flat on it and arrange cushions to provide specific underpinning to the right areas of your body. If the seat is too deep then you will perch on the edge, sit back and tuck your legs underneath you to provide an anchoring point or dangle your legs, unsupported, in the air. If two people sit beside each other on an overlarge sofa they tend to 'sag' towards each other or end up slumped up against an arm at one end, which means that their spines will be curved and unsupported as a result.

A smaller two seater sofa with a seat that is just deep enough to accommodate you comfortably in the sitting position it a better choice. It may not look as inviting as an oversized three seater, but it can be more comfortable and ultimately more relaxing too.

Armchairs and footstools

Similar criteria also apply to a single armchair. Big, deep, cosy chairs may look the best but in fact a neat, upholstered and well proportioned chair will be better for you in the long term as it gives you good support.

The ideal relaxing sitting position should allow the feet to rest lightly on the floor, with an angle of slightly more than 90 degrees between the hips and the lumbar region of the spine. The back of the chair should support the whole length of the spine as well as the base of the head. If the seat is too low you will feel the need to cross your legs, which is bad for blood circulation.

Upholstered furniture with arms not only makes you feel more enclosed and secure in the seat but also helps you get in and out

Below: Choose a sofa carefully – it mustn't be too big or it will overpower the room, but at the same time it mustn't be too small or it will look lost or insignificant in a large space. The most important thing, however, is to choose one that has proper lumbar support for the spine.

of a chair. For older people, a chair with a high frame and raised arms that meet the elbow will make it easier to get in and out of.

'Putting your feet up' has long been an expression used in conjunction with having a rest, and there is a lot of truth in it. For those who spend a lot of time standing at work or around the house, or people with leg problems such as varicose veins, putting their feet up while sitting is beneficial. An ottoman or footstool at the same height as the edge of the seat of the chair is ideal as your legs will be straight out in front of you. If you have a circulatory problem in your legs it can be beneficial to raise the height of your extended legs above your hip level for some time to help blood flow. There are a number of chairs designed with retractable footrests, which slot neatly into the base of the chair when not in use, but are easily raised by means of a lever at the side of the chair when wanted.

Electrical considerations

Television and video equipment are almost always located in living rooms today. The positioning of such equipment is very important, not only for aesthetic reasons but also for your health. Firstly, try to avoid glare on the screen, which can cause eye strain and headaches. Also, reduce the effect of the radiation given off by the screen by sitting well back from it. Radiation diminishes by the square of the distance and a minimum of 180cm (6ft) is suggested. The level of light when watching TV should also be regulated. The intensity of light in the room should be similar to that emitted from the screen. It can be detrimental to your vision to watch TV in a dark room (see Lighting your living room, pages 134–5).

Another electrical consideration is the management of wires and cables in living rooms. There will be flex for table lamps and lampstands, for TV, hifi and other electrical items, which all require access to a socket and a clear route to their base. Never overload a socket, especially with adapters – by all means use one single adapter to extend the use of a single socket to two plugs, but don't put one adapter into another because you may not only overload the circuit and cause the power to trip the fuse,

Above: A sofa with high arms is easier to get in and out of. Cushions on sofas can be used not only to provide colour but also support.

Above: Fun fabrics, such as this Dalmatian print, are ideal for accessories where they can be used in moderation.

Right: A simple, bucket chair offers good support and has a raised shape.

Below: *Raw silk cushions have an interesting slub texture and a soft sheen.*

Below right: *By mixing shapes, you will bring a change of emphasis.*

but you may also, inadvertently, cause an electrical short circuit, which could start a fire.

If running electrical wire, such as a flex for a side light, under a rug or carpet, ensure that the cable is properly insulated and that it does not run directly under a wheel, castor or any other sharp or heavy object that may cut or damage the wiring or its casing.

Textiles

Textiles and textures play a vital part in encouraging relaxation. However, the practical element of wear and tear must also be kept in mind.

Upholstery

Soft and sensual fabrics such as silk, velvet and wool can be comforting, especially in the autumn and winter when it is icy and dark outside. However, these fabrics are very delicate and

so are best used for incidentals and accessories where they will not become worn.

An increasingly popular material for upholstery and even floors and wall panels in living areas is leather. Leather can be used to cover traditional as well as more

contemporary furniture. This material is great for upholstery as it is soft but hardwearing.

If you choose to upholster your furniture in pale shades, ensure that the fabric has a stain-retardant or repellent finish. Light colours can form a good neutral background to a room but will easily become stained and marked. These protective finishes create an invisible coating on the fabric, preventing spillages from soaking into the weave or texture of the fabric and making it easy to wipe them clean.

Another option is to have loose or removable covers. These are fitted to the shape of the chair or sofa but can be removed by unzipping or untying. Depending on the fabric, loose covers can be machine washed or dry cleaned. The main thing to be wary of with loose covers is to check that they are prewashed or shrink tested. There is nothing worse than trying to refit a loose cover after it has been washed and discovering that it has shrunk! Dry cleaning is usually the safest option. Manufacturers make many textiles suitable for upholstery in heavier weight such as woollen weaves, jacquard and damask self-

patterned designs as well as textured cotton or canvas. When looking in a fabric shop or department, ask to be directed to the fabrics that are specifically designated for this type of use.

Floor coverings

These days living room floors are most often carpeted or covered in a hard surface such as wood. A luxurious, wool or wool-mix pile carpet is still among the most popular of finishes but is best used in a room that is not subjected to heavy use as the pile will eventually wear. Heavy traffic areas or main walkways can be

protected by a rug or runner or by rearranging the furniture from time to time, to expose different parts.

If you use a hard floor such as wood, tiles or stone, you may want to soften the overall appearance by adding a decorative Oriental flatweave mat or rug, such as a kelim or dhurrie. (Remember to include a non-slip backing onto the rug.)

Another popular way of covering a large wooden floor is with a substantial square or rectangle of carpet. This will cover the majority of the floor but leave a rim of wood exposed around the edge of the room.

Curtains and cushions

The fabric used on curtains does not need to be as hardwearing as that for upholstery. However lightweight curtain fabrics usually need to be interlined and lined, and even heavier ones hang and drape more easily if they have a light backing or cotton lining.

Scatter cushions can be round, square, rolled or even triangular. They are decorative, fun elements that can be made from leftovers of material, which links them in to the other furnishing fabrics in the room. Alternatively, they can be made in dramatic, contrasting colours and patterns.

felt rug and

floor cushion

Felt is an increasingly popular furnishing material. It has many advantages as it is naturally eco-friendly (made from boiled wool scraps), warm and does not fray when cut. Felt is not often considered as a flooring material but 6mm (¼in) thick industrial felt is an ideal choice as it is warm, hardwearing and soft underfoot. This patchwork style rug is stitched together using a traditional blanket stitch. It is important to use a non-slip underlay if the rug is to be used on wooden or laminate flooring. For a co-ordinated look add a comfortable floor cushion made using the same method.

Materials

6mm (¼in) felt in three colours (2 x 2m/6½ x 6½ ft of each colour is sufficient for the rug but ensure you also have enough to cover your cushion if required)

Black tapestry wool

Non-slip backing strips (optional)

A cushion pad

Hook and eye fastenings

Tools

Soft pencil

Metal rule or set square

Sharp scissors

Tailor's chalk

Hole punch

Darning needle

Making the squares

1 Mark out three squares of each of the different coloured felts using a pencil and metal rule or set square to ensure they are identical sizes (we have made ours 50cm/1½ft).

2 Cut out each of the felt squares carefully using a pair of sharp scissors.

3 Mark the position of the stitching holes at 1cm (½in) intervals along all of the sides of each piece of felt using a soft pencil or tailor's chalk (see picture bottom left, page 128). Check that the holes will line up.

4 Use a hole punch set on its smallest hole setting to cut out the holes you have marked on each piece of felt (see picture bottom middle, page 128). (The felt is too thick to be pierced with a darning needle.)

Stitching the squares together

5 Thread a darning needle with a double thickness of black tapestry wool. Sew the squares together using a simple over stitch, making sure that they butt

Measure each felt square using a pencil and set square to make sure they are all the same size.

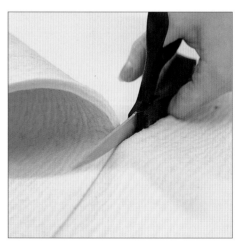

Using sharp scissors, carefully cut out each of the felt squares.

Know your materials

Because of the thickness of the felt used in this project it is essential to punch holes in the material before sewing. We have joined the squares of felt with a simple over stitch that, when pulled taut, tightly butts the two pieces of felt together. This is simply formed by passing the needle from one piece of felt and into the other (see picture bottom right). Traditional blanket stitch has been used to bind the edges and give them a neat, finished appearance. This is formed by passing the needle through the fabric then under the loose thread (see picture bottom left, page 129).

together closely. Alternate the colours of the squares in order to build up the required chequerboard pattern over the surface of the rug.

6 When all the squares have been joined together use a blanket stitch to finish off the outside edges of the rug. Make sure that you join the wool with a neat knot on the underside of the rug otherwise it will eventually work its way undone. You should then position self-adhesive non-slip backing strips onto the back of the rug if it is going to be placed on a hard surface, as it would be difficult to walk on without slipping otherwise.

Making the floor cushion

7 Use the same technique to make the co-ordinating, large floor cushion. It is very

simple to do this: first, cover a large cushion pad with two squares of felt and then join them together securely using the blanket stitch once again. You should then make a slit down the

centre of one side of the cushion using a sharp pair of scissors.

8 On either side of the slit sew on hook and eye fastenings using a darning needle.

With a soft pencil, mark out the position of the holes on each piece of felt.

Use a hole punch set on its smallest setting to cut out the holes.

Use black tapestry wool to over stitch each of the squares together.

Alternative

If your style is more opulent than the simple, understated look of felt adapt the design to use luxurious fabric with beautiful glass bead trims. Affordable beaded trimmings are now available in haberdashery departments and work well alongside rich velvets and silks.

To make an opulent patchwork throw cut out six equally sized velvet squares, with 1cm (½in) seam allowance all the way round. Press them and then pin them together before machine stitching them. Cut a piece of silk or satin backing fabric and a lightweight lining fabric to the same dimensions as the velvet top section. Sandwich the layers right side facing inward. Place the bead trim in-between the layers, lining up the flat edge of the trim with the raw fabric edges. Carefully pin it in place so that when it is turned right side out only the beads are visible. Machine stitch all the layers together almost all the way around, leaving enough of an opening to turn the throw the right side out. Hand stitch this closed using slip stitch.

Finish off the outer edges of the rug using blanket stitch all the way round.

Once you have made the basic cushion, use scissors to cut down the middle of one square.

On either side of the opening, sew on hook and eye fastenings.

Display and storage

Different sizes and types of objects should be treated in various ways to suit their purpose. It is best to store useful, but not necessarily attractive items, out of sight or in an orderly way, while interesting and decorative pieces should be grouped attractively and given prominence.

Storage choices

In a living space storage is important, as it helps to keep order and to make movement around the room easy. Bookcases, freestanding or built-in, are the most usual way to contain books, CDs, videos and general household artefacts. Open shelving gives the easiest access, but is also the most dust-prone arrangement. Shelves contained in cupboards, whether glass or wood fronted, will keep the contents within cleaner for longer.

The secret to success in clutter management is to edit the amount of things you possess to a controllable number, selecting those that you really need or want and then allotting them to a specific space or area. Throw or give the rest away.

Simple shelving systems

Modern storage is usually practical as well as aesthetically pleasing. Even shelves can be of interest in their own right.

Purpose-built and contemporary shelving often appears to hang magically in the air, although it is in fact attached to the wall by concealed pegs and brackets. The most basic, ready-made shelving systems have open, usually prefixed shelves and are made of a cheap timber such as pine, which can be painted or stained for a more decorative finish. Adjustable shelving with support brackets that slot into regularly spaced niches in the uprights are also available.

As well as shelving systems you can buy single shelves with individual supports such as gallow brackets. These are triangular wooden supports that are screwed into both the wall and the base of the shelf with a cross support between the two right-angled legs. Another single shelf option is the fixed steel shelf bracket that consists of two metal legs at a right angle to each other. These strong metal brackets are screwed into the wall and the base of the shelf.

Alcove supports are lengths of wood, preferably with a sculpted or finished front end, that are

Right: This wall mounted CD rack is very striking but also displays the CDs in such a way that they are easy to identify, remove and return.

Left: *A row of small cubic storage spaces makes use of what otherwise would have been an empty space.*

Above: *The upper surface of storage units can be used to display favourite ornaments.*

Decorative shelving

Shelves need not be dull – they can be beautiful architectural features. They can be cut and arranged to form a shape, such as a pyramid, or be 'sculptures' in their own right.

Shelves can be painted the same colour as the wall so that they almost disappear, or painted in a vibrant contrasting colour so that they become a definite feature. Polished or varnished wood can also be used and the wood can be chosen to highlight or emphasize the wood elsewhere in the room.

You can also embellish shelves with a fringe, panel or cut-out, attached to the front edge of the shelf. Another option is a beaten metal strip, such as copper.

screwed into the wall with a glass or wood shelf resting on top. Finally, you can make the support invisible by using a timber or laminated shelf that is grooved or drilled along the back surface. This hollow section slips over dowels or fixed supports into the wall.

Specialized shelving

As well as single or purpose-built shelves there are also more specialized modular and flexible systems, which can be bought from good furniture and office storage suppliers. Many have fine metal frames with adjustable brackets and shelves but will come with additional features such as angled display shelves so that a flat object such as a book or plate can be supported but easily seen on a shelf that is raised at the back. Other options such as cabinet and roll front enclosures are also available. This type of system is usually attached to the wall by brackets and screws so it is fixed and secure.

When planning a set of fixed shelves, calculate the distance between them carefully because once they are in place they are there for good. For example, if a mid-height shelf is to support a TV or hifi system, measure the depth and height of the piece of equipment and allot the appropriate amount of space. Also, look at your collection of books and artefacts and see if they fall into height categories so that you can allocate two narrow shelves for small paperback books and one taller shelf for hardback, glossy art books.

Another popular modular system comes in cubes. These wooden cubes can be empty, with one shelf, two shelves, three drawers or a door. You select the

Right: *The different coloured interiors of this storage system, and the objects within, form several small 'pictures' or points of interest. The concealed internal lighting also highlights objects such as the glass balls and the pyramid.*

Concealing or decorating radiators

Radiators are rarely elegant or attractive, so they are best disguised. Radiators are often placed under windows and, if the window is long and elegant and the radiator small and painted the same colour as the wall, the window will be the eye-catching feature and the radiator hardly noticeable. At night curtains may also be drawn over the radiator.

On the other hand, if the radiator is in a prominent position you may want to cover it up or disguise it. Do this by boxing in the top and sides using MDF or wood. The front should not be completely obscured, so that heat can still flow, so choose an open mesh or decorative fret cut panel.

number of cubes you need to fill your area and then pick the arrangement of storage you want, so tailor making your own system. This style of unit is usually connected across the back so that the units are interlocked, and will form a single freestanding block but for safety, especially if you have an uneven or irregular floor surface, you may also want to secure them to a wall.

Displaying objects

Some of the shelves in your room will probably house small objects and photographs, arranged in a set piece display. These items should be carefully chosen as they are going to be in such a prominent position.

When arranging items you should also think about height and depth – try to avoid having everything at the same level as

this can appear monotonous. A group can be placed so that a taller item is to the back, with a mid-height and small item in front. This sort of display could include a plate propped up against the wall with a bottle in front and a little dish or bowl in the foreground. Above all you should try to avoid clutter – don't let your shelves become places where general household mail,

matchboxes and unframed photographs build up as they will detract from the display items and make the area look messy.

Storage systems can also make wonderful room dividers. A set of freestanding shelves can provide a screen between one part of a room and another without permanently blocking it off.

Open shelves will also allow light to pass through them from one side of a room to another, so maintaining an open and airy feel. Conversely, a shelving system with a solid back will provide a dense screen, which will make a space feel more enclosed and much more private. Bear in mind, however, that unless the shelving unit reaches right up to the ceiling, sounds from each area will still carry.

Practical considerations

When deciding on the type of storage for your room try to identify what belongs where. In the case of a living room this will depend of the amount of space available and the allocation of tasks to the room (see Planning your space, pages 102–3). If it is a multi-purpose room you will need practical elements such as bookcases or shelves and cupboards but you may also be able to introduce decorative storage, for example an antique wooden box or chest, a decorative chest of drawers or a console table with drawers. Consider what your shelves will be supporting – lightweight objects only need light shelves, but heavier things need robust shelving and secure wall fixings.

Try to keep things that you use frequently to hand, and other items that are used occasionally can be stored in a less accessible area or even in another room or the attic. For example, place video and DVD storage next to the TV and CD racks near their player. If the living area is a place for plants and displays, but may also be a space for children to play in, it can be worth providing some higher level shelves or storage so that fragile or breakable objects are placed out of the reach of small hands.

Think about subdividing storage to fit objects into a container of an appropriate size. For example, if you are putting a number of small things into a drawer, consider subdividing the space so that you have several small compartments each containing one or two things that are easily accessible rather than a jumble of objects.

Finally, beware of providing too much storage because any resulting empty gaps in your room will probably have an ominous ability to become full, and not necessarily with useful or beautiful objects either.

Left: *The niches in this decorative display unit are painted in bright colours to create a feature out of them.*

Below: *These deep boxes slot neatly under the coffee table but keep magazines and books close to hand.*

TV cabinets

For those who find the presence of a large black TV screen offensive or distracting, there are purpose-built cabinets and tables that will conceal the box when it is not in use. Behind the doors there is usually a sliding shelf on which the TV rests and beneath are shelves for storing tapes and videos.

Another option is a deep chest, like an old-fashioned blanket box or travelling chest. This unobtrusive oblong box can house a concealed lift, which is operated by remote control.

Or, you could use a console or side table with a lower shelf. Place your TV on the shelf and conceal it with a cloth that hangs to floor level over the table.

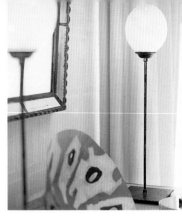

lighting your living room

The lighting in the living room should be variable and flexible so that during the daytime task or reading lights can be focused for close work, while at night decorative and ambient lighting may be used to create a relaxing mood and atmosphere.

Types of lighting

Background or ambient lighting is a substitute for natural light, providing a general level of visibility. On its own this type of lighting is fairly uninspiring.

Task or work lighting has specifically directed beams that provide a localized light in a prescribed area where an activity such as reading takes place.

Accent lighting is a creative light used to highlight colour, texture or objects. It can range from a pin hole fine beam to a broad spot.

Decorative lighting covers anything that is attractive but not necessarily useful as a main source of light, such as candlelight.

Effective lighting

The real skill of lighting design is to have a good balance so that the light can be adjusted to suit every action or event that takes place under its beams. The colour and finish on walls, floors and furniture will also have an effect on the lighting you need in a room. For example, in a room with white walls and few pictures or additional wall decoration, plain light carpets and natural or neutral upholstery, a lot of light will be reflected, so fewer and less high-strength lights will be required. However, if a room has dark walls, a heavy rich carpet and heavily upholstered furniture then more light fittings will be needed, as each of these dark-coloured items will absorb a certain amount of the natural light.

Matt finishes tend to absorb light whereas shiny ones reflect it. Therefore fabrics such as suede, felt and tufted coverings will reduce the effectiveness of electric lighting whereas silk, lacquer work and chrome will give a limited, but useful, amount of light amplification.

Planning your lighting

You need a central or main light that illuminates the room when you first enter it. In a traditional setting this is usually a pendant light. In modern homes, however, this is often replaced with a number of recessed ceiling spotlights or wall lights.

In a living room a general scheme usually includes three or four levels of lighting. The first is general ambient light, which is provided by the pendant and other elements such as wall lights. These can also be wired to a dimmer switch so that the level or brightness can be lowered to alter the atmosphere of the room.

In order to choose the other levels of lighting, you first need to identify specific areas of use in the room. Task lighting may be required if there is a table or a desk in the room, or close to the CD and TV so that you can see the controls. It will also be

Right: Instead of having one small wall light that might get lost in the centre of a vast wall, this group of three forms a sculptural feature.

needed placed near chairs and sofas where newspapers and books are read or knitting or sewing occurs.

You may also want to include accent lighting to highlight a certain feature or collection in the room, such as a picture, glass or a particular plant. These accent fittings can vary from a specific wall mounted picture light to a recessed, ceiling spotlight that has its beam directed onto the chosen object.

The adjustable spotlight gives a broad spread of light to the immediate area but draws the eye to its focus. A strip light or picture light runs along the width of a picture and casts an even light from top to bottom, so illuminating the whole of the picture but not the space around it. Another option is a specialist framing light with adjustable shutters that train the beam of light exactly onto the picture.

Architectural features, such as decorative arches, pillars or a series of beams can also be 'painted' with light. Halogen spotlights or eyeball downlighters are useful to pick out this type of feature and can be particularly effective if the ambient lighting is dimmed to a level lower than the spot.

Using light as a disguise

Although light is usually seen as a way of illuminating things and making them easily visible, it can also be used to disguise areas and, surprisingly enough, to make a room seem more spacious.

By placing larger pieces of furniture away from the walls and locating a couple of tungsten uplighters behind them, the light will reflect off the walls and make the place look larger. You can also focus light away from an area that you don't want to be seen, leaving it in shadow and making it retreat into the background.

Above: *By opening up the roof and installing laminated glass panels the amount of natural light in this room has more than doubled.*

Left: *Classic white plaster uplighters can be painted to blend in with the colour of the wall. Church candles provide additional decorative lighting.*

135

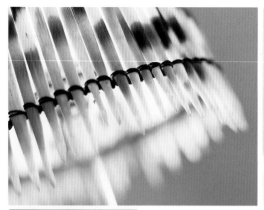
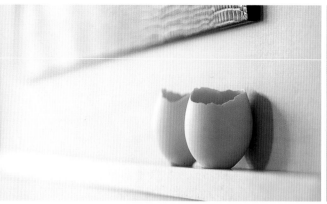

Living room accessories

Accessories are the finishing touches that bring personality and individuality to a room. In a living room these small items all add up to create a complete interior and should be selected for their individual merit as well as their contribution to the overall effect. The choice of accessories will be influenced by your chosen colour and theme, but there may also be architectural limitations to consider, for example, small windows and a deep sill may point you in the direction of blinds rather than curtains; a large expanse of wall may call for decorative, wall mounted lights and a dark or richly coloured room will require more light than a light coloured, bright and sunny room. Even practical aspects such as radiators, door handles and light switches should be thought through as these will all contribute to the general appearance of the room. Radiators, for example, need not be ugly or dominant. There are many discreet low level radiators to choose from and if you already have an large featureless style then it can boxed in and disguised.

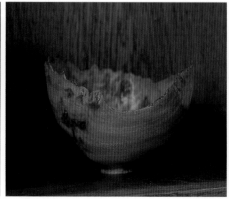

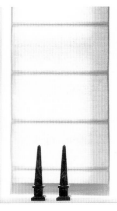

CLOCKWISE FROM TOP LEFT:

An ornate lampshade made from porcupine quills creates an unusual pattern and colouring when the electric light passes through it.

A mantelpiece is often a place where cards, letter and general paperwork accumulates – try to keep it clear and choose just a few, special pieces for arrangement and display. The mantle and fireplace are usually the focal point of a living room and therefore the first place that someone entering the room will look at.

In a room with a low ceiling a neat, close fitting lightshade like this will provide light but not restrict head room.

This magazine storage is made out of leather. Although unusual, it still provides ample space to keep magazines and other papers tidy.

If you have small windows, a well tailored set of blinds will be more space effective than a large pleated curtain.

The lighting in this living room has been carefully planned to focus on this magnificent statue.

Door and cupboard handles should not be overlooked because the sum of these small details is significant.

Dimmer switches can be used to lower the lighting and instantly change the mood of the room. It is a good idea to cover all light switches with a protective shield that can be wiped clean easily.

Textured fabric can add a luxurious finishing touch to your living area.

Bookshelves are a neat storage solution but can also become an attractive feature in a living room.

Pieces of craft or artwork should be displayed to look their best. Here the grain of the wood shelf supporting this bowl accentuates its shape and texture.

Photographs that have been mounted and framed in a similar way can be arranged together on a wall.

This twisting glass lampbase is topped with a plain but pleated shade, which does not distract from the intrinsic beauty of the base.

A whimsical plain and coloured glass chandelier adds an opulent decorative touch.

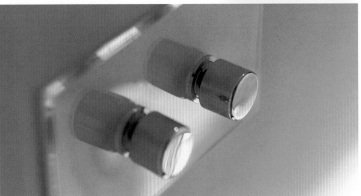

Bedrooms

Planning your
bedroom

We spend a third of our lives in bed and so the bedroom is an important part of the house and should be a space where you feel comfortable and can retreat to after a busy day. Above all it needs to be warm, inviting, relaxing and quiet.

Below: Wood panelling such as this will provide a certain amount of sound insulation for your bedroom.

Below right: As well as creating a tranquil scheme for your room, ensure that it is located in a quiet part of the house.

Opposite: The leather panelled wall acts as a screen for the bathroom and doubles as an attractive headboard.

Planning your space

The quality and quantity of sleep that you get has a profound effect on the way that you function both physically and mentally. During periods of deep sleep the body restores and heals itself. Sleep also affects the body's ability to process and store carbohydrates as well as regulate hormone levels. And during the day the spine is compressed by gravity but at night it is given the chance to recover. So it is important that the room where you rest at night is designed to encourage good sleep.

The bed is one of the most important pieces of furniture in the home and so the general advice given is to spend as much as you can afford on a good quality bed (see Choosing the right bed, pages 148–50). And don't think that a bed is for life – you should replace it every eight to ten years.

Finding the right location

Almost more important than the amount of sleep you have is the quality of it, so ensure that you are not disturbed unnecessarily. If you have a choice, locate your bedroom at the back or on the quietest side of the building, away from traffic noise.

If you are in a block of flats check out what rooms are above and below you. Also, investigate what happens on the ground floor of your building – you may have moved away from traffic noise at the front only to have repositioned yourself above the kitchens of a restaurant or the doors of a nightclub where activity carries on until the small hours of the morning, or begins at daybreak.

To ensure a quiet space you may need to install double glazing, double doors or other forms of soundproofing.

Above: *If the best position for your bed is close to the door then a screen can provide a useful shield creating privacy.*

Above right: *This clever sliding wall panel has been covered in fabric to link with the rest of the room. It can be pulled across to conceal the storage when access is not needed.*

Safety tips

Those who follow the eco and environmental researches believe that synthetic materials, such as nylon carpet, encourage static electricity, which can be potentially harmful, especially in a bedroom.

It is also best to keep electrical appliances to a minimum because of radiation or electromagnetic fields and to avoid running electrical cables under the bed. Therefore, ensure that the flex for bedside lights runs along the skirting boards or edge of the wall to the bedside table.

Double glazing will muffle exterior noise while double doors help reduce noise by creating a small lobby or barrier between you and the outer elements. Sound insulation between you and a lower area can be improved with good underlay beneath a carpet or with insulation boards or cork tiles.

An effective bedroom layout

More often than not it is the shape and configuration of the space that dictates how the bedroom is laid out, and particularly where the bed can be set. If you have a window in the room it is pleasant to have it at the foot or side of the bed so that you can look out at the sky or view beyond, but avoid sleeping with your head directly under a window because you may be subjected to draughts of cold air while you are asleep, which can cause stiffness in the neck and shoulders.

The door to the room will also influence where the bed is. Try to allow adequate space for the door to open and for the person entering the room to have a clear margin to turn around, without walking straight into the bed. Some people prefer to place their bed behind a door so that it is hidden or shielded from view. This is because a bed is the most personal and intimate piece of furniture in the home, and one that some people prefer to keep as private as possible.

The position of cupboard or wardrobe doors will also have to be considered, and if the wardrobe is built-in then the location of the bed will have to be fitted around it. There should be enough space for the wardrobe door or doors to open and give adequate access to the contents without having constantly to move other pieces of furniture or battle with the bed.

Creating the right environment

Once you have decided on the layout of the room, there are other important considerations, such as good ventilation and maintaining the right temperature. There is a tendency to make the bedroom too warm as people feel that this is a place where they are naked or only lightly clothed, but an overheated bedroom may cause the sleeper to dehydrate. The ideal temperature for a bedroom is 13–15°C (55–60°F), though it should be slightly warmer for children and older people.

A humidifier helps keep a little moisture in the air, especially during the height of the summer. You don't need an expensive humidifying machine, just a good sized, shallow bowl of water, with a reasonable surface area. Wash the bowl and replace the water everyday so it does not become stagnant. Although it is best to sleep in a well ventilated room, do be careful to avoid draughts.

It is also beneficial to air the bedroom each day by opening the window and door to get a flow or circulation going. If you live in the city or close to the road leave a washable cotton sheer or voile curtain over the window while it is open to help reduce the amount of smog and grime that will inevitably come in through the window. Bedclothes should be turned back each morning so that the bed can be well ventilated.

Bedroom flooring

Floor coverings in a bedroom are important because they help dampen noise and also because they usually come in contact with bare skin. Wool carpets are the softest and warmest under foot but, if you suffer from allergies or are dust sensitive, a carpet can be a place that harbours fine particles and produces fluff.

Wooden floors are quite warm on bare skin but need to be well sealed to prevent splinters. Wood is also easy to clean. To soften the area around the bed you can use rug or mat made from cotton or other washable fibre. Stone is not usually a good bedroom floor covering as it is hard and, unless under heated, also cold.

Above: *Warm colours can be enveloping and soothing when used in a bedroom.*

Left: *In this attic bedroom mirrored panels on the cupboards reflect light and create the illusion of depth.*

Positioning pictures and mirrors

If a mirror is to be used for applying make up and for checking clothing then it should be positioned so that it benefits from a source of natural light.

Some people find it disturbing to have a mirror directly opposite or over the foot of the bed because it reflects their image and shadow play makes them think that there is someone else in the room. But in a small space a large mirror can help to reflect light from a window and make the room seem larger.

Right: *This basement
bedroom is painted a
bright, warm vibrant colour
because there is little access
to natural light.*

Below right: *This young
girl's bedroom has soft
decorative touches, such as
the painted wardrobe, and is
not overtly childish, making it
a comfortable and enjoyable
room for an adolescent too.*

Colour and style

The bedroom is often the room
where people indulge in decorating
fantasies, opting for a favourite
colour or theme, something with
richly coloured Victorian overtones
or a Zen-like, cool space.

If a husband and wife, partners
or young children share a
bedroom then it may also be a
place where a compromise has
to be reached regarding colour
and style that it is neither
overpoweringly feminine nor too
masculine. Many people prefer
to keep the decoration of the
bedroom simple so that it is easy
to clean and maintain. Swags and
frills tend to be dust stores and a
plethora of knick knacks and
decorations just adds to the
burden of cleaning.

Clear space is also more therapeutic and relaxing than a cluttered room. A bedroom should be comfortable and an enjoyable place to be, but not a dump for unwanted collections of clothes, shoes and books. Well placed and plentiful storage is extremely necessary in a bedroom (see Display and storage, pages 164–7).

Using colour

Good colours for bedrooms are those from the neutral and pastel range of the spectrum. Warm soft yellow, watery blue or pale green are all worth considering.

Yellow is a sunny colour, which is cheerful and heartening on winter mornings. Choose your tone of yellow carefully – one with a paler, white base can be more comfortable than one with a red/orange emphasis, which might make you feel overheated. Some sludgy yellows with green overtones also look slightly grubby in low electric lighting, which is not an inspiring or appealing sight in a bedroom.

Some people find blue cool but it is the colour of natural elements (water and the sky) and it is said

At-a-glance colour guide

Light pastel colours are good for bedrooms because they are relaxing and calming. Yellow is a warm colour at night but sunny and bright in the morning. Blue can be cool and refreshing but may need elements of pink or lavender to prevent it from making a room seem cold.

Green is a colour associated with renewal and rebirth and it can be invigorating and refreshing to wake up to in the morning. Red is a bold colour that is rarely used in quantity in a bedroom because it can make a small room feel very claustrophobic and overheated.

Opposite: This child's bedroom has been carefully planned to fulfil changing needs. The fabric around the bed can be pulled across while the room is used as a play area during the day. And as the child gets older a quiet study area will be needed. The desk will provide that but for now, it is a display area for the child's doll house.l

Below: This young girl's bedroom is warm and comforting with soft peach coloured walls with a delicate print, which is repeated in the curtain at the small window above.

Below right: Timeless pieces, such as this brass bed, look good in a traditional setting. The cool blue used in the room has been warmed up by the brass fixtures and fittings.

to be a colour that can aid relaxation. Cool blues can be warmed by a touch of red taking them to the lavender side of the colour wheel or with the addition of accessories and bed throws that are decorated with patterns that include various warmer shades.

Green is said to be a colour of rejuvenation and growth and the right shades can be bright and fresh. But be wary of teaming it with its contrast colour of red in a bedroom as these colours are diametrically opposed and in certain strengths and shades can appear to 'fight' or clash, which is neither calming nor relaxing. Soft almond or pale mint green can be used successfully with wooden bedroom furniture as green and brown have a natural earthy affinity. These colours together can be used to create a pleasant and tranquil room.

Potent, strong colours may be used to create a bedroom with impact. You can create an

interesting scheme using one wall of strong colour or pattern and then decorate the rest of the room in a soft, plain colour. The wall that is often chosen to make a feature of is the one behind the bedhead. This is because the colour creates an impact on entering the room and highlights the bed, which is the main feature and purpose of the space.

The other advantage of putting strong colour or pattern behind the bedhead is that you don't see it when you are in the bed, unless you deliberately turn your head round. In this way the colour and fun are there but when you are lying on the bed or are in it, unwinding or going to sleep, your eyes focus on the soft, plain colour that has been used on the other walls.

Using fabrics to create mood

Light and decorative fabrics such as toile de joey can be attractive in a bedroom. These prints are generally in red, blue or grey and on a white or off-white background. They depict cameo scenes and views – many are inspired by 18th century pastoral paintings, but modern interpretations can also be found.

When using fabrics in a bedroom try to keep the words 'fresh and simple' in mind. If you are keen to have a multi-floral material or dense pattern restrict it to curtains and perhaps a bed cover or maybe a single chair or cushion but avoid teaming it with a floral or similarly busy wallpaper. If you cover every surface with a dense pattern the room will appear small, overcrowded and stifling.

Secondary uses

In an ideal world the bedroom would be a single, dedicated sleeping space but in reality, and particularly in metropolitan living, the bedroom may need to double up and be used as an exercise facility, dressing room and clothes storage area, or even a place to study or work in. It would also be great if every child could have a large playroom and garden den, but modern homes rarely provide this luxury.

Instead space often has to be found within their bedrooms. Whether in an adult or children's bedroom, making the secondary function fit in around the main one will require careful planning. For example, in one-room or studio apartments it may be worth considering a foldaway bed that pivots back against the wall. This sort of flip-up bed is generally housed in a purpose-built cupboard so that when it is not in use its presence in the room is unnoticed. Other options are foldaway sofa beds and futons.

Another solution that works well in tall, high-ceilinged rooms, and provides a dedicated bedroom space, is the sleeping platform. This is a purpose-built mezzanine level, which needs only to be the width of the bed plus a metre (a few feet) around it. This can be installed against an end wall, leaving the floor space underneath free for use as an office or living area. With sleeping platforms it is important to have enough head room above to make it comfortable. To save even more space on the lower level a sleeping platform may be cantilevered or supported on brackets, therefore negating the need for pillars. This sort of structure should be devised by an engineer or architect.

In children's rooms space can be invented by the installation of a platform bed with a play area

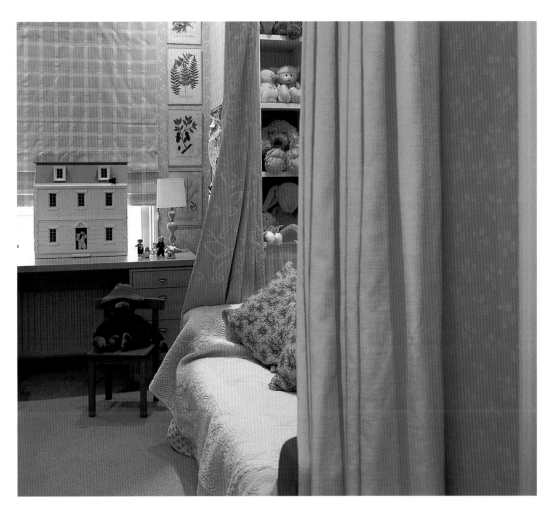

underneath it. Of course, this is only suitable for older children who will be able to climb up and down a ladder. By raising the height of the bed to the level of the upper bunk of a bunk bed, a desk or den area can be created underneath. The newly reclaimed floor area can house a desk or work station, with a chair. To save more space the desk could be built-in against a wall and a set of shelves constructed to one side, for storing books, crayons and other items (see Display and storage, pages 164–7).

Elsewhere in this under-bed zone there could be a curtain so that the lower area can be screened off from the rest of the room. A couple of floor cushions could be introduced as these take up less space than rigid chairs and can be easily stacked one on

top of another when not in use. Whether the space is used for play or study, your child will love having such a unique room.

Another option is to raise the floor level by building a row of deep steps up to a bed platform. This does not need to be so high off the ground as the other option, because the room underneath will be used for general storage rather than a built-in desk.

By raising the bed to about 90cm (3ft) off the floor you will gain copious amounts of storage underneath. The access to the bed is by two or three long, but shallow, steps. These steps can, when not needed for access to the bed, be softened with cushions and be used for sitting. The space under the steps, accessed by doors in the side, will provide valuable storage.

Containing a work area

A specially devised cabinet or cupboard is one way of containing your work area. This type of cupboard is deep and opens in half – one side contains shelves for storing files and paperwork and the other forms a desk with a computer. When it is not in use, one half folds over the other to conceal the contents.

A deep wall cupboard can also be kitted out in the same way with a desk shelf or platform on a slide or pivot base so that it can be pulled out on a runner. The shelf may be folded back and closed up out of sight in the cupboard door when work time is over.

Furnishings and textiles

The golden rule for a relaxing and calming bedroom is to keep the furnishings and decoration simple. The cleaner and more accessible the space the more enjoyable it will be to live in. Natural, soft and absorbent fabrics are ideal.

Choosing the right bed

The major piece of furniture in a bedroom is, of course, the bed. On average, we spend a third of our lives in bed so it is vital that you try out plenty and then buy the one that is right for you.

Below: This traditional-style bed is raised off the floor, which ensures all-round air circulation.

There are those who strongly advocate a firm mattress for a good night's sleep but that may not be the best type for you, especially if you already suffer from aches and pains.

What you really need is a bed that offers the right support for your spine while allowing the hips and shoulders to lie comfortably in their natural curvature. Your spine should form a shallow 'S' shape when you lie flat, and a straight horizontal line when you lie on your side. Use a pillow, neither too thick nor too thin that supports the nape of the neck correctly and aligns the head.

It is also advisable to raise the bed or mattress off the floor, to enable adequate air circulation around the whole bed. Also sleeping on the floor puts you closer to dust and fluff and can make it more difficult to get in and out of bed.

The standard bed available today comes in three main parts: the mattress, the base and the head- and footboards.

Mattresses

On the surface most mattresses look the same, but there are a number of different interior constructions on offer. Foam mattresses are made from different layers and densities of material that 'give' when a body

lies on the surface. This type of mattress is best suited to a slatted base.

The most popular type of mattress on the market today is the pocket sprung. A good bed will have a high number of tightly packed springs, as many as 1,500 in a double, which offers great individual support. Pocket sprung beds don't have completely flat surfaces – there is a slight undulation – so the bed moulds itself to the body shape.

Futons, originally Japanese mattresses used for sleeping on the floor or low wooden platforms, are another bed option. The traditional futon is unsprung and offers a firm place of rest. It is a space-saving option because it can be rolled up after a night's sleep and stored in a box or cupboard.

Base options

The base of a bed is usually a divan or slatted. Some old-fashioned beds have a frame with springs, but these are rarely found at modern retailers.

The divan base is the most popular type. It is a box-shaped construction with a slightly padded top. It is generally upholstered in the same fabric as the mattress and is fitted with castors for mobility. Some even come with deep drawers, which is

Left: *The walls of this Scandinavian-style bedroom have been covered, above dado height, with a fresh blue and white gingham material, which creates a soft and cosy environment.*

Below left: *The bedcover and cushions here are quilted. Fabric can be quilted by sewing along the lines or motifs of a printed pattern – this insulates the piece, making it warmer.*

useful for storing spare bedding. A divan base generally comes without a head- or footboard but these can be bought separately and added as necessary.

Slat bases have flexible slats made from laminated wood and supported on a frame. These offer a certain amount of 'give' and in some systems the tension can be adjusted for firmer/softer support. A slatted base is recommended for foam mattresses.

When buying a mattress and base make sure that you try the two together before purchasing to ensure that they are compatible.

Bed frames and boards

The most traditional bed dressing is the four poster. This dates back to the time when curtains were

Adjustable beds

A fairly recent introduction to the mass market is the adjustable bed. Adjustable beds usually operate electrically and in the case of a double width bed there are two single mattresses and bases so that individual arrangements can be made for each sleeper.

The adjustable bed allows you to raise the head of the bed, or the foot or both ends at the same time. By raising the head it can be more comfortable for reading or drinking tea and raising the feet slightly may help people with digestive or circulatory problems.

Above: A cushion echoes the trim and fabric of the quilt.

Above right: Neutral furnishings, such as this lamp, work well next to simple, understated bedlinen.

Below: This tone-on-tone scheme is lifted by a variety of textures from waffle to slub linen.

Looking after your mattress

Mattresses should be replaced every 10 years because they will have deteriorated as much as 75 per cent. Many mattresses need to be turned over regularly to spread the wear and tear and give springs a change to rebalance.

A mattress protector is also important. This can be a simple calico or cotton cover that is pulled on over the mattress's own ticking cover and can easily be removed for regular washing. There are also special dust mite protective covers that people with eczema and asthma find particularly helpful.

hung around the bed so that they could be drawn to keep the cold at bay. Now, in the days of central heating, the curtains have a purely decorative purpose. The traditional four poster has turned wooden posts and a frame over the top. The back panel is sometimes hung with a thick or tapestry style material between the two posts at the bed head. Then a canopy is placed over the top and curtains are draped around the side.

This ornate and heavy dressing has, in recent years, been refined and simplified into a simple, plain wooden frame over which a single length of cotton voile is draped. In country style bedrooms gingham and printed fabrics may be used on the voile.

The simplest dressing option is the covered headboard that can be attached, with long screws and washers, directly into the divan base. When choosing a headboard, whether it is fabric-covered, wood or metal, find a style that is best suited to your overall decorative scheme. If your room is to be simple and Zen-like then a natural cherry wood, panelled or rail-topped headboard or a waxed pine surround would be in keeping with the overall mood. On the other hand if you are opting for a scheme that is more decorative and colourful then a padded headboard covered in a bright fabric with contrasting piping of decorative quilting is a good option.

There is also the contemporary padded cushion or long tabard arrangement with tab or tie-tops – these are hung from a pole fixed to the wall so that there is a buffer between your head and the wall (see Removable bed head tabard hangings, pages 152–5).

Tall people often prefer to have a bed without a footboard so that they are not restricted by it, but for many traditional styles of bed surrounds, such as those wrought from iron, wood and copper, matching head- and footboards are part of the overall effect.

Although there are many antique bedsteads to be found in specialist shops they tend to come in smaller sizes and may require custom-made mattresses and bases. There are, however, many modern copies of these traditional designs. These brand new versions are made in contemporary bed sizes and will most likely be coated or treated to make them rust resistant and, in the case of brass bed frames, tarnish resistant.

Traditional materials are also used to create modern steel and iron bedsteads. These can be simple, following traditional wooden designs, or they can be more ornate and fanciful with frond and tendril Art Nouveau-like decorative features. Many can be custom made to your own specific design by a blacksmith or forge owner.

Bedlinen

Dressing the bed is also an extremely important decorative element. There is such a wide choice of bedlinens that it is often difficult to choose what you want. Changing your bedlinen can also be a simple but very effective way of ringing the seasonal differences in a room, keeping deep colours for winter and white or lighter colours for the summer. There are many reversible duvet covers and pillow sets on the market today that are designed specifically to help create this very type of mood change.

Although coloured and patterned bedlinen has been popular since the 1960s the classic white, crisp cotton bedlinen has been a perennial favourite and suits every scheme and style, from simple to ornate. White bedlinen does not have to be boringly plain; the small details are what make it special. For example piping, broderie anglaise trim, a self pattern or monogram will all lift the appearance of a white linen covered bed.

A range of pillows and cushions can make a bed attractive and contribute to the overall decoration of the room. There are many different shapes and sizes – some pillows are large and square, others long and rectangular. The old-fashioned bolster is a long cylindrical pillow, which was traditionally placed across the top edge of the bed providing an angled support for a second pillow. Try experimenting with variously shaped pillows to find an arrangement that suits your bed.

You can also use different coloured pillowcases or slips to emphasize a scheme in a room. For example, you could use a dark shade on large square pillows in the background and a paler cover for the oblong pillow in the foreground.

Curtains and blinds

Curtains and blinds are a great way of pulling the overall colour scheme in the bedroom together. When choosing the shade, look at the fabrics that have been used elsewhere in the room, such as the bedlinen or cushions, and try to find a tone that will complement them.

Make sure that the style of curtains you choose fits with your decorative scheme. Light sheer voile curtains work well in a contemporary bedroom, while heavy rich coloured curtains, complete with swags and tails create an opulent ambience, which would complement a traditional period scheme.

Below: It is important that the fabrics that you choose for your curtains and bedlinen are complementary. Here simple white cushions work well with the neutral curtains that have a colourful trim.

Below left: White bedlinen is not boring. The details, such as broderie anglaise or a raised pattern, make it special.

removable

bed head tabard hangings

Calico tabard hangings sit comfortably in a modern interior and also provide useful storage space for bedtime reading matter. Adding embroidered monograms gives a personal touch to a utilitarian bed. We used strong deckchair canvas, which was the ideal width to fit our bed. Basic sewing skills are needed to secure the storage slots, then chunky bamboo was slotted through channels at the bottom of the tabards to weight it down into place. Mother of pearl buttons provide a decorative touch and secure the tabards over the bed post.

Materials

12m (39ft) of natural deckchair canvas

Cotton thread to match

Grey silk embroidery thread

Nine large mother of pearl buttons

One 1.5m (5ft) length of 50mm (2in) diameter bamboo

Tools

Sewing machine (or needle and thread for hand sewing)

Calligraphy book

Photocopier or computer

Tracing paper

Soft pencil

Embroidery hoop

Needle

Tailor's chalk

Set square

Tape measure

Craft knife or stitch ripper

Preparing the fabric

1 Cut three lengths of deckchair canvas to fit the drop between your bed post and mattress. Allow half a drop extra on one piece for storage slots and a couple of centimetres (about an inch) hem allowance on each end. Press and hem. Fold two of the lengths of fabric in half and position these over the bed post. Choose some initials from a calligraphy book and enlarge them on a photocopier or size and print them on a computer. Trace the initials onto a piece of tracing paper to form a monogram pattern.

Sewing the monograms

2 Transfer the monograms of your choice onto the tabards using a soft pencil. Secure an embroidery hoop in place over the monograms and use satin stitch to form the letters. Choose a colour that complements your bedroom scheme.

Transfer the monogram onto the fabric using tracing paper and a soft pencil.

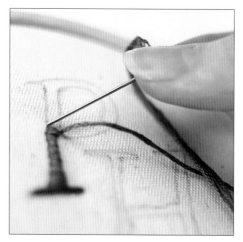

Use satin stitch to form the letters of the monogram pattern.

Know your materials

Canvas is a strong, utilitarian material that is available in a number of different weights, which makes it suitable for many different uses. Deckchair canvas is available in widths suitable for re-covering deckchairs with prefinished edges. It can be found in various striped colourways as well as the natural colour used here. Its main advantage in this project is its strength, as it can easily support the weight of books and magazines. It is readily found in large department stores and at scenic (theatrical) suppliers.

Making the pockets

3 Take the third piece of fabric and fold the front section of fabric forward to form a loop, and pin in place. With the tailor's chalk and a set square mark out two channels using a folded magazine as a guide. Pin in place, then sew.

4 Use a couple of paperback books or magazines to measure the required depth for the top pockets. Pin the fabric in place, then sew using a medium length straight stitch.

Hanging the tabards

5 Drape the fabric loosely over the headboard ensuring all three pieces are level, mark four equidistant points across the top of the fabric, 4cm (1½in) down from the pole. Measure the buttons and mark the positions of the button holes with tailor's chalk.

6 Machine sew the button holes or, if you prefer to hand sew them, then cut horizontal slits that are slightly smaller than your chosen buttons. As a finishing touch, neaten the edges with a button hole stitch.

7 Pin both ends of the buttons and slit with a sharp craft knife or stitch ripper.

8 Stitch the buttons on the insides of the tabards, secure and slot the bamboo into place.

Use a magazine to measure the size of the looped pocket and then pin in place.

Make sure that you leave enough room to store books in the bottom pocket.

Measure the position of the button holes and mark with tailor's chalk.

Alternative

Canvas is also an ideal material to make sturdy hanging storage from, as it can be folded up when not in use. The shelves are made from thick cardboard covered in canvas. These are stitched to each side panel, giving a concertina effect. It is essential to measure the depth of your hanging space before you begin and to consider the dimensions of the items you wish to store so that you make your unit to the correct size.

Cut two equally sized side panels, press and hem with a sewing machine. Decide on the number of shelves you require – don't forget the top and bottom pieces. Cut these all from sturdy cardboard using a craft knife and set square. Cut pieces of canvas to cover each and machine stitch in place. Mark the position of each shelf in tailor's chalk on the inside of each side panel. Machine stitch in place then add two flaps to the top of the unit with sturdy velcro fastenings that fit over the wardrobe or hanging rail. Finally, machine stitch the top and bottom panels in place.

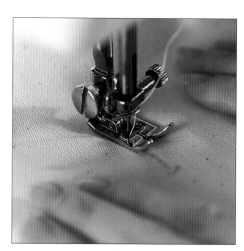

It is easiest to use a sewing machine to make the button holes.

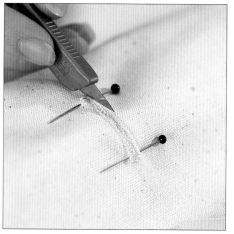

Use a sharp craft knife carefully to slit open the button holes.

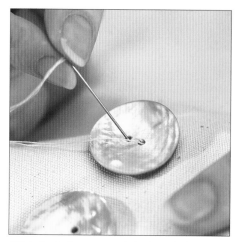

Stitch the buttons securely in place before hanging the tabard on the wall.

white washed cork

headboard with decorative niches

This simple, minimal headboard is designed to look as if it is a built-in piece of furniture. The dimensions are dictated by the size of the sheets of plywood, which come in 2.5 x 1.25m (8 x 4ft) sheets, making it perfect for use behind a futon bed. The cork covering is an ideal surface for pinning up mementos while the shallow niches hold bedtime essentials like alarm clocks. The open sides of the headboard are ideal for storing magazines. Due to its height and weight it requires careful handling and should be firmly secured to the wall using mirror plates.

Materials

5cm² (2in²) square section planed timber cut to the following sizes: 4 lengths of 2.5m (8ft), 5 lengths of 1.1m (3ft 10in)

Wood glue

Wood screws

2 sheets of 6mm (¼in) thick plywood

Cork tile adhesive

Cork tiles

White wood wash

Quick grip adhesive

Satin acrylic varnish

Tools

Pencil

Set square

Handsaw

Chisel

D cramp

Electric drill

Jigsaw

Metal ruler

Craft knife

Abrasive paper

Mitre saw

Making the framework

1 Begin by marking up the halving joints on the timber in order to make the framework. To form the centre use one length of 2.5m (8ft) long timber. Use a pencil and set square to mark the positions of five equally spaced horizontals (remember to take the thickness of the wood into consideration when doing this). Use a handsaw to make two parallel cuts halfway through the thickness of the wood. Then use a sharp chisel to remove the waste wood, leaving a U-shaped notch. Do the same to three of the 1.1m (3ft 10in) lengths, laying them across the centre vertical and marking the corresponding notch on them.

2 With all the halving joints cut, spread a layer of wood glue in the notches before slotting them together. Grip each joint in turn in a D cramp, drill a hole and

Using a chisel, remove the wood so that you end up with a U-shaped notch.

Apply a layer of glue into each notch and then slot the halving joints together.

Know your materials

Mitre cutters and saws are useful tools that enable you to cut a perfect 45-degree angle, which is essential for neat frame-making joints. If you do not want to buy one they can be hired on a daily basis from all good hire shops. Alternatively you could use a more primitive mitre block, which consists of a U-shaped trough made from wood or plastic with precut 45-degree slots. Your timber can be placed in the trough and then the slots used to guide a handsaw through to cut the angle.

then screw in place, making sure that the heads of the screws are countersunk below the surface. Fix the surrounding battens in place using simple butt joints.

3 Lay the framework onto each sheet of hardboard in turn and mark the positions of the battens on it using a pencil. Clamp the marked side of the plywood onto the front of the frame and drill through the thickness of the plywood into the timber frame using a wood bit. Use countersunk screws to attach.

Marking out the niches

4 Mark the positions of the cut out square niches on the remaining piece of plywood using a pencil and set square. Make sure that each niche will sit just above a timber batten, which will provide the shelf.

5 Cut out the niches from the plywood sheet using a jigsaw. Attach the sheet to the front of the frame, screwing it into the battens with countersink screws.

Applying the cork tiles

6 Spread adhesive over the front piece of plywood and lay the tiles. Cut where necessary with a metal ruler and craft knife.

7 Lightly sand the cork tiles then paint with a couple of coats of white wood wash.

8 Finish off the edges of the niches and the headboard by cutting an L-shaped trim with a mitre saw. Attach this with quick grip adhesive and hold in place with a D cramp until set. Varnish with a satin acrylic varnish.

Drill through the plywood into the timber frame and hold in place using screws.

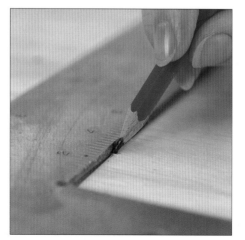

Mark the positions of the niches on the remaining piece of plywood.

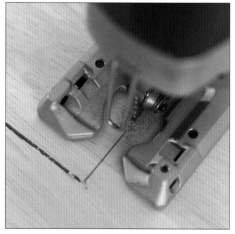

Using a jigsaw, cut out the niche squares from the plywood sheet.

Alternative

If you prefer a softer, tailored look then why not create a padded headboard instead? Keep the dimensions tall and square to ensure a contemporary look. Upholstering a headboard in soft suede or leather is the ultimate in luxury and it will last for years, but for a budget version try suedette or moleskin in a subtle colour.

Decide on the dimensions you want your headboard to be. Get your timber merchants to cut two pieces of 12mm (½in) thick MDF then sand the edges lightly. Get two firm pieces of thick foam cut to the same size as the MDF boards then stick them in place using strong white adhesive. Cut two pieces of fabric large enough to cover the foam-covered boards. Use a staple gun at the back to anchor the fabric cover in place, pulling it tightly over the foam as you do this. Staple opposite sides at the same time so that you achieve a good, even tension. Attach the boards to the wall just above the mattress using mirror plates to fix them.

Glue down the cork tiles over the whole surface of the front piece of plywood.

Lightly sand and then paint over the cork tiles using two layers of white wood wash.

Hold the L shaped trimming around the niches and headboard in place using a D cramp.

159

framed

linen blinds with decorative panels

These panel blinds are a great tailored alternative to fussy, frilly window treatments. Natural linen is sheer enough to let plenty of light in while still maintaining privacy. We have added a woven linen ribbon cross motif that is fixed in place with a no-sew bonding material. Fixed on a light wooden framework, the blinds can be made to fit any size of window and can be mounted on the window in a variety of ways. We used a sliding mechanism but if you have a window that is flush with the wall, simply attach the panels with hinges to the frame and add a hook and eye fastening.

Materials

1.5cm² (½in²) section planed timber

Wood glue

Panel pins

White emulsion (acrylic)

Natural linen or similar weight material

Linen or 'linen-look' ribbon in two different widths and colours

Pins

Fabric bonding

Fabric glue

Tools

Tape measure

Mitre saw

Pin hammer

D cramp

Paintbrush

Scissors

Iron

Staple gun

Hinges or sliding door kit

Making the frame

1 Work out the size of frames you will need to make by measuring your window accurately. Next, cut the timber to make the frames using a mitre saw. Apply wood glue to the mitred pieces, then fix them in place using panel pins and a pin hammer. Clamp them using a D cramp until the glue is firmly set. Repeat the process in all four corners of each frame, leaving them overnight to set.

2 Paint over the surface of the frames with a coat of white emulsion (acrylic) paint.

Preparing the panels

3 Cut panels of linen material that will be large enough to stretch around the frames. Next, cut the lengths of your widest ribbon and arrange them so that you form a cross on each panel. Add narrower ribbon over the top to form a border. Use pins to hold

Glue the mitres together using wood glue and then secure them with panel pins.

When the frames have been constructed, paint over them with white emulsion (acrylic).

Know your materials

Fabric bonding consists of a thin material and backing paper in sheet or tape form that has been impregnated with fabric glue. It is used in sewing and dressmaking as a quick way of hemming a garment or applying an applique patch without actually sewing. It comes in a variety of different widths and strengths suitable for bonding different weights of material. The glue is activated by pressing the fabric with a warm iron. Then the backing paper is peeled away. The bond is made by sandwiching the two layers of fabric together and pressing them, again with a warm iron.

all the ribbon in place while you turn it over.

4 Iron on lengths of fabric bonding to the back of the ribbon, following the manufacturer's instructions.

5 Spread the linen panels on a large, flat surface that has been protected with a heatproof cloth and iron the ribbon trim in place. The fabric bonding will cause it to stick to the linen.

6 Stretch the linen panels taut over each frame, folding the raw edges under. Staple these in place, making sure the fabric is pulled taut in each direction.

7 Use a non-staining fabric glue to fix the ribbon trim around the edges of both frames, hiding the staples for a neat finish.

(We also added an optional border of ribbon to frame the panels.)

Attaching the panels

8 Attach your linen panels in the most suitable way. If you want the panels to swing open, screw hinges to the sides of the panels and fix to the window frame. For panels that slide sideways use a sliding door kit, which consists of a channel fixed to the wall or ceiling. Then attach wheels or runners to each panel.

Make a cross pattern with the two sizes of ribbon and pin them together.

Turn all the ribbon over and iron on fabric bonding to the backs.

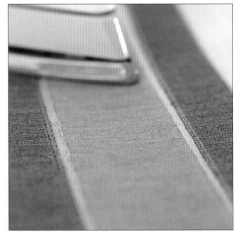

Put the ribbon back on the linen and iron it into its final position.

Alternative

If you do not have space for linen panels, or prefer a simpler window treatment, make a pull up blind. These blinds are less structured than Roman blinds; rather than forming stiff folds they are gently gathered. They look particularly effective when made of a soft natural fabric and hung unlined so that the light can filter through them.

Measure and cut a piece of fabric approximately 10cm (4in) larger all round than the dimensions of your window. Turn over the edges, press and hem with a sewing machine. Machine stitch a channel at the top of the fabric and feed in a wooden batten the same width as the blind – hand stitch to enclose it at each end. Stitch three vertical rows of small brass rings at regular intervals (of about 30cm/1ft) along the back of the blind. Attach three brass screw eyes along the back of the batten. Feed a length of cord through the screw eyes then along the rings. When pulled, this will raise and lower the blind. Attach the batten with 'L' brackets to a second batten fixed just above the window.

Staple the linen onto the frame using a staple gun. Ensure the material is pulled taut.

Hide any staples by gluing on ribbon trim around the edges.

Fix the panels to your window using an appropriate method. One way is to use hinges.

Display and storage

The more efficiently your wardrobe is arranged the easier it will be for you to see what is there and to select your clothes. Bundles of jumpers stuffed at the back of a shelf and odd shoes hidden under the bed slow down the process of dressing and make it a difficult rather than pleasurable task.

Below: Built-in wardrobes can be tailored to fit in and around even the most awkward spaces. The interiors can also be arranged to provide hanging and storage to suit your clothes and accessories.

Below right: This wall of wardrobes was built around a fireplace. The shelves above the fireplace are less deep, but are still perfect for smaller items such as folded T-shirts or knitwear.

Storage furniture

Effective storage in your bedroom is essential to keep it tidy and inviting. When planning your bedroom, consider what storage option would be most suitable to meet your requirements.

Wardrobes and cupboards

Division of wardrobe space is important – keep one section for long coats and dresses but subdivide the rest of your hanging space into two levels to double the capacity. Shirts and skirts can go in one half and jackets and half-folded trousers in the other.

Wardrobes come in a variety of styles and shapes. The most common these days is the built-in wardrobe or prefabricated fitted wardrobe, which stretches across one wall or is built into niches on either side of a chimney breast. Nowadays the freestanding wardrobes that are available are usually either the traditional heavy wooden closet style or the more contemporary MDF variety.

If space in the bedroom is limited then you could use a simple metal rail fixed to the wall or on its own supports, with a fabric curtain to cover the clothes and prevent dust from gathering on them. Sliding doors also work well on wardrobes in a small room where there may not be enough room to open hinged doors fully.

On the other hand, if space is not a problem, divide off a section of your bedroom and create a walk-in wardrobe. You can install directional, recessed spot lights into the ceiling so that the light is good and everything is visible.

In a child's bedroom the divides between hanging and shelving can be smaller because children's clothes need less space. A recess could be fitted with a deep drawer at the base for shoes and boots, a couple

Seasonal storage

The majority of storage in the bedroom revolves around seasonal changes, between the spring/ summer and autumn/winter divide of clothes and bedlinen. The most storage space will be needed in the summer months when bulky winter duvets, overcoats, puffa jackets and thick jumpers are not in use.

The simplest way, once they have been dry cleaned or laundered, is to zip them up into large plastic clothes and storage bags and put them at the top of your wardrobe or in drawers in the base of your bed. You can also buy storage boxes on wheels that are specifically designed to slip easily under the bed.

Left: *A walk-in wardrobe combines hanging and storage space with a dressing room.*

Below: *By subdividing a drawer with a storage tray you can keep small items such as socks and tights neat so that they are easy to find.*

of narrow shelves for small jumpers, T-shirts and shirts and then a hanging space incorporated above. If you use curtains instead of doors to cover this space then use a bright, fun fabric to reflect the child's interests.

Chests of drawers

The other main area of storage in a bedroom is usually a chest of drawers. Drawers can benefit from being subdivided so that things are kept in separate niches instead of in a jumble. Small items such as socks and tights can easily be

rolled up into a ball and slotted into individual sections of a drawer divider.

When planning your shelf storage think carefully. Some people opt for fewer big deep shelves, but in fact they would be better with more narrow shelves as you tend to end up with two piles of clothes with a deep shelf. This means that the ones at the back are difficult to get at without removing everything in front. Narrow shelves allow the clothes to be positioned in easily accessible stacks.

Bedside tables

A bedside table or tables are also practical. These can be freestanding units or in some cases are an integral part of a headboard. As the bedroom is a place for relaxing, books, a radio and CD player may be placed on these tables, along with a telephone and bedside light. Then there are all the things that may be needed – a box of tissues, alarm clock, a glass of water.

This essential night time equipment can build up and up until it eventually overflows onto

Above: *These units are ideal for storing folded shirts.*

Below right: *This wall mounted bedside table takes up a minimal amount of space but provides neat storage for essentials.*

the floor or under the bed. Therefore you should try to make sure that your bedside table is commodious enough to house all the things that you need. Look for something with shelves or a cupboard underneath so that there is plenty of storage for different-sized objects.

To ease the pressure on the limited space of a bedside table you could use a wall light instead of a table lamp – something with an adjustable head or arm so that the light can be positioned for reading. If you have a tabard cover for your bed head (see pages 152–5) you could also sew pockets at the edge to hold small light useful objects such as tissues and a pocket alarm clock.

Additional storage items

If your room is spacious you may like to add a blanket box or chaise to the end of the bed. The blanket box provides more storage but is also a useful place to lay clothes and sit on.

An easy or occasional chair, whether it is a small armchair or a more genteel style such as a slipper chair, can also be an asset in bedroom. As well as being attractive to look at it is useful.

Storage solutions

Another consideration in bedroom storage is the diversity of size of things that are kept there. Items range from earrings to overcoats and from flimsy lingerie to boots and shoes. Each requires special containers to suit its size and shape.

Shoes and boots

Boots and shoes take up space and are awkward to store unless placed in a specially designed container. You can buy or make hanging shoe pockets. These have a banner-shaped backing with rows of deep pockets sewn on the front. Each pocket is long and deep enough to hold a pair of shoes.

Another alternative is a shoe rack or drawer that can be stored in the lower part of the wardrobe. Shoe racks come in two main styles, a metal version that has upright loops onto which the shoes are slotted so that the toe of the shoe points upwards and the heel down. The second style is made of wood and a simple, narrow, two shelf construction onto which the shoes are lined in

Scented liners

Both wardrobes and drawers can benefit from the introduction of scented liners. In wardrobes, especially where men's clothes are stored, the woody, slightly musky aroma of cedar blocks can be most attractive. These can also be slotted among shoes and boxes at the base of the wardrobe.

Liners are decorative paper sheets, impregnated with scent, that are placed at the base of a drawer to gradually release their scent and keep clothes resting on top of them lightly perfumed. Some people also put bars of good quality soap in drawers to perfume the contents.

However, you may prefer to use a mirror in the bedroom that is adjacent to a window in order to benefit from the daylight.

Decorative storage

Large boxes that may be used for storing blankets and thick jumpers can be made to look more attractive and more an integral part of the room's scheme if you cover them so that they co-ordinate. If you are wallpapering the room you could simply use excess paper to cover the boxes. Otherwise simple and inexpensive lining paper is a plain alternative.

For a more ornate finish you could staple or glue on remnants of material, such as pieces of left over curtain material or upholstery. For a really simple finish, you could paint the boxes the same colour as the walls, or cover them with a couple of layers of gloss paint to make them look like a lacquer chest or container.

Above: Perfume bottles are attractive items to display.

Left: These are specifically designed shoe drawers in a bedroom cupboard.

Below: This cupboard has been fitted with narrow shelves where shoes are stored in neat rows.

pairs. Another option is to store your shoes in bags or shoe boxes – label these on the outside for easy identification.

Boots are usually best stored with boot trees. Another option is to hang them from coat hangers with clips at the end. The weight of the base of the boot helps to pull the boot straight.

Jewellery and ties

Jewellery is generally small and delicate so it needs to be stored extremely carefully to avoid any damage. Long chains or necklaces may be best arranged in curls or circles in a deep box or hanging from a coat hanger. Earrings should be stored in pairs. You can buy boxes that are subdivided into small compartments and these are ideal. Otherwise visit a jewellery wholesaler or jewellery shop where you can buy specific earring boxes.

Ties and belts can be hung on small brackets or racks fixed to the inside of a wardrobe door,

once again keeping them in groups and subdividing them into colours so that they are easy to select and remove.

Cosmetics and toiletries

As well as clothes storage there will be a certain amount of space needed for cosmetics, hairbrushes, hairdryer and other toiletries. A collection of little bottles and pots may be best stored on a tray or in a small box that is kept in a cupboard or dressing table. The tray or box will enable them to be easily lifted out together.

A few decorative bottles and attractive pieces can be left on show, but remember that perfume is adversely affected by exposure to direct sunlight. Therefore, even though the bottle may look pretty on your dressing table its contents will go off if it is left out in the bright sunlight for too long.

If you have an en-suite bathroom a certain amount of cosmetics and toiletries can be stored and used in there.

ighting your
bedroom

Lighting in a bedroom should be on two levels, a general central light or wall lights that illuminate the whole room and small bedside lights that can be used for reading. Remember to position the main light switch beside the bed so that you can turn off all the lights without having to get out of bed.

Planning your lighting

The lighting that you use in a bedroom can play a fundamental part in creating a relaxing atmosphere. For general points about lighting design, see Effective lighting on page 134.

Bedroom lighting needs to work on two levels. Firstly, you need to have an efficient ambient lighting system. This light needs to be powerful enough for you to see clearly when selecting clothes or

Below: A decorative Devoré velvet shade softens and diffuses the light.

Right: An adjustable task lamp, attached to a bed head, provides a light to read by.

applying makeup. Secondly, the bedroom is the room where you wind down and read before you go to sleep. As such, your use of task and decorative lighting is key.

Ambient lighting

In most bedrooms ambient lighting is provided by a pendant or by a series of recessed lights in the wall or ceiling. The decoration of these central lights can be as ornate or as simple as you wish. Chandeliers and pretty decorative

shades work well within a traditional scheme, while recessed ceiling lights complement the contemporary bedroom.

When planning the wiring of these lights, make sure you have switches by the door and the bed, so that you can illuminate the room as you enter, but also turn off all the lights in the room without having to get out of bed.

To make a bedroom a really relaxing place to be in you may also want to add a dimmer switch

an evening meal with friends. In addition, the table setting style and the overall décor of the room will also be influential.

A change of flooring may also help to delineate the food preparation part of the room from the entertaining section. In the kitchen, the floor should be hardwearing and practical, so stone, linoleum or terracotta tiles are ideal, whereas in the dining area the floor could be warmer, welcoming and stylish, so wood or a high quality, polished limestone, perhaps with a rug or kelim, would be appropriate.

In many kitchens, a section of work area – an island or length of units and worktop – creates an actual, physical break between the two areas. This works well and creates the impression of having a distance between the dining and food preparation zones.

The dining table

The configuration and layout of the dining space should allow for a certain amount of flexibility, so that a family of four will be comfortable having lunch there, but a dinner party for eight will feel equally at home. An extending table will help to accommodate this, whether there are separate leaves to be inserted, or adjustable flaps that fold down.

There are some ingenious round table designs that enlarge by the addition of segments, like putting pieces into an orange. A simpler method is to have a larger disc, made in a cheap material such as MDF or chipboard, that clips on top of the smaller table and can be disguised by a generous round tablecloth. The larger disc can be hinged in the centre so that it may be folded in two and stored in a cupboard, under a bed or in a garage, until it is required.

Seating arrangements

Dining room seating is an important consideration. It is one thing perching on the edge of a wooden stool when you are gulping down breakfast, but quite another to be expected to sit through a lengthy dinner party on a hard stool with no back support.

Dining chairs should have a back to provide some bracing for the diner, and if made of wood or metal, a cushion is important. You can also dress chairs up to give them a more formal appearance by adding a tabard or slip cover (see box, right and pages 184–7).

Another option is to build a well-upholstered window seat or bench style arrangement along a wall. This is ideal for children and will enable you to seat more people than you could in separate seats. The table can be placed in front of the window seat and extra chairs lined up around the edges.

Above: *A low wall separates the dining and kitchen area from the seating space beyond.*

Covering chairs

High-back padded dining chairs are comfortable but can be decoratively covered to make them a feature. The most simple dressing is a long panel of fabric, the width of the back and base of the chair. This drapes over the front and down the back of the chair and is held in place with simple ties at the top and base of the seat back. More tailored covers with skirts that cover the legs are also popular. These can be held in place by bright buttons or contrasting ties of cord or tape.

Above: The way you dress the dining table is as important as the decoration of the room as a whole. It should echo the style of the meal being served, whether it is formal or informal.

Below right: This dining area is at the front of this house, overlooking the street. However, clever use of half shutters and crisp white linen curtains means that the view is obscured but natural light can still come into the room.

At-a-glance colour guide

Eating Room red is a traditional colour for dining room walls – it is a rich period colour and looks opulent in candle or electric light. Chocolate brown, which has an element of red in its composition, is also a luxurious colour against which crisp white linen and sparkling glassware looks good. However, these rich, lavish colours loose something of their intensity in daylight so are best used in evening only rooms.

Colour and style

When considering what colours or style options to use in a dining room, look at the other functions that take place in the space, and also how natural light and artificial lighting will affect the colour and décor at different times of day.

Using colour

If you have a separate dining room you may like to look at richer, darker, more dramatic tones. Dining rooms are most often used at night so you can afford to indulge in a real splurge of jewel shades.

Dark red, rich emerald green and even chocolate brown can look wonderful under muted electric light and candles. Even minimalist and contemporary schemes can include a panel or single wall of these rich colours, to spice up a simple setting.

For a living/dining area choose a scheme that is suitable to both day and night time living. Again, table dressings and lighting can help transform a dining area, but the wall colour and floor covering should be compatible to both functions. If in doubt opt for a neutral or plain scheme and then add details such as pictures, table lamps and patterned cushions.

For a kitchen/dining arrangement the emphasis should be on practicality – fabrics and dressings should be easy to remove and washable. In general stick to light colours as they enhance a feeling of cleanliness and productivity. Choose a darker tone of the same colour for the dining area because this will create a division but retain a link between these parts of the room. Or, paint the kitchen in a single pale colour and then incorporate this colour into the dining area in conjunction with a darker tone of the same colour or a paint effect combining the two shades.

There are certain colours that have an affinity with food and others that don't work so well. Deep purple is a colour seldom found in kitchens or dining rooms, the sludgy shades of olive green, mouse brown and mid-grey are also rarely seen. They may appear as part of a pattern or in a

worktop material such as slate or granite, but in quantity and on their own they can give an impression of grubbiness.

Even though you may vary the floor covering from one area to another and even dress up plain walls in the dining section, it is advisable to keep the ceiling in a uniform plain colour, providing continuity and reflected light.

Style and furnishings

As well as linking shared spaces with colour it is advisable to keep to a similar style of furnishings. If the kitchen is futuristic in steel and glass, then the dining area should have complementary elements to reflect that look. If the sitting area of the room is in a neoclassical style then the dining area should follow suit with columns, pilasters and furniture in a similar vein. But, if you have a separate dining area, in a room by itself, then you can opt for whatever style you like.

tiled tabletop

with limed driftwood edging

This tabletop can be teamed with the legs of your choice and used as a dining, coffee or even outdoor table. Its tiled surface makes it practical to care for as well as heat resistant. We used ceramic tiles, which mimic more expensive sandstone or marble. Their irregular edges give them a handmade appearance and blend well with the driftwood finish of the wooden edging. To give new planks a weathered finish, we first raised the grain of the wood using a blowtorch then toned down the effect with white liming wax. The wax protects the surface too.

Materials

9mm (⅜in) exterior grade plywood for the base

Planks of wood slightly thicker than your tiles

Wooden trim deep enough to cover the plank wood and edge

Liming wax

PVA adhesive

Panel adhesive

Screws

Tile adhesive

Small 'stone' ceramic tiles

Sandstone grout

Panel pins

Tools

Tape measure and pencil

Set square

Handsaw

Mitre saw

Blowtorch

Fine-grade steel wool

Soft cloth

D cramp

Electric drill

Notched spreader

Spirit level

Flexible grout spreader

Calculating the framework

1 Sketch out the dimensions of your table, making sure that you will not need to cut any tiles. This will give you the measurements for the plywood base and the lengths of plank, which will form the frame. Use a set square or the edge of a handsaw to mark the 45-degree corner angles and use the mitre saw to cut out your wood to form the four pieces for the frame.

Preparing the frame

2 Gradually singe the surface of the plank frame using a blowtorch on a low setting. The patterns in the grain will emerge gradually as the surface singes. Make sure that you don't forget to do the sides of the frame too.

3 Apply liming wax to the surface of the wood using fine-grade steel wool, working it well into the grain. Allow this to

Measure the size of the table, marking the 45-degree corner angles before cutting.

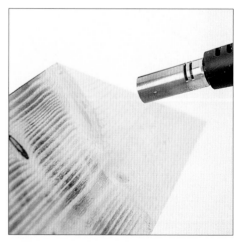

With a blowtorch, singe the surface of the plank frame until the patterns in the grain show.

Know your tools

• When using a blowtorch you should light it with care, following the manufacturer's instructions. Always wear heavy-duty gloves and a protective eye mask. To get the hang of the scorching method described in the project, practise on wood offcuts. This will allow you to see the length of time it takes to raise the grain without burning the wood.

• Always use a notched spreader when applying tile adhesive. This provides a grooved bed of adhesive, which grips the tiles more effectively than a flat surface would.

• Flexible spreaders are used to apply tile grout once the tiles have stuck firmly to the adhesive. The flexible blade of the spreader is used to force the grout into the spaces between the tiles. It can then also be used to remove any excess grout from the surface of the tiles.

dry then polish the surface with a soft cloth to remove any excess liming wax and to ensure you create a neat finish.

4 Seal the surface of the plywood with a coat of diluted PVA adhesive and allow this to dry for approximately half an hour. Anchor the frame in place on the plywood base using panel adhesive. Clamp the frame with a D cramp until it sets, then drill a hole through the back of each corner and put a screw in place to ensure that you create a very firm fixing.

Preparing the surface

5 Apply a thick layer of tile adhesive to the plywood using a notched spreader. Cover the surface up to a height that will ensure that the tiles all sit level with the surface of the frame.

Laying the tiles

6 Bed the tiles firmly into the adhesive, checking regularly with a spirit level to ensure that you achieve a level surface. Then make sure you allow the tiles to set overnight.

7 Use a flexible spreader to work the grout well into the tiled surface, making sure that

there are no gaps. Allow this to set then polish off the excess with a soft cloth.

8 Singe and lime wax the flat edge trim before mitring it to cover the edge of the table. Stick in place using a thick layer of panel adhesive. Position small panel pins at regular intervals to give it an extra firm fixing.

Apply liming wax to the surface of the wood using steel wool. Work it into the grain.

Glue the frame and plywood base together, clamp them and fix screws in the corners.

Apply an even layer of tile adhesive to the surface of the plywood, which will be tiled.

Alternative

If you would like to make a tiled table suitable for outdoor use, then buying a ready-made metal frame is the best option. Many small metalworking companies will be happy to make a table base to your dimensions. To apply an intricate design to it you should use the indirect mosaic method.

Get your timber merchant to cut you a piece of exterior grade plywood to fit snugly within the table frame. Seal both sides with PVA glue diluted one part glue to two parts water. Use coloured pencils and a piece of graph paper to plan your design, working out the exact number of mosaic tesserae needed. Cut a piece of sturdy brown paper to the size of your tabletop, and scale up and transfer your design onto it. Stick individual tesserae, grooved side up, onto the paper using PVA adhesive. Spread tile adhesive onto the plywood surface. Carefully lift the paper and apply to the tabletop, paper side up. Allow to dry before wetting the paper in order to peel it away from the surface. Finally, grout around the tiles.

Lay the tiles in place and use a spirit level to check you are achieving an even surface.

Grout over the surface of the tiles, making sure that you fill in all the gaps.

Glue the singed and limed trim to the sides of the tabletop to finish it off.

suedette

dining chair cover with decorative trim

Any straight-backed dining chair can be instantly transformed with a simple slip cover. For a really luxurious look we have used a chocolate brown suedette, which is an imitation suede. Suedette is far more economical than the real thing, is easy to cut and sew and will not fray. The trick to getting a really good fit is to make a calico or paper 'toile' or pattern first. The leather thong lacing allows the material to be adjusted around the chair legs and also minimizes the amount of sewing involved. Decorative punching along the skirt and colourful feather trims provide a final flourish.

Materials

Calico or newspaper to make toile

Pins

Suedette (around 1.5m/5ft)

Card

Eyelet kit (consists of eyelet punch and rivetter)

4m (13ft) leather thong

Beads to trim

Tools

Scissors

Tape measure

Pinking shears

Sewing machine (or needle and thread for hand sewing)

Pencil

Hole punching tool

Tailor's chalk pencil

Making a template

1 Drape the calico or newspaper over the chair and use scissors, a tape measure and pins to cut and form the shape of the cover. For a snug, tailored fit, one long piece should be folded over to cover the front and back of the chair back. The seat and skirt can then be formed by using additional pieces of calico or newspaper.

2 Remove the paper from the chair and pin the pattern onto the suedette. Cut the pattern out of the material using pinking shears. Leave just over a couple of centimetres (about an inch) allowance all the way round in case there are any necessary final adjustments.

3 Turn the fabric inside out and pin it onto the chair, marking the position of the seams along the sides of the seat and back.

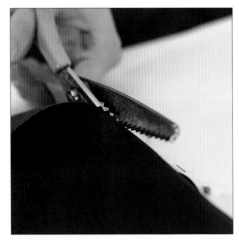

Lay the template over the suedette and cut out the material using pinking shears.

Once the fabric is pinned on the chair, mark the position of the seams using pins again.

Know your materials

Making a paper pattern or calico toile is useful because it allows you to make slight adjustments as necessary on a cheap material, before committing yourself to cutting the final, more expensive material. If you have never cut a pattern before then practise by cutting and pinning a cheap calico toile over a simple shape, such as a footstool or cushion. This will help you get a feel for the technique. You should soon be able to cut an accurate pattern with the right seam allowances, which will mean you are confident enough to move on to work on the proper fabric.

Sewing the cover

4 Sew the pieces together using a short straight stitch. Then press the fabric while it is still inside out using a cool iron. Turn the suedette back the right side out and place it over the back of the chair to check the fit again. Make sure that the flaps meet neatly. Use scissors to trim any excess fabric as necessary.

Creating a pattern

5 Make a pattern of carefully measured holes with a pencil on a piece of thin card and then use a hole punching tool set on different settings to punch out the design. Use the card as a template, placing it on the suedette. Mark the design on each flap using a tailor's chalk pencil.

6 Turn the suedette over and use the hole punch on different-sized settings to punch out the design on the skirt.

Lacing the skirt

7 Using the tailor's pencil, mark six eyelet positions on each side of the skirt at 2cm (just under 1in) intervals. Punch these out with the hole punch. Thread lengths of leather thong through the holes to 'lace' the skirt together.

8 Cut the ends of the thongs to length. Thread a silver bead onto each one, tying knots to secure the beads in place.

Sew the pieces of suedette together using a short straight stitch – by hand or machine.

Once you have a template, mark your design onto the fabric with a tailor's chalk pencil.

Punch out the design using the various sizes on your hole punch.

Alternative

If you prefer a more traditional look then why not adapt the pattern to add stylish covered buttons that fasten along the side of the chair? Covered buttons come in two parts; you simply cover the front piece in your choice of fabric before snapping the back in place.

Measure your chair and cut the fabric following the steps given in the main project, but add a slightly larger seam allowance. Then cut two additional pieces of fabric that will form side flaps to cover the back of the chair. Pin together inside out. Machine stitch the pieces together, hem the back piece neatly and then turn the cover right side out. Position the cover in place over the chair and carefully work out the positions of the buttons, ensuring that when done up they will provide a snug fit. Hand stitch them along the side of the cover. Stitch small loops of elastic in the corresponding positions along the length of the back flap. Slip the buttons through the loops to secure the cover in place.

Punch holes along the sides of the skirt and then lace them together with leather thongs.

Place a silver bead at the end of each leather thong and secure it by tying a knot.

Know your materials

Saris are excellent value for money, when used to decorate a home, as a single one provides around 10m (33ft) of good-quality fabric. They also come in stunning colours. They can be purchased from Indian and Asian fabric merchants, but are increasingly available in large department stores too. Many saris have ornate woven metallic borders, which add extra interest to the material and can be used as a feature in your design.

Saris make great lightweight curtain panels, simply draped or clipped onto a pole. For additional privacy, and to soften the light, you can also use them in conjunction with a blind. They can be used to dress a bed canopy or create a wall hanging, in order to bring some instant colour to a room.

Decorating the pockets

3 Cut lengths of bead trim to fit around the squares, which will make up the pockets, and then pin the trim in place.

4 Sew the bead trim onto the pockets (you will need to position the machine foot on the left or right setting to avoid crushing the beads). Pin the pockets in place at equal intervals on the fabric panels then sew them on to secure.

5 Sew gold mirror trims onto the centre of each pocket.

Fixing your panels to the wall

6 Cut the flat timber battens to the correct length with a hacksaw and feed them into the channels at the top and the bottom of your fabric panels. Hand stitch the channels closed.

7 Use a bradawl to make small holes that drive through the fabric right into the battens. Then carefully screw brass rings so that they sit along the top of each of the panels.

8 Attach the panels to the wall using small brass picture nails or picture hooks, which you can either decorate with tassels (as we have) or glue paste gems into the centre of each one.

Pin the bead trim in place around the top of each of the organza squares.

Sew the trim in place, taking care that you do not damage the beading.

Now hand sew the gold mirror trims onto the centre of each square.

Alternative

If you prefer to create a more permanent fabric wall covering there are various methods to choose from. It is possible to buy textile wallcoverings from specialist wallpaper suppliers. They are fairly expensive but hardwearing – which means that they are often used in commercial interiors. Suitable fabrics include those with heavy weaves like hessians or slubby linens with a high natural fibre content. They consist of a textured fabric surface with a paper backing, which is hung in a similar way to standard wallpaper.

Another option, which provides a quick solution to a poor wall surface, is to fix slim battens along the top and bottom of the wall. The fabric should then be stretched taut and stapled or tacked top and bottom onto the battens. Each width of fabric should be overlapped slightly so that no gaps appear. Canvas or fabric with a high natural fibre content is an ideal choice for this. Once stretched it can be sprayed lightly with water, to cause it to shrink taut.

Feed your timber battens through the channels at the top and bottom of your panels.

Use a bradawl to make holes in the top of the fabric, then screw brass rings along the edge.

Use picture hooks to attach the panels to the wall. These can then be decorated.

ighting your dining room

Lighting a dining room requires several levels of illumination and ideally a dimmer switch so that the intensity of light can be fine tuned to create the right ambience to suit different occasions. The focus should be on the table and the light must be distributed so diners can see each other and what they are eating.

Using candles

Great care should be taken when using candles, especially in glass containers because they may overheat and shatter, so only use containers that are specifically designed to hold candles and are wide enough not to be in direct contact with the flame. Never leave a naked flame unattended in a room. Scented candles are best avoided in a dining room or eating space because their perfume may interfere with the aroma of the food. The senses of taste and smell are closely linked and sweet perfume and savoury aromas may conflict and be unappetizing.

Right: *Light passing through this segmented lampshade creates a swirling pattern on the ceiling.*

Far right: *Nightlight candles in decorative glass containers and taper candles in classic sticks are an effective way to provide atmospheric lighting at the table.*

Creating a mood

For general points about lighting design, see Effective lighting on page 134. In dining areas lighting plays an important role in creating the right mood. For breakfast time the light needs to be bright and invigorating to get sleepy people going. In the summer natural light is best, so windows should have dressings that can be pulled well back to allow the light to pour through. In the winter artificial light takes the place of natural, so it is best to allow curtains and blinds to block out the dark and cold.

Lighting for different occasions

A central light over the table can help to focus attention on eating and will illuminate the food and related items on the surface. Wall lights may also help to bring up the overall level of light in the room. Breakfast and lunch time should not need much artificial light, apart from during a very dull day, when lights can be used to top up the amount of light present in the room.

A retractable centre light over a table is a great way of changing the feel of a meal time. If the light is pulled up close to the ceiling the spread of light is wide, covering most of the table with a

fan of illumination. On the other hand if the light is pulled down closer to the table the beam will be concentrated on a smaller area making the atmosphere more intimate, ideal for a dinner party.

Dimmer switches are another useful way of changing the mood. For breakfast and family meal times the light should be bright and clear so that the food and utensils are clearly visible. However, for smart lunch parties in the autumn and early spring or an evening meal for adults, the lights can be dimmed to a low level and also be augmented by candlelight and low level wall lights.

Reflected lights

In a dining situation reflected light is subtle and attractive. This can be achieved in a number of ways, the most obvious being with a mirror. If you have one over a mantlepiece or on the wall behind a console or side table you can arrange a group of candles so that the flames are reflected in it. This doubles the impact of the light from the flames and also creates an interesting feature.

Candles can be used in wall sconces too. These are wall mounted candle holders that have a back plate, which was originally used to prevent fat and wax from splashing on the walls as well as increasing the efficiency of the light. The back panel of a sconce is usually made from polished metal, copper, brass or steel and it is sometimes made up of a shaped piece of glass or mirror.

Plain glass can also reflect a certain amount of light. If you place a small table lamp or candle in front of a window at night, the polished surface of the window will reflect light back into the room. The darkness outside will also make the light stand out as a feature in its own right.

Light shades

The shades you use on the lights will influence the level of light that comes through them. If you opt for a yellow tinted glass shade then the light will assume a golden hue, while a white shade may mute the strength of light slightly but in general it will still be bright and clear. A dense shade will restrict the flow of light through the sides and concentrate the flow directly downwards.

If the base of the shade is open, as in a standard coolie-hat shaped shade, then the light will shine out of the base, and a small amount through the narrow top, in an increasingly wide triangular pool. A tubular shade will direct the beam in a downward direction while a round or ball shade will not create a direct beam at all – the light will be emitted through the sides of the shade and will create a soft, overall glow, although there

will be an opening at the top of the shade to accommodate the light fitting and to allow heat to escape.

Light bulbs generate heat and therefore will increase the ambient room temperature during the course of an evening. Light bulbs should never be in direct contact with a shade or covering because, as they heat up during use, they may cause the material in contact with them to burn or melt.

Above: *These Chinese ceramic bowls, with patterns created by grains of rice, make an attractive table decoration when they are lit up with candles.*

Left: *In a large room a chandelier, such as this one with its ornate iron structure, can be a focal point and help to reduce the feeling of height and distance in the room.*

Dining area accessories

Accessories for the dining area really revolve around the tabletop and will reflect the type of dining, and maybe even the food that is being served. For casual meals the dressing can be less formal; maybe bowls for pasta or noodles, a knife and fork, a side dish for salad and glasses for water and wine. Mats can be used instead of a cloth and colourful napkins are fun and functional. For more formal entertaining, however, the table is likely to be set with a cloth and a full complement of cutlery, crisp white napkins and several glasses for water and various types of wine. The addition of candles, flowers and other table decorations will depend on the amount of space you have on the tabletop and the time of day that you are entertaining. All these things will add to creating that special sense of occasion. Seating around a dining table should be chosen for its comfort as well as appearance. A rigid and upright chair with little or no back support will make diners restless during the meal, whereas a padded seat and flexible back will help them to relax and enjoy their time with you.

CLOCKWISE FROM TOP LEFT:

Decanting mineral water from commercial plastic containers into decorative coloured glass bottles will add to the attractive appearance of your table.

Trays are old-fashioned but are still useful for carrying items to and from a table.

Various sizes and shapes of glasses are appropriate for different wines and drinks.

Table surfaces such as glass and wood may need to be protected from sharp blades and hot dishes, otherwise they could get marked and damaged.

Don't make a table centre decoration so big that people sitting opposite have to strain to see each other or find it difficult to hold a conversation.

The other furniture in a dining room is as important as the table – think about co-ordinating the materials they are made from as well as using the same handles on all storage items.

This voile envelope contains the cutlery for a single place setting. It can be a useful way of allocating cutlery for a buffet party, so that each guest has their own special container to pick up.

In a more informal dining area, perhaps one that is off of a kitchen, stools and a breakfast bar work well for everyday eating.

Don't forget to think carefully about every aspect of your dining area – even light switches can be chosen as decorative embellishments.

A small plant such as this cactus can be made more dramatic and have larger impact if set in an outsized dish or bowl.

Think about the type of seating that will suit your dining space – stools are an effective way of making the most of limited space.

This table setting has modern elements with leather mats and napkin rings, yet still retains classical feel.

A decorative gilded Moroccan tea glass makes a perfect holder for a night light candle.

Candelabra can add a touch of romance and glamour for evening dining.

Kitchens

Planning your kitchen

The kitchen is the heart of the home – it is where people tend to congregate and have coffee and chat, but it is also where food is prepared, stored and cooked. Standards of hygiene in a kitchen should be rigorous and safety is a factor that must be taken into consideration both in planning and decoration.

Kitchen layouts

Galley kitchens are long, usually narrow, passageway-like spaces where work surfaces and units are lined up along opposite walls, as in the galley of a ship.

Island kitchens are generally found in large rooms where a central block of units and worktop has been installed to make it easier to create the work triangle. The block of units is referred to as the island, because it sits alone on the floor area and is not attached to any other section of work top or units.

Planning your space

The role of the kitchen has changed in the last 30 years. It used to be a room with just one function but it now often has to be multi-functional.

Whether you are designing a kitchen from scratch, altering or adapting an existing one it is best to be aware of the basic rules. The most important of these is that you should always take professional advice and help with plumbing and electrical wiring.

The work triangle

It takes time and effort to create a well-designed layout for a kitchen. Each one is unique in shape and size and will also have its own variety of problems that have to be solved. The standard rule to use as a starting point is to ensure that you create the work triangle. This maps out the three main working areas in a kitchen – the sink, the oven/hob and fridge. These areas should be sited at the points of an imaginary triangle so that you work efficiently and effectively between each point during the preparation of a meal. Beside each point on the triangle it is advisable to have some sort of worktop.

This work triangle should not be interrupted by main traffic thoroughfare so don't position it between two main doorways. The space between each point should be easily accessible and they should not be too far apart. If the distances between the fridge and

Right: *There is easy access between the different working areas of the kitchen and the island unit provides plenty of work surface.*

Opposite: *The design of this small kitchen makes the most of all available space. The sliding panel at the back of the room folds back and connects to the living room.*

Appliances

When choosing appliances, you should be guided by the amount of space you have and the way that you eat and entertain. If you are mainly a takeaway eater then you probably won't make much use of a semi-professional cooker. If you live alone and have a dishwasher then a double sink with integral waste disposal outlet and double drainer may be beyond your needs.

Right: *Here the upper units are long and narrow, which makes the room seem taller. The glass fronts stop the units from being too heavy.*

Below: *Where wall space is at premium this type of open shelving, with a row of hooks for mugs underneath, is effective.*

cooking and washing surfaces are substantial and you cater for a large family or regularly entertain lots of people, you may find a trolley useful to bridge the gap. A butcher's block or island is another option.

It is also wise to keep the fridge/freezer and oven apart because, although both white goods are already insulated, the heat emitted by a high-temperature oven may affect the freeze and chill mechanisms and efficiency of the cooler machines.

Storage considerations

When planning your storage, be sure to take into consideration the doors on the units and appliances. Allow plenty of space for each one to open and to ensure you have easy access to the inner depths.

Ensure that you allocate suitable storage beside each element of the kitchen. By the fridge/freezer you could, for example, have storage for fresh fruit and vegetables in wicker drawers or racks. By the dishwasher you may find cupboards to stack china and drawers for cutlery and glass useful (see Display and storage, pages 218–19).

Fitted or unfitted?

There are two basic types of kitchen units, fitted or unfitted. You can choose whichever you prefer, or opt for a combination of both. The fitted kitchen generally gives a more tailored appearance to the room, whereas the unfitted allows more versatility and variety.

In small kitchens, fitted units can be structured to make the most of all the limited space available. Freestanding units usually look best in a large kitchen. Here a dresser can be placed along one wall and a collection of cabinets and tables used to create a variety of working areas. Freestanding furniture can be a good option if you live in rented accommodation, because you can then take the units and fittings with you when you eventually move.

Unfitted schemes allow you more time to accumulate the various pieces you want. With this type of kitchen you can freely add to it as and when your budget permits and when you come across an attractive piece. A fitted kitchen, on the other hand, is usually bought and installed in one go so you need to ensure that you have the money to pay for it all at once or commit to a monthly payment scheme.

You may decide that you want a combination of fitted and unfitted furniture. It is usually best to ensure the areas where

Filling the gaps

Very few kitchens are perfectly symmetrical and able to accommodate a precise number of regularly sized units. The basic units are base- and wall mounted and these come in standard sizes but most manufacturers produce fill-in units such as broom cupboards, spice cupboards and wine racks, which can be used to complete a scheme.

Most of the standard, factory-made units have a chipboard, plywood or MDF carcass with a melamine or similar facing on the side. Drawers and door fronts can be made of a wide variety of finishes – they are simply attached to the standard carcasses. Inside the carcasses you can have a fixed shelf, or variable shelves that can be moved up and down to meet your storage needs. Corner units come with a number of special fittings including swing shelves that pivot around a central pole – these enable the full depth of the corner to be used. Some units come with a single drawer while others have a complete set that run from top to bottom.

Left: *One of the advantages of a fitted kitchen is that you can have cupboards specially made to fit the space available, such as the narrow corner units in this kitchen.*

Below: *These stylish fitted kitchen cupboards are tailored to follow the line of the opening that leads from the kitchen to the dining room.*

the larger machines or major plumbing is involved are fitted. For example, items such as a wall mounted oven and the sink need to be in a stable unit to support the plumbing and waste points. However, general storage and a table/worktop area can easily be unfitted.

Installing your kitchen

Unless you are a competent DIY enthusiast leave the installation of a kitchen to the professionals. The process is often fraught with problems and requires technical knowledge.

Consult the electrician, plumber and unit fitter before they start and make sure that each knows what the other is up to. If they work individually, rather than being employed by the same company, try to get them to work out a timetable so that they don't get in each other's way and so that they work in a logical order.

When installing a kitchen you should do all the groundwork first and then add decoration. This is because the wiring and ducting for pipes and vents are best done before any flooring or tiles are put in place. Get the cooker, extractor fan and hood, hob, sink and radiators plumbed and wired in before you paint and tile. The fridge/freezer can be put in later as it only requires an electrical socket, and, sometimes, access to a water inlet.

Most fitted units have a base plinth, which can be put in place after the flooring has been laid. The plinth fits between the base of the unit and covers the adjustable legs that support most base units.

Below right: This kitchen is typical of the domestic-professional style – its focal point is the large steel clad hob and industrial style vent. By raising the solid unit on tall legs, it appears less dominant because there is space and light beneath.

Styles of decoration

Once the practicalities have been sorted out you can turn your mind to colour and decoration. There are various styles of kitchen to choose from so you need to think carefully about the look you want to create and how this fits with the various roles your kitchen needs to be able to fulfil.

Domestic-professional kitchens

The domestic-professional style of kitchen is modelled on the steel-clad industrial kitchens of professional chefs. In its ultimate form the scheme is white, steel and clinical, but it is easily adapted to a domestic setting by using colour, wood and softer elements.

The primary pieces of equipment are the industrially inspired cooker, large fridge/freezer and clean, long expanses of work surface. This is a kitchen for keen cooks. The professional oven usually has double the capacity of the standard appliance and you can add a plate warming cabinet and eye level grill.

Keeping your kitchen safe

Ensure that you always have a fire blanket and a small handheld extinguisher near the hob and oven. Also fit a smoke detector or alarm in an area away from the main cooking facilities.

If children have access to the kitchen fit door-fastening devices to cupboards. Fit guard rails around hobs and cookers and, if possible, fit a safety gate across the door.

Don't keep sharp knives in a cutlery drawer. Wall-mounted magnetic bars are a good idea. Another option is a knife block, which keeps knives in order with the blades covered but the handles free.

Left: *This metal-clad kitchen has a sleek, modern style.*

Below: *One way of softening the industrial look is to introduce wood, such as this work surface.*

Bottom: *This single sheet, steel splashback is easy to wipe and polish because it has a continuous smooth surface.*

To go with these large and serious pieces of equipment you need an equally large fridge, again steel clad. Large American-inspired designs are now available on the retail market.

To link these steel-clad machines, the work surface and splashback of the kitchen is often made of steel as well. This type of worktop usually has to be specially made, ideally from a single steel sheet so that there are no unsightly lumps or joins in the middle of a run of working area.

This style of kitchen is very hardwearing and long lasting due to its industrial background. The domestic versions of the appliances are not made to such high mass-catering, specifications but they are still sturdy and will therefore also have a long and productive life in the average domestic kitchen.

Using such a large amount of steel in a room can make it feel cold and hollow so it is important to balance this by introducing natural elements. An occasional warm, wood unit front, wooden flooring or a panel of colour will help. The colours you choose should work with the coolness of the steel so blues, soft shades of lavender and even orange can look good. The flooring can be wooden but if you want to keep strictly to the industrial feel look at polished cement, grey slate or stone or a textured, industrial rubber sheeting.

If this style of kitchen is part of a kitchen/dining room try to avoid too many soft and fluffy elements in the dining area. Echo the clean, uncluttered lines of the kitchen and use similar colours. Simple geometric patterns will complement the modern, no-nonsense look.

Above: Bright colours in a kitchen work well to soften the sometimes clinical look of modern design.

Right: The Belfast sink and traditional style lever taps are typical elements of a country style kitchen.

Simple modern kitchens

A less severe version of the domestic-professional kitchen is the simple modern style. This creates a light and airy surrounding with colour and space. It is still streamlined but has a certain softness to it. Here the layout is practical and functional but elements of colour are encouraged. The doors of the units are generally plain or have a minor panel detail, but they are dressed up with interesting and functional knobs or handles and a colourful laminate or finish. The flooring may also be colourful but washable – for example, a lino in a complementary shade to the unit doors, which incorporates a patterned layout of chequerboard tiles or a laser-cut overall pattern may be used.

This style can be based on a palette of two or three colours, or two colours and a lighter or darker tone of one of them.

If you are in any doubt when you are first devising a scheme, you should start by keeping it very simple. You can always add more decorative elements later but if you put too much in to begin with then it will be much more difficult to subtract any of it later. Simple is usually best.

Country style

Another look that is popular is the country style. Even in city centre homes there are kitchens that look as though they have doors that open out onto green pastures, rather than a two-lane highway. The rural idyll provides inspiration for a number of interpretations. For example, Folk style incorporates tongue and groove panelling, brick or flagstone floors, the dominant enamelled range or Aga cooker with a shelf or fire surround and plenty of utensils, crockery and items on show.

Country style can be pared down to a neater, more spartan Shaker or Scandinavian interpretation or taken to Mediterranean climes where the walls are roughly plastered and painted. White teamed with cobalt blue accessories follows a Greek influence while terracotta and brightly hand-painted plates evoke Italian or Spanish settings.

Two areas that are usually constant in the country genre are the oven and sink. The oven is often an enamel-fronted range cooker or Aga, and dominates a wall of the room. The sink should be a deep, oblong, white ceramic Belfast sink. With this type of sink you may also go for the old-fashioned style of taps.

The colour schemes you choose for the kitchen should complement the genre of country style that you have chosen. Cooler shades such as grey, muted green and pale grey blue indicate a more Scandinavian approach. Stronger tones such as deep greeny blue or ox blood red mixed with warm cherry wood and a leaning toward the neat and tidy indicate a Shaker style kitchen. A more cluttered and colourful range of inspirational pictures with a cottage garden feel and a diverse range of colours is of the English rural vein. Terracotta mixed with either green, red, yellow and strong blue will hint at more distant shores and the warmth of the Mediterranean lands.

For a contemporary take on this old-fashioned style, and to avoid creating a pastiche, extract the elements that you like best and work around them. For example, warm colours and textures, especially those like the adobe walls of traditional south American homes, will suggest heat. Instead of putting your bottles of olive oil in the cupboard leave them on a

shelf. Pots of fresh basil and oregano on the window sill will provide a subtle hint and some nice, clear glass Kilner jars with various dried pastas will also allude to their country of origin.

Traditional kitchens

The last style is the traditional kitchen, which relies mainly on a long-standing, tried and tested formula. In its purest form this is a working kitchen like the semi-professional, but instead of taking stainless steel as its main feature, wood is dominant. The wood can be natural, painted or even stained and is mixed with other established materials and finishes such as ceramic tiles. Slate, stone and glass are also present.

In some cases wood and even old wood is simulated with modern materials and finishes to create a viable traditional appearance. MDF units can be routed to create a faux tongue and groove and paintwork may be rubbed down around the corners and in areas where, over many years, signs of wear would naturally appear.

The basic traditional kitchen is once again a simply decorated room, but it is up to you to accessorize and embellish. However, although this type of kitchen is meant to feel 'lived in', you should never let the amount of accessories you have get to a level where they begin to interfere with the functionality of the room.

Left: A Scandinavian country setting where the dominant material is wood.

At-a-glance colour guide

Kitchens are best decorated in light, fresh colours on the walls – secondary colour can be introduced in units and soft furnishings.

The domestic-professional kitchen (see pages 214–15) is usually white with plenty of stainless steel, but to soften this look for the home add elements of wood and splashes of colour such as orange or blue.

The simple modern kitchen (see opposite) can incorporate a scheme of two colours and tonal variations of the main colours.

The country style kitchen (see opposite) generally mixes white or cream with pea-green, sky blue, cherry-red or sunflower yellow, unless you go for a Mediterranean scheme where terracotta takes the place of the white and lavender blue and olive green become the complementary colours.

Traditional style (see left) often mixes wood with slate, stone, glass and ceramics and revolves around a natural colour palette rather than fashionable colours.

Display and storage

In a kitchen storage should be allocated so that the items are close to the place where they will end up being used most often. For example, keep spices near the hob where they will be shaken into dishes, and spatulas and wooden spoons near the work surface where you stir ingredients.

Storing pots and pans

Care should be taking when storing pots and pans. If you stack frying or shallow pans on top of one another, fold a double thickness of kitchen towel and place it between the two to prevent damage to the enamel or non-stick surface of the lower pan. Before storing woks and cast iron pots, dry them thoroughly and brush over the surface lightly with cooking oil.

Storing and displaying kitchen equipment

Kitchen cupboards are important areas for storing equipment, pots and pans as well as tinned foods, but there are also many display opportunities around the kitchen.

Storing utensils

In most kitchens a number of frequently used utensils are kept out so that they are always to hand, so this inadvertently leads them to being on display. The way

in which these things are contained or shown will depend on the style and decoration of kitchen that you have chosen, but here are a few suggestions.

Spatulas, wooden spoons and light wooden utensils can easily be kept upright in a glass, ceramic or metal container that is positioned on a worktop.

Rails or rods and butchers' hooks are popular hanging options. You can use a wooden pole in a country or traditionally

decorated kitchen or steel in a more contemporary one. Butchers' hooks are S-shaped, made of steel and come in two sizes – the large is big enough to support pots and pans whereas the smaller size is ideal for hanging spoons, spatulas and whisks from.

When hanging heavier items you should ensure that the rail is strong enough to support the weight. If you use a long rail that is holding heavy weights then you may need to put a couple of extra support brackets, fixed to the wall or ceiling, along the rail.

If you want an alternative to a rail then you can use a chain. This chain should be made of a strong metal with good size links. The chain can be hung horizontally between two points or cut in varying lengths that are individually hung and allowed to fall vertically.

Storage containers and units

Storage jars need not always be shut away in a cupboard. Think about displaying them on a shelf to add a decorative feature and also to allow easy access to the items stored within them, such as tea, coffee and sugar. Give such jars a sense of unity by choosing a matching set such as steel and glass or white ceramic containers.

Above right: Butcher's hooks are used to hang steel utensils close to the hob where they will be most frequently used.

Glass containers are extremely good for display as they show the contents from top to bottom.

Traditional wicker and reed baskets are fine for general storage but they do hide most of their contents behind dense sides so you should only use them in cases where you don't mind concealing what is contained within them.

Plate racks can be fitted inside a cupboard or on the wall over the work surface. These enable you to slot washed, flat tableware in between the sections in order to leave them there to dry (see Storing plates, page 193).

Displaying equipment

Although the clean worktop approach is advocated in modern kitchens, a few useful pieces of equipment can be left on show to soften the edges and provide the feeling of a lived-in space.

Salt and pepper mills are often placed on an open shelf so that they are easily accessible because they are in constant use. Mills come in a variety of shapes and sizes but a matching pair of chrome, glass or wood pieces will look very appealing in any kitchen. Choose a pair that will go with your overall colour scheme.

Classic pieces of equipment such as the Philippe Starck Alessi juice squeezer, a cafetière or French coffee percolator are common show pieces. A neat espresso coffee maker and a kettle are also fashionable kitchen equipment.

The rule with this sort of accessory is that it should be both useful and beautiful. If you are leaving it on display then make sure that you choose the nicest shape, the best finish and also the one that has the most interesting lines, because it will become part of the look of the kitchen.

Storing and displaying food

Fresh fruit and vegetables can bring a pleasant splash of colour to a kitchen and will also be a constantly changing embellishment as you replace what you have eaten from the display. To display fruit and vegetables well look at open weave metal baskets, which allow the fruit to show through and also breathe, and glass bowl containers. The disadvantage with glass

bowls is that they restrict the airflow to the lower fruits, which means that they will ripen and rot much more quickly. Make sure that you use fruit and vegetables within a few days, before they start to go wrinkled or mouldy.

Left: Plates can be neatly stored away inside a drawer. Wooden dowels prevent the plates from moving around and getting broken.

Below left: Frequently used and stylish equipment can become part of your display.

Below: Glass is effective as a display because it reflects light back into the room.

wall writing

paint effect

Painted lettering is a cheap and effective way of adding wit and humour to a wall. Writing in a foreign language always looks far more stylish than your mother tongue, which will also add a touch of glamour and mystery to something as mundane as a recipe. The writing is achieved by using cotton buds and wet acrylic scumble glaze. If you are confident of your own handwriting style you can work freehand but for a neater, more controlled look use an overhead projector, which will allow you to project a guide onto the wall. Projectors can be hired from most good tool hire firms.

Materials

Pale blue emulsion (acrylic) for your base coat

Acetate projector paper

Acrylic scumble glaze in slate blue

Cotton buds

Satin acrylic varnish

Tools

Paintbrush or roller

Computer

Marker pen

Soft-bristled brush

Overhead projector

Varnish brush

Preparing the surface

1 Apply the pale blue base coat to the wall and leave it to dry.

Creating the recipe acetate

2 Type out your chosen recipe on a computer using a suitable font and print it out on acetate paper. Alternatively, you can handwrite onto the acetate

using permanent marker pen, which is what we did here.

Transferring the recipe

3 Use a broad, soft brush to apply the scumble glaze to the wall using random strokes.

4 Place the acetate sheet on the projector and adjust it so

that the recipe fills the wall space. Work quickly, 'writing' in the glaze with a cotton bud. Take a fresh bud as soon as the one you are using becomes clogged.

5 Once dry, protect the recipe wall by applying a coat of satin acrylic varnish using a varnish brush.

Apply the base coat over the whole wall using a brush, or roller if you prefer.

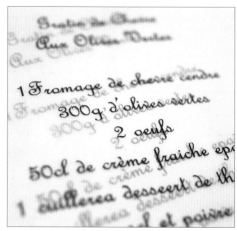

Type your recipe and print it out onto acetate paper, or write directly onto the acetate.

2 oeufs.

50 cl de crème fraîche épaisse

1 cuillerea desseert de thym frais,

sel et poivre

Coupez le chèvre en tranches puis, en mor

Battez ensemble la crème fraîche et les oe

ajoutez le thym frais, du sel et du poi

Dans, quatre ramequins, disp

fromage puis versez des

With a broad, soft-bristled brush, apply the scumble glaze in random strokes to the wall.

With the writing on the acetate projecting onto the wall, 'write' in the glaze with a cotton bud.

Once the writing is dry, protect the wall with a coat of satin acrylic varnish.

revamped

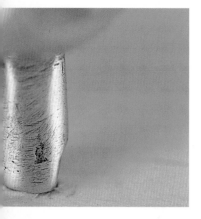

kitchen cabinets with wood veneer

If you are fed up with your existing kitchen units or have inherited units that are not to your taste you can revamp them in a number of ways. A simple way of giving plain flat doors a quick facelift is to stick thin wood veneer over the melamine surface. The beauty of this treatment is that the doors look as if they are solid wood. There are also a huge variety of different veneers available so you can choose the colour and grain that most appeals to you. A couple of coats of yacht varnish gives the veneer a tough surface. Simple chrome pebble handles provide a contemporary touch.

Materials

Wood veneer

Contact adhesive

White spirit

Yacht varnish

Knobs or handles of your choice

Screws

Tools

Flexible sanding block

Pencil

Metal ruler

Sharp craft knife

Adhesive spreader

Pile of books or something similar

Cloth

Fine-grade wet and dry paper

Varnish brush

Drill and wood bit

Screwdriver

Preparing the doors

1 Clean each melamine door well to remove any grease and grime. Use a flexible sanding block to 'key' the surface.

Cutting the veneer

2 Place each door face down on the sheet of veneer and, using a pencil, draw around the doors to mark their outlines on it.

3 Carefully cut out the veneer using a metal ruler and a sharp craft knife (see picture bottom left, page 224). Handle the veneer with care as you do this – it is brittle and marks easily.

Attaching the veneer

4 Spread a thin, even layer of contact adhesive over the front of one door and the back of its corresponding veneer and allow to dry until just tacky. Carefully lower the veneer into place over the door. Accuracy is very important at this point as the

Once you have cleaned the surface of the doors, use a sanding block to create a 'key'.

Place each door in turn on top of the veneer and draw around it with a pencil.

Know your materials

The best way of fixing veneer panels in place is to use contact adhesive. This is a very pungent glue that should be used in a well ventilated space. (Always wear a face mask for extra protection against fumes.) It is important to spread a thin layer evenly on each surface to be stuck, as the bond is instantly formed between the two layers. This does mean that repositioning is impossible so take great care when placing the veneer on the door. Once stuck, even pressure should be applied over the whole surface to stop areas rising or 'bubbling' – use a layer of heavy books or magazines and leave for the manufacturer's recommended drying time.

glue forms an instant bond, making it difficult to reposition the veneer. When in place cover with a cloth to avoid marking the surface and weigh the veneer down evenly with piles of books.

Finishing touches

5 When the front of the door is dry cut thin lengths of veneer

that are slightly wider than the sides of the doors. Spread both the door side and thin strip with glue and stick the first one in place. Use a sharp craft knife to trim away the excess for a perfect fit (it is a good idea to use a new blade for each cut). Wipe away any residue of glue with a cloth dipped in a little white spirit as this

will mark the finish if left. Continue this process until you have covered all of the doors.

6 Sand the veneer using fine wet and dry paper for a super smooth finish and wipe it down with a little white spirit (do not use water as this will cause the veneer to swell). Use a clean varnish brush to apply a thin layer of yacht varnish over the surface and sides of each door. Allow to dry then sand lightly with wet and dry paper before adding a further two coats of varnish for an extra hard finish.

7 Mark the position of your knobs or handles, then drill using a wood bit.

8 Screw the knobs in place. Hang the doors back up and tighten the hinges.

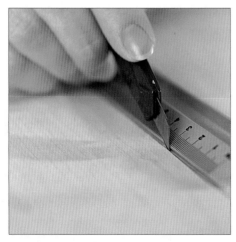

Use a metal ruler and sharp craft knife to cut out the various pieces of veneer.

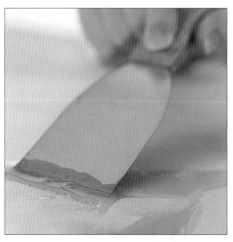

Cover the veneer surfaces with contact adhesive using an adhesive spreader.

Create thin strips of veneer to cover the door sides. Glue, stick in place and trim to fit.

Alternative

For a more industrial look, you can use a similar technique to cover existing cabinets in sheet metal. This is not a cheap option and should only be considered if your cabinets are of high quality and are still in good condition. For a really professional finish it is best to take your cabinet doors to a specialist metal supplier who will be able to 'wrap' the cabinet doors in thin metal sheeting, to give a perfectly smooth finish.

If you want to have a go at doing it yourself get your choice of sheet metal cut to fit the front of the cabinet doors. A solid metal sheet can be stuck in place using contact adhesive applied to both surfaces. It should then be weighted until dry. If you have chosen a pierced design this method will not work so you should use small tacks or screws to secure the metal sheets along the edges of the cabinet doors instead. Make sure that the metal you have chosen is rust resistant – if in doubt seal with a coat of clear lacquer varnish. Finish off with contemporary knobs or handles.

Once you have created a smooth finish, apply a thin layer of yacht varnish to the veneer.

Drill the holes for your knobs or handles using a wood drill bit.

Screw all of your chosen knobs into position on the doors before rehanging them.

toughened

glass splashback with tile design

Toughened glass provides a good alternative to tiles acting as a splashback in a kitchen or bathroom. Glass merchants can cut glass to your measurements and bevel or polish the edges to make it safe to handle. Ask for the glass to be drilled so that you can secure it in place. You can back the glass with the design of your choice. Here we used a chequered aluminium leaf design, which gives a modern tiled appearance echoing chrome utensils. Rubbing the leaf with fine-grade steel wool gives the leaf a distressed look, allowing the backing to show through.

Materials

Length of predrilled toughened glass

Lining paper

Water-based gold size

Sheets of aluminium transfer leaf

Fine-grade steel wool

Clear wax polish

Blue emulsion (acrylic) paint

Rawlplugs

Mirror screws

Tools

Soft cloth

Scissors

Set square

Pencil

Small paintbrush

Drill

Masonry bit

Screwdriver

Preparing the glass

1 Clean the piece of glass thoroughly to ensure that there are no greasy marks on it, then polish with a soft cloth.

Designing the backing

2 Using a pair of scissors, cut a length of lining paper the same size as the splashback. Mark out a grid of squares about the size of kitchen tiles with a set square and pencil. Make sure that there are no cuts in the design.

3 Place the glass splashback carefully over the grid, making sure that all the edges line up exactly. Use the grid as a guide and, with a fairly small paintbrush, apply a thin layer of water-based size over each alternating square.

4 Allow the size to dry for the recommended time until it becomes clear. If necessary cut

Clean the glass to remove all greasy marks and fingerprints, then gently polish with a soft cloth.

Using a paintbrush, apply a thin layer of water-based size over alternate squares on the glass.

Know your materials

Glass provides a hygienic, easy-to-clean alternative to tiles in both kitchens and bathrooms. Although it needs to be handled with care, glass is also extremely resilient when used correctly. A good glazier should be able to recommend the correct thickness for your project and cut and drill it to the size that you require.

All interior glass must carry the safety mark to prove that it is toughened for use in the home. It is important to ask for glass that has a polished or bevelled edge, as this removes any sharp edges. You could try using glass with an etched pattern or Georgian wired glass, which would make attractive alternatives.

the aluminium transfer leaf to the required size with a pair of sharp scissors. Apply the sheet of aluminium transfer leaf carefully, making sure that it lines up exactly with the square that you have already marked on the lining paper.

Applying the transfer leaf

5 Rub the back of the sheet of aluminium transfer leaf carefully. You must make sure that it adheres firmly to the water-based size. Then gently peel off the backing paper, ensuring that you leave the aluminium transfer leaf in place.

6 Dip a small piece of fine-grade steel wool in a little clear wax polish and use it to rub the back of the aluminium transfer leaf gently. This action will lift away small areas of the

transfer leaf and will allow some of the backing to show through.

7 Using a small paintbrush, apply the blue emulsion (acrylic) paint over the back of each square of the aluminium leaf and then allow the leaf to dry.

Fixing the splashback

8 Position the glass against the wall and use a pencil to mark the drilling point. Use a masonry bit to drill a hole and fill with a Rawl-plug suitable for your wall. Screw the splashback in place using a mirror screw with a chrome cap.

Apply a sheet of aluminium transfer leaf to the lining paper making sure it adheres to the size.

Peel back the lining paper carefully making sure the transfer leaf remains in position.

With a piece of fine-grade steel wool dipped in clear wax, rub the back of the transfer leaf.

Alternative

To create a traditional tiled splashback you could use irregular broken tiles or small mosaic tesserae cut with tile nibblers to form organic patterns. You will need to start with a completely smooth, clean wall. Plan your design first by producing a sketch with coloured pencils on graph paper. Use the direct mosaic method, which involves transferring your design directly onto the wall in pencil. Apply waterproof tile adhesive, 'buttering' it onto the back of each tesserae or tile fragment to build up the design one piece at a time. You will find it easiest to start by sticking down the pieces that form the outlines of the shapes within the design – then fill in large blocks of colour around them. Place whole tesserae first then use tile nibblers to cut smaller shapes to fit the design.

Using broken tiles or pieces of china is a good way to achieve a design on a budget. Break them up by placing them in a strong plastic bag or wrap them in a tea towel. Use a hammer to break the items into small irregular pieces.

Paint the back of the transfer leaf with some blue emulsion (acrylic) and allow to dry.

Finish off by screwing the glass splashback to the wall using mirror screws with chrome caps.

lighting your kitchen

Task lighting that illuminates the work surfaces of a kitchen is a top priority – after all, this is the place where you will pour hot liquids and use sharp knives. But the kitchen may also be used as a dining area or place to have coffee with friends, so a softer, more ambient level of lighting will also be required.

Natural and artificial light

It is extremely important to provide effective lighting in every part of the kitchen. For general points about lighting design, see Effective lighting, page 134.

Using natural lighting

It used to be a rule that kitchen designers invariably put the sink in front of a window so that the person washing up had something to look out on, but with the advent of the dishwasher this is no longer a priority. Daylight is still a prized commodity because its access and flow is usually restricted by wall mounted units and machines. To get around this an increasing number of people are putting velux or glass roof panels and windows in the kitchen ceiling. This is a perfect solution in an extension or single storey dwelling.

In an apartment block or house with upper levels over the kitchen it is often not possible to carry out this sort of improvement so other options have to be explored. Shiny surfaces are good at reflecting light but they can be hard to keep in good condition. Pale and white-based colours will help, as will tidy worktops. By keeping clutter to a minimum you will make your room appear to be lighter.

Right: A large window can be an asset in a kitchen because it allows plenty of natural light in. An adjustable blind will help soften the light if it is too bright.

Below: This lighting feature at the base of an island unit faces towards the dining area and creates an unusual display in the evening.

Window treatments can also contribute. Opt for blinds or sheer curtains, which can be pulled back rather than heavy window dressings, which restrict light and may also be a haven for grime.

Artificial lighting

An overall ambient light is useful – when first entering the kitchen this will give you a general view and be adequate for a simple or direct assignment. To work within the kitchen you will need task lights that focus a steady and even beam of light on the work surface.

Task lighting is usually positioned under the lower edge of wall-mounted units and should run the length of the unit in order to allow the light to be distributed across the whole, lower surface.

Spotlights or recessed ceiling lights provide a good level of light over large areas such as an island or hob area. This type of light needs to be carefully positioned and angled to avoid the beam casting a shadow of the person over the work area. Pendant lighting is also a useful addition, if placed over an eating area.

Light fixtures, fittings and accessories

Under-unit lights are often small strip lights. Fluorescent tubes were once the main source of light here but now mains voltage halogen tubes are more popular.

For pendant and wall lights, it is best to avoid shades that are delicate and fragile because they are difficult to clean, whereas metal, enamel, glass and ceramic can be easily washed down.

If the kitchen is a large room or a kitchen/dining space it may be worth having two or three different circuits of lights connected to individual switches. Then you can turn off the main kitchen lights but leave an ambient lighting level in the dining area. It is also a good idea to have a switch by the main door that turns off all the lights.

Above: *Fibreoptic lighting set into the glass work surface and lower edge of the cabinets gives a constant level of light over the whole area.*

Left: *The linear lighting along the side walls illuminates the worktop from both sides, rather than from directly overhead. This type of lighting will mean that you can avoid casting shadows over food while you work.*

recycled

slate and zinc noticeboard

This stylish and useful noticeboard exploits the beautiful weathered finish of old roofing slates, which make an ideal chalk board frame. Within the frame there is a zinc panel onto which postcards, recipes, invitations and other stray pieces of paper can easily be attached with magnets, making it ideal for use in the kitchen or the office. Let the roof slates dictate the size of your noticeboard so that you will not have to cut them down to size. The predrilled holes can then be used to anchor the slates in place on the backing with a few galvanized 'clout' nails used for roofing.

Materials

Slate roof tiles

Plywood

Abrasive paper

Slate grey paint

Sheet of galvanized metal

Contact adhesive

Screws

Clout nails

Chalk

Kitchen string

Magnets

Tools

Pencil

Metal ruler

Jigsaw

Medium paintbrush

Electric drill

Screwdriver

Tile adhesive spreader

Pair of gloves

Piece of wood

Small hammer

Measuring the frame

1 Work out the dimensions of the frame by laying out the slate roof tiles on to the piece of plywood. With a pencil, draw around the slate tiles as a guide, then using a long metal ruler, measure 1cm (½in) in and mark out the frame.

2 Cut out the frame carefully with a jigsaw and then with a piece of abrasive paper, sand to remove any rough edges.

Painting the frame

3 Using a medium-sized paintbrush, paint the entire frame with a couple of coats of slate grey paint and then allow to dry for a couple of hours.

4 Once the paint is dry, turn the frame over and place the sheet of galvanized metal over the hole (it should be large enough to overlap the edges of the hole by a couple of centimetres – about an

To measure the size of the frame, place the tiles on the plywood and then draw around them.

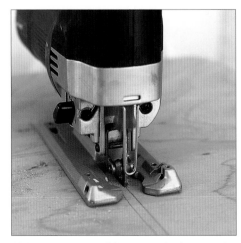

Using a jigsaw, carefully cut out the frame and then gently sand to get rid of any rough edges.

Know your tools

Power tools make most DIY projects quicker and easier. If you do not own any, then it is a good idea to borrow them from a friend or hire them from a tool hire outlet. This will help you to get a feel for them before you invest in tools of your own. The most useful power tools are the jigsaw and electric screwdriver/drill.

Jigsaws have detachable blades that can cut various materials with accuracy. (When cutting most materials, it is advisable to wear eye protection and a dust mask.)

A combination electric screwdriver and drill is a dual purpose tool. Detachable drill bits are available for making holes of various sizes in different materials and a range of screwdriver bits can also be attached for speedy screwing. It is useful, when choosing, to pick a model that has a reverse action so that you can unscrew with ease too.

inch). With an electric drill, drill then countersink a hole in each corner and screw in place.

5 Using a tile adhesive spreader, spread some contact adhesive onto the front of the frame and also onto the back of the slate tiles. When using contact adhesive make sure you use gloves to protect your hands. Allow the adhesive to partially dry (it needs to be tacky in order to carry out the next step).

Assembling the frame

6 When the adhesive is still tacky, position the slate tiles onto the frame and press firmly in place with a piece of wood. Ensure that you wear gloves to do this. Allow the adhesive to dry then, with a small hammer, tap a clout nail through the holes in each slate tile.

7 Attach a large piece of white or coloured chalk to a medium piece of kitchen string or twine and then tie the string around one of the clout nails to secure in place.

8 The frame is now ready to be used. Using magnets of your choice, position postcards, recipe cards, pictures and any other pieces of paper that are lying around onto the frame.

Paint the plywood frame in a couple coats of slate grey paint and allow to dry thoroughly.

Using a screwdriver, screw the sheet of galvanized metal firmly in place.

Apply some contact adhesive to the back of the frame and the slate tiles and allow to dry.

Alternative

As an alternative, you could create a stencil design on your kitchen noticeboard. In this dramatic piece, the elements of air, earth and water are represented by doves, grapes and fish. To make this, choose an appropriate size of 12mm (1/2in) MDF board. Use a mini roller and tray to apply two coats of blackboard paint or black matt emulsion. Leave to dry. Stencil a flock of doves at the top of the board. Place a grape leaf stencil in the top left-hand corner. Stencil a bunch of grapes underneath and repeat two thirds of the way down the board, then create the shoal of fish. To protect the pattern, gently brush on a coat of acrylic dead flat varnish using a nylon decorating brush. If you want to use different colours, experiment with variations in pearlized colours, such as jades, pinks and silvers.

As soon as the adhesive is tacky position the slate tiles onto the frame and press in place.

Once the tiles are in place, tap a nail through the tile holes to fix them securely to the frame.

Kitchen accessories

These are mainly practical pieces of equipment that are constantly on display in a kitchen. This could be because they are frequently used and need to be easily accessed or because they are bulky, heavy and difficult to store and retrieve. Where possible keep kitchen accessories off the worktops as they will restrict the amount of surface you have to work on and may also become splattered with ingredients when you are preparing food. Store your utensils and equipment in good working order so that they are always ready for use. If items are left out long term, cover them with a cotton cloth or washable cover to protect the working parts from general kitchen grease and condensation. Small items such as knives should be kept in a knife block or on a wall mounted magnetic strip, as leaving sharp knives in drawers can be dangerous. Wooden spoons and spatulas can be kept in a ceramic or metal holder with the handles downwards and the ladle or paddle section upwards so that it is easy to identify each one.

CLOCKWISE FROM TOP LEFT:

Retro-style products, such as these chrome pieces, look as though they are vintage but are in fact manufactured to the highest modern standards.

Traditional wooden chopping boards are still very popular. You should have separate ones for cutting different types of food such as raw red meats, chicken, onions and garlic, and fruit, so that tastes, aromas and enzymes don't transfer.

Clean, sparkling glassware is attractive and may be left on display, but be aware that it could become smudged and marked if left too close to a cooker.

Items that are in daily use, such as a toaster, may be left on the work surface for easy access.

Lever taps are very easy to turn on when you have sticky or flour-covered hands.

It is best to keep all your knives in a wooden knife block, out of harm's way.

Stainless steel utensils can be hung from a simple rack near to where they will be used.

This old butcher's block has seen many years of use but is still a welcome addition and feature in most styles of kitchen.

Copper pans are treasured by professional chefs because the metal conducts heat quickly, but they must be kept well polished if they are to be left on show.

A draining rack or surface is extremely useful positioned next to a sink.

Store like things with like so that you automatically know where they are. For example place teapots beside the cups and saucers, as you will need them all at the same time.

Coloured glassware adds an unexpected decorative element in a practical environment.

Simple handles are best in a kitchen because they are easy to hold and pull when your hands are wet or greasy. They are also easy to wipe clean.

Pepper and salt mills do not need to look mundane. There are so many to choose from so find one that echoes the style of your kitchen.

Bathrooms

Planning your bathroom

The bathroom is more than just a place to carry out your daily washing and cleaning ablutions – it doubles as a sanctuary of rest and relaxation into which you can withdraw after a busy day, a place in which you can unwind and pamper yourself.

Planning your space

The bathroom needs to be an adaptable space, with chameleon qualities. A well-designed bathroom should be a bright, invigorating and a high-speed cleansing space in the morning, but also a calming, tranquil oasis

Below: Bathrooms planned on a linear scheme, so that all the main appliances run along one wall, make the best use of long, narrow spaces.

for a soak in the bath later in the day. So, planning the design, layout and decoration of a bathroom is important.

First, identify your needs. If you prefer a shower, fit a separate shower cubicle into the bathroom or another space and leave the bath-only bathroom as a back up or visitors' facility. Or, if you have a limited amount of space in the bathroom, plumb the shower in over the bath providing a two-in-one resource.

Where possible try to alleviate the pressure on a single bathroom with the sole lavatory by installing another lavatory and a small handbasin elsewhere. Handbasins can be installed into bedrooms and even self-contained shower cubicles may be plumbed into an alcove or a fitted wardrobe space in the bedroom to take more pressure off the main bathroom.

When planning the layout and design of your bathroom, first find out and locate the following utilities because the plumber is bound to ask. Where is the access to mains water and drains? What is your tank capacity and where is it situated?

Family bathrooms or main bathrooms need to be practical and easy to maintain. It is a busy room where steam and damp are present on a daily basis so good ventilation is important. Ventilation

can be provided by gadgets such as a panel fan, which is inserted in a window or ducts recessed into a false ceiling – this will disperse the dampness as well as preventing mould from growing on grout or the shower curtains.

An effective bathroom layout

The main bathroom should be planned so that there is space to move without bumping into things. The layout of traditional bathrooms is usually worked out around the largest piece of fitted furniture, the bath.

The bath is often plumbed in at the far end of the room with its longest side running parallel to the longest wall. At the foot of the bath is the toilet and beside that the handbasin. The basin and toilet are usually located nearest the door as they are used most often. This linear layout provides a corridor of space in front of each item making them accessible.

In a square room the bath could be along one wall with the toilet and basin opposite, leaving the third wall free for the door and the fourth for storage or a shower.

Space saving ideas

There are two types of bathroom suite – floor standing and wall hung. With floor standing units, the basin, toilet and bidet are mounted on co-ordinating

Left: In an en-suite bathroom such as this ventilation is very important so that humidity is quickly and efficiently expelled and does not damage the fabrics and finishes, or make clothes in the bedroom damp.

Safety features

Light switches need to be carefully positioned to comply with building safety standards. Standard panel switches should be installed on the outer wall, not in the bathroom. If the switch is in the bathroom it should be activated by a string pull from a socket set into the ceiling. The lights themselves should be contained in sealed units.

Only use electrical appliances that are specifically designed for use in a bathroom, such as designated shaver sockets.

Non-slip mats and textured tape strips that adhere to the base of the bath are ideal for households with young children or older people. If children have access to the bathroom, make sure that medicines and cleaning agents are placed in a wall mounted cupboard that has a child-proof catch on the door.

pedestal bases, while with wall hung items, the fixtures are attached directly to the wall, which leaves the floor space much more clear.

Wall hung items can make a small room feel more spacious because of the empty floor area – also you can allow for some overlap, which may just help you squeeze in an extra item. For example, a handbasin can overlap with the edge of the cistern of the toilet, or can edge out over the end of the bath.

The small, modern cisterns now made for toilets mean that you can hide the unprepossessing water container behind a wall panel or a tongue and grooved section, so that it is not on view. With a panel, marble slab or any such covering it will, however, be necessary to make a section removable to gain access to the cistern.

Another option is to mount the basin on or in a cupboard, which provides extra storage space too. The basin can rest on top

of the surround or surface, or even be countersunk so it lies beneath.

En-suite bathrooms

The en-suite bathroom has also risen in popularity. This linked facility provides a direct connection to the bedroom. In some older homes people sacrifice a second bedroom or study to have the luxury of this extra bathroom and in modern apartments they are often standard in the main bedroom.

Below: Double basins can streamline preparation time for a busy working couple.

En-suite bathrooms are often linked to, or part of, a dressing room or wardrobe area and in these cases the decorative theme can take a lead from the bedroom and continue into the bathroom, so keeping a common or complementary colour and pattern theme.

If space is at a premium consider sliding doors instead of conventional opening doors between the bedroom and this space. Sliding doors or panels take up less space and can be made with an opaque section at the top so that natural light from the bedroom can filter through to the bathroom, making it feel more light and spacious.

Wet rooms

Another recent trend is for wet rooms. These are small or modest-sized rooms that are completely tanked and tiled. A waterproof liner must be laid before tiling and a gentle slope

built into the floor so that the water will drain away easily through a single outlet. Wet rooms are large showers without the restrictions of doors, curtains or panels. They can also be fitted with steam attachments so that they can double up as a steam room. In this type of setting it is common to find a small wooden stool or built-in, tiled bench area so that the bather can relax in the warm, moist environment.

Decoration and style

A bathroom is a private space where you can indulge your fantasies and decorate in a style that gives you pleasure.

Practical decorating

Whatever style of decoration you opt for, make sure that you bear in mind the practicalities of cleaning and the main purpose of the space. A quantity of fancy or ornate decorative objects will be time-consuming to clean, and thick pile carpet will be difficult to vacuum thoroughly. There are specially designed acrylic carpets, but it is a floor covering that is best avoided for the bathroom.

Good ventilation is paramount because the fabrics stored and displayed, such as curtains, upholstered furniture and clothes, can be ruined by steam and damp. This also applies to linen cupboards or storage where towels and bedding are kept, as warmth and damp can give rise to mildew.

Waterproof and water-resistant materials play a major role in bathroom décor. These used to focus on the standard ceramic tiles and mirror, vinyl paints and papers as well as reinforced glass, but some industrial materials have also made their way into this domestic setting.

Stainless steel is now used to form baths and basins, as well as panels and shower trays. Polyurethane sheeting, even corrugated as in the roofing building material, can make an unusual panel for the side of a bath or even a sturdy door to a shower enclosure.

Acrylic, fibreglass and resin mixes are used in the construction of preformed units such as the all-in-one basin and surround or bath with integral shelf or wide lip around the perimeter. Materials once regarded as cold and uncomfortable in the bathroom have also had a reprieve – underfloor heating makes stone and even marble a viable floor covering in this space.

Tiles have also developed from the plain-coloured square or those with a transfer motif. Nowadays there is a wide interest in mosaic, whether laid randomly in a mixture of several shades of one colour, or pictorially. There are metallic and iridescent finishes, tiles with insets of metal and relief patterns and encaustic tiles with flat matt finishes, all available in a wide variety of shapes and sizes.

Large sheets of reinforced glass are now very popular as splashbacks around basins and baths. Curved opaque glass panels are used to create shower cubicles and basins. Wood that is specifically dried and finished for bathroom use is also gaining recognition – it has long been used in saunas and spas because it adds a warm and earthy element to what could be a cool and clinical room.

Using colour

The colour scheme that you use in your bathroom is a personal choice, but blues and greens are

and Victorian interiors – dark wood and rich colours were in vogue then. Art Deco style with its angular shapes and black, white and chrome schemes can also be attractive and opulent or you could go back to the founding fathers of the bathing culture and study Roman references, with details such as mosaics and sunken baths. Your bathroom could also be inspired by the style of other countries and cultures. For example, Turkish and Moorish civilizations made great use of colourful and decorative ceramic tiles. Turkish steam baths are found around the country and many are decorated with blue, white, green and brown tiles in delightful geometric designs. Moorish tile work can be seen in homes in southern Spain and north Africa, and again pattern and colour are dominant.

Modern indulgent schemes tend to be more streamlined than traditional styles – lighting plays

Left: The minty green colour used here adds a fresh touch to this contemporary white and stainless steel bathroom.

Above: In a wet room you can install a bench along one wall, and then cover it with tiles.

Below: A timeless, classic roll top bath, with central tap and overflow fitting, rests on a rich blue ceramic tiled floor.

generally regarded as appropriate watery colours, reminiscent of sea, sky, lagoons and other aqueous features. Yellows and oranges are bright and warm, while deep colours can be dramatic and indulgent in a bathroom setting. Although coloured bathroom suites were all the rage during the 1960s and 70s there has been a return to white ceramic, which is fresh, clean and adaptable. White bathroomware is also safe – it will work with every colour and is compatible with every style or decorative theme.

Indulgent style bathrooms

Traditional indulgent bathrooms can follow a period style, with features such as a roll top bath, a Victorian basin on a pedestal with an integral decorative splashback and shell-like soap recesses, and a high flush lavatory with wall mounted tank. These items are all available, either as reproductions

or second hand through antiques merchants and specialists.

To create an indulgent traditional style, look at Edwardian

Above: *This classic tap and shower unit would complement a traditional style bathroom suite.*

Below right: *The towel rail around the side panel of this bath is adapted from a shower curtain pole.*

Opposite: *The water tank for this lavatory is concealed behind a slate-clad box. Slate is also used to line the shower enclosure.*

an important part in creating the indulgent mood, as will the accessories. The finish and fittings should be luxurious as the setting will be plain.

Streamlined style bathrooms

In a traditional streamlined bathroom, the basic furniture designs may still allude to an historical period. But in this case, the room will be decorated with lighter, brighter colours and adequate storage will ensure that surfaces are left clean, uncluttered and easy to wipe down. Additional furniture will be kept to a minimum and the layout designed specifically to assist quick and efficient use. However, in the evening, lights can be dimmed, candles lit and the atmosphere changed to one of indulgence and relaxation.

The modern streamlined bathroom is almost clinical in its efficiency and minimal lines. The materials used are business-like and utilitarian and there are absolutely no fancy frills or floral prints. This is a place where morning ablutions are carried out at top speed and there may be a floor area where an exercise mat or equipment is used. In the evening, this space can be made

softer by dimming lights and putting aromatherapy oils in the bath or steam shower but it will retain its minimal, uncluttered appearance, creating a restful and undemanding environment in which to unwind.

Bathroom fixtures

The first elements of your bathroom that you need to plan are the fixtures. Be aware of plumbing and space limitations as you make these plans.

Baths

There is a wide variety of different styles to choose from. Baths are usually plumbed along one wall. If, however, your room is spacious you may choose to have a freestanding bath in the centre of the room. A freestanding bath is luxurious in its use of space, giving a feeling of opulence simply by taking up so much room. However, with a free-standing bath the plumbing and

waste pipes must be laid under the floor as they cannot be run along a wall.

Sunken baths are an alternative option. You will need to consult a professional if you plan to install this type of feature. Jacuzzi, whirlpool and spa baths are luxurious choices for those who like to spend many hours soaking in a bath. Again, these systems need to be installed by a professional.

There are also smaller than standard baths: these half or Stiz baths are popular in Europe. The Sitz bath is designed so that it is short but deep, with a step or seat cast into the centre. The half bath is a compromise but, with a shower overhead it can be used as a deep shower tray or an occasional rather than regular bathing place.

Handbasins

The handbasin that you choose should complement the style of bath that you select. Basins come

and a glass door then there are a number of screen options available.

For a shower over a bath you could opt for a fixed screen, standard or bifold doors or a series of sliding panels. These will be made from textured plastic or reinforced glass. To make these screens watertight there needs to be a flexible rubber seal along the bottom edge of the section that meets with the bath.

For a freestanding bath in the centre of a room or a corner bath, a separate screen or screens makes a sensible option. The showers for these baths can either be ceiling mounted or on a stand or rod that comes up from the centre of the tap fitment.

Another option is a ring, like a mosquito net arrangement, suspended from the ceiling. From the ring the curtain or curtains are suspended and the bottom edge of the plastic liner is tucked neatly inside the edge of the bath so that the water is contained.

There are a number of standard fittings that can be fixed between two opposite walls or a straight wall and an adjacent one. The basic shower rail fitting is either straight (to be attached to facing walls), or L-shaped (so that it can be attached around a bath with access to adjacent walls).

The simplest of these fittings is a telescopic, extendible tube with suckers at each end. You simply pull out the pole until it is the right length for the gap, lock in place and then slide it into position on the wall – no nails or screws are required. The other option is the fixed pole, which will need to be secured with screws.

Toilets and bidets

An unlikely area for decoration but one that should not be ignored is the toilet seat. The standard seat is a dull, plain plastic rim protector and lid, and the classic version is of polished wood, which provides a warmer and more comfortable surface to sit on.

Above: Bathroom design is now focusing more on style and aesthetic appeal than just utilitarianism. This fine wood basin and elegant chrome stand are an interesting sculptural feature for a bathroom as well as being somewhere to wash.

Right: Ladder style, wall hung, radiators not only heat the bathroom they also double as a towel rack.

in a wide range of different styles, either floor or wall mounted. A popular shape for the contemporary bathroom is like a large bowl, which sits on a support. Basins are also available in different materials, such as wood, which has to be treated so that it doesn't warp or bow when it comes into contact with water.

In small or second bathrooms you can use 'rinse' basins – these are just large enough to be used for handwashing or teeth rinsing, but not hairwashing. There are certain styles that have an integral return or splashback so tiling is unnecessary.

Showers and screens

If you don't have a preformed shower enclosure or a shower built into a corner with two tiled walls, a fixed glass panel

In the traditional style bathroom there are a number of options for the arrangement of taps and related hardware, but the accepted layout in this setting consists of separate hot and cold taps each with a spout, and a plug on a chain. The classic tap design is the cross bar often with ceramic hot and cold discs.

The modern bathroom pares down this equipment and can be as minimal as a lever with an integral spout with the waste lever included in the back of the spout arch.

In contemporary bathrooms these fixtures are most often in chrome but in the traditional bathroom brass is an option. These days many reproduction brass taps come with a lacquered finish, which means that the shine on the metal stays bright and does not need to be polished.

Towel rails

Another element of bathroom fixtures is the towel rail, which now falls into the useful and beautiful category. Towel rails have gone from being a necessity to being a star feature in the bathroom, with a wide selection of attractive designs to choose from.

There are also an amazing variety of heated towel rails available. The most popular and straightforward style is the wall mounted ladder, which supplies heat and provides a place on which to hang and dry towels. These come in a variety of colours and finishes and have horizontal bars that are grouped in sections of varying widths.

Another design is the S or snake. This can be either attached to the wall so that it is fixed in position or on brackets so that it can be swung out at a right-angle to the wall. Make sure that the towel rail is not positioned where you may brush up against it while drying and burn yourself.

Left: *This polished slate panel acts as a splashback as well as a surround for the wall mounted taps and spout.*

Above: *The sandstone walls used here mellow the overall sleek look created by the stainless steel fittings.*

Below: *Many contemporary bathrooms feature basins that are styled like bowls sitting on a tabletop or surround.*

The current vogue is for more decorative finishes on toilet seats and these range from gimmicky, with beer or wine labels suspended in clear, solid plastic, to photographic images such as tropical leaves or blooming flowers. There are also photographic techniques that reproduce images of materials such as marble or granite onto a plastic or resin surround.

Another item of bathroom furniture that is popular throughout Europe is the bidet. This is an underrated piece of equipment, which can be useful in households where there are young children or elderly people who find a bath or shower too difficult. It can also provide an effective footbath for refreshing your feet at the end of a long day.

Taps and other fittings

In the modern bathroom the taps and other fittings are an important part of the overall design. They make a statement because the rest of the fittings and fitments and the general decoration are usually very simple and plain.

Among contemporary designs there are many taps that have utilitarian roots, for example, the lever. This simple metal paddle, which is connected to the spout or water faucet, has been refined from the originals found in industrial washrooms and at hospital sinks.

Taps have also migrated away from the basin surround and are now likely to be wall mounted directly above the basin and accompanied by the spout, which arches gracefully at the end.

framed mosaic
splashback panel

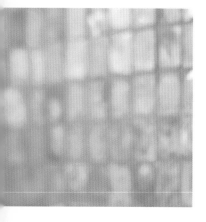

This mosaic panel is an attractive alternative to tiled walls, and can be positioned behind a bath or basin or simply hung on the wall like a picture. Any type of mosaic tile can be used – we chose an unusual iridescent glass mosaic, which catches the light beautifully. Although the materials of the panel are quite pricey, one of its main advantages is the fact that it is portable, meaning it can be repositioned with ease. You can choose a trim to complement your design; we opted for a simple wooden frame stained with a dark walnut varnish that offsets the pale colours of the tiles.

Materials

Waterproof plywood

Abrasive paper

PVA bonding agent

Sheets of mosaic tiles

Grout

L-shaped trim

Panel adhesive

Walnut satin varnish

Tools

Metal ruler

Pencil

Jigsaw

Tile adhesive

Paintbrush

Notched spreader

Sponge

Flexible spreading tool

Soft cloth

Small paintbrush

Mitre cutter

D cramp

Preparing the panel

1 Firstly, plan the size of the mosaic panel carefully so that you can avoid cutting any mosaic tiles. With a long metal ruler and a pencil, mark out the dimensions of the panel onto a sheet of plywood, making sure you allow for a border trim all the way around the panel.

2 Cut out the panel carefully using a jigsaw and then, using a piece of abrasive paper, sand to remove any rough edges from it.

3 Seal the plywood with a solution of two parts PVA bonding agent to one part water and allow to dry.

4 Using a notched spreader, apply a layer of tile adhesive to the sealed sheet of plywood. (Make sure that you wear gloves when you do this.)

Fixing the mosaic tiles

5 Place the sheets of mosaic tiles face down into the adhesive, pressing them down

Using the mosaic tiles as a guide, mark out the dimensions of the panel onto the plywood.

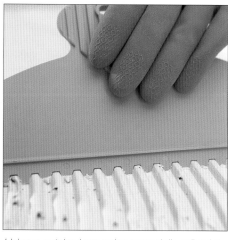

Using a notched spreader, spread tile adhesive evenly over the sealed sheet of plywood.

Know your tools

• Having a set of good quality cramps is essential for many woodworking projects as they hold glued joints together, exerting pressure until the glue has dried enough to form a strong bond. (Confusingly, they are known as G, D or C cramps.)

• The mitre cutter used in this particular project is the type often used by picture framers. It allows for fine adjustments of the blade, so ensuring a perfect angled cut. Mitre cutters can be bought from all DIY outlets.

firmly to make sure they adhere to the panel. Allow the mosaics tiles to dry overnight.

6 Use a wet sponge to thoroughly soak the paper backing of the mosaics. Allow the water to sink in for a few minutes before peeling away the backing.

7 With a flexible spreading tool, force the grout well into the gaps between the tiles. Wipe away any excess grout then allow it to dry completely.

8 Polish the mosaic tiles with a soft cloth until they shine.

9 Using a mitre cutter, cut an L-shaped trim to form the frame, stick in position with some panel adhesive and clamp in place until dry. Colour with a varnish or stain of your choice.

Place the mosaic tiles carefully onto the tile adhesive and press them firmly into place.

Soak the paper backing of the tiles, then let the mosaics sink in before peeling off the backing.

Using a flexible spreading tool, force the grout well into the gaps between the mosaic tiles.

Alternative

You may prefer to tile directly onto your bathroom wall. To do this, you must first ensure that your wall is perfectly smooth and that the surface has been sealed with bonding adhesive.

Mosaic tiles are usually supplied with paper or mesh backing, which enables you to work with squares of about 30cm (1ft) at a time. If you are tiling behind an existing basin it is advisable to start in the bottom right-hand corner and work your way along and then up. If you are tiling an entire wall then use a level batten tacked to the wall as a guide. Always order ten per cent more tiles than you think you need, to allow for mistakes or breakages. If you are using blends of more than one colour it is wise to mix the sheets up well to ensure a good colour mix.

When your tiles are hung and grouted you should seal the gap between any bathroom furniture and tiles with silicone sealant. This forms a flexible watertight seal between the fittings and the tiled surface.

Wipe away any grout, allow to dry and then polish the tiles with a soft cloth until they shine.

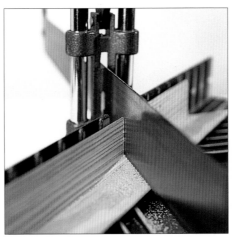

Using a mitre cutter, carefully cut an L-shaped trim to fit around the border of the panel.

exotic fabric
shower curtain

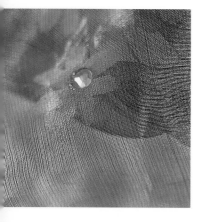

Shower curtain designs only seem to cater for lovers of shiny plastic with wacky or nautical themes – there are few that add instant glamour to your bathroom. This painted organza shower curtain is both pretty and practical as it is backed with clear PVC. The two materials are joined at the top, allowing you to separate them so you can shower with the plastic layer inside the bath or shower cubicle while the delicate fabric remains dry on the outside. For added glitz we used iridescent fabric paint to attach small glass and diamanté beads all over the surface of the fabric.

Materials

Organza fabric

Clear PVC

Ribbon

Curtain weight

Iridescent fabric paint/glue

Small glass beads

Small diamanté 'gems'

Curtain rings

Tools

Pins

Tailor's chalk

Metal ruler

Scissors

Sewing machine (or needle and thread for handsewing)

Punching tool

Riveting tool

Eyelets

Measuring the shower curtain

1 Measure the 'drop' (this is the distance from your shower curtain rail down to the floor) and then add a couple of extra centimetres (about an inch) to allow for the hem. Pin both materials together, making sure that the clear PVC is on top. Next, use tailor's chalk and a long metal ruler to mark a straight line and then cut the material to the required length using a pair of sharp scissors.

Sewing the shower curtain

2 Turn over the bottom edge of the material and press down on it to flatten it. Next, use a sewing machine set on a medium straight stitch or a needle and thread to sew a length of ribbon along it. This will then form a channel along the bottom of the material.

3 Cut a length of curtain weight and feed this through the channel. Secure the curtain weight with a couple of small stitches by hand at each end. Carefully trim the sides of the shower curtain.

Using a pair of sharp scissors, cut the material carefully along the marked straight line.

Pin the length of ribbon along the bottom of the material and sew in place to form a channel.

Know your tools

• Clear PVC is sold in large fabric stores and is often used as a table covering.

• Organza is a lightweight material woven from metallic threads, which gives it a shimmering quality as it catches the light. It is quite slippery, making it tricky to sew. Set the tension on your machine to a setting suitable for lightweight fabrics and use a needle designed for metallic thread. When sewing the layers of PVC and organza it is best to practise on some scrap pieces first until you find the ideal tension settings.

Decorating the shower curtain

5 Using an iridescent fabric paint or glue, attach some small glass beads and diamanté 'gems' to the organza. Because it will come in contact with a lot of water, make sure that the fabric glue is waterproof.

Fixing the shower curtain

6 Use the punching tool to make holes at even intervals along the top of the curtain.

7 Using the riveting tool, fit small eyelets into each of these holes.

8 Thread the curtain rings through the eyelets and hang the shower curtain from the shower rail. We used rings with decorative glass droplets here to provide an extra glamourous finishing touch.

4 Turn over the top edge of the shower curtain material and once again press down on it. Then cut another length of ribbon to fit over it. Make a sandwich of the ribbon, the organza and PVC material and pin them all carefully in place. Stitch along the top and bottom of them with the sewing machine set on a medium straight stitch. Alternatively, use a needle and thread.

Cut a suitable length of lightweight curtain weight and thread through the ribbon channel.

Turn over the top edge of the curtain and stitch the ribbon, the organza and PVC together.

Using an iridescent fabric glue attach some diamanté 'gems' and glass beads to the curtain.

Alternative

Simple recessed shower units with sleek glass doors look particularly effective in contemporary surroundings where a fussy shower curtain would look out of place. Many homes have a cupboard or alcove that could be transformed into a showering area. Take advice from a reliable plumber who will guide you through the process. Ventilation and ease of running pipes to the site are the most important things to take into consideration. It may also be worth installing a pump to increase the water pressure.

To make the area watertight you will need to fit a shower tray or tile the floor area and add drainage. For the walls use conventional ceramic, mosaic or stone tiles (you could consider waterproof lining panels in a number of different materials, including hardwood or glass).

If you cannot find an off-the-shelf glass door to fit your alcove many bathroom manufacturers have a bespoke service and will be able to make a frame and door to fit.

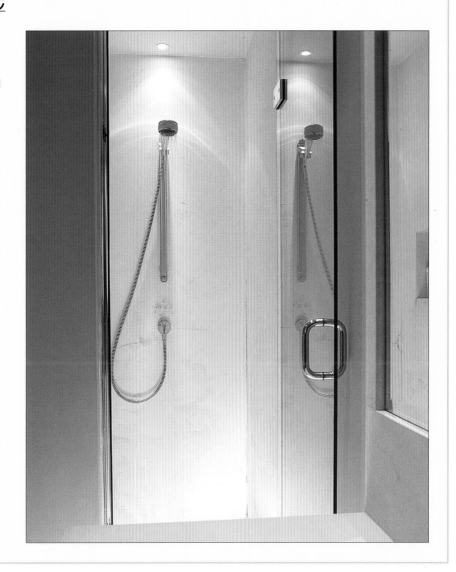

Make holes at even intervals along the top of the shower curtain with the punching tool.

Use the riveting tool to fit the small eyelets along the top of the shower curtain.

Thread the curtain rings through the eyelets and then hang the shower curtain from the rail.

recycled glass
bead curtain

Bead curtains make a delicate alternative to lace or voile curtains, and catch the light beautifully. Their moisture resistance makes them an ideal choice in the bathroom. We chose beautiful recycled beads in watery shades of blue and green. It is important to ensure your wire or string is sturdy enough to support the weight of your beads. We used a fine-gauge heavy-duty wire alongside small 'crimping' beads to hold the glass beads in place. Use a strong piece of dowelling or metal pole to hold the individual strands and hang from curtain pole brackets.

Materials

Glass beads
Strong bead wire
Crimping beads
Dowelling
Silver spray paint
Wood drill bit
2 long nails
Metal washer

Tools

Pliers or scissors
Handsaw
Pencil
Drill
Pin hammer

Measuring the drop

1 Measure your window or doorway in order to work out the exact number of bead strands that you will need for the curtain. Next, work out the necessary 'drop' or length that each strand should be and then cut the appropriate number of lengths of wire by using your pliers or a pair of scissors.

Threading the beads

2 Use a glass bead in order to anchor the bottom of each length of wire, threading it through a loop and then securing a crimping bead with pliers to hold it in place.

3 Thread the remaining beads in place. While doing this you can either build up a pattern or use them completely randomly if preferred. When you reach the end of the bead string use a crimping bead to secure the last glass bead in place (see picture bottom left, page 258).

Preparing the dowelling

4 Use a handsaw to cut the dowelling to the length that you require.

Cut out the number of lengths of wire that you need with scissors or pliers.

Anchor the bottom of each length of wire with a glass bead. Secure it with a crimping bead.

5 Use a spray paint to apply a coat of silver paint to the dowelling and allow it to dry.

Fixing the strings in place

6 Mark the position of the bead strings at intervals along the length of dowelling. Grip the dowelling in a vice and drill the required holes using a wood bit.

7 Thread different-shaped beads onto a slim nail and then tap the nail into the end of the dowelling with a pin hammer to form a finial. Do the same the other end.

8 Anchor the bead strings by feeding them through the hole in the dowelling, add a metal washer then loop the wire around a small glass bead and hold in place with a crimping bead.

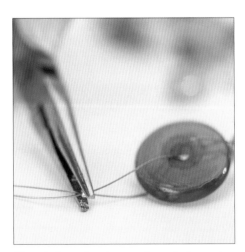

Thread all your beads on a piece of wire, and use a crimping bead to secure the last one.

Once you have cut the piece of dowelling to length, spray it with silver spray paint.

Measure and drill holes in the dowelling for the lengths of bead to be suspended from.

Alternative

When it comes to screening windows and doors anything goes. You could combine traditional wooden slatted blinds with an elaborately decorated sheer curtain to create a multi-layered effect. Dress the curtain by stitching decorative beads or mirror pieces at random intervals or attach tassled hems along its lengths. The light will be reflected off these decorative features back into the room.

Use your imagination to come up with your own ideas when dressing windows. You could use any material that can be attached to a length of string or wire. For a hi-tech solution try shiny compact discs threaded onto strong nylon – their shiny surface reflects coloured prisms onto the walls of the room. For a whimsical, nautical look try decorating with shells, sand dollars and small pebbles gathered from the beach. Use a small drill bit on a low speed to drill holes in shells carefully. Use rustic garden twine to complete the look.

Thread beads on a thin nail and then hammer it into the end of the dowelling as a finial.

Once the bead strings are in place, attach a metal washer and crimping bead to secure.

lighting your bathroom

Bathroom lighting needs to be focused on individual areas, for example, the mirror over the handbasin where shaving or make-up applications takes place. There should also be lighting focused on a shower enclosure or bath so that you can see gels, soaps and shampoos.

Right: As well as a good-sized normal mirror, it is useful to also have a magnifying mirror in the bathroom.

Below: Lights can be placed directly over a bath and shower – such fixtures will need to be installed by a professional electrician.

Planning your lighting

For general points about lighting design, see Effective lighting, page 134. Lighting in a bathroom needs to be located so that it focuses on the needs and moods of the person using the space. In the morning and evening good lighting above or around the mirror is a priority for shaving, applying makeup and cleaning.

Practical lighting

Even if there is a good-sized window in the room you will most probably need additional electric lighting. This can be provided by targeted spot or task lights on the ceiling that are directed onto the mirror in front of the basin. Make sure these lights are directed to shine into the

mirror so that it is reflected back at your face. If the light shines down too steeply it will light your back.

A strip or row of bulbs may also run along the top and sides of the mirror so that the light is evenly distributed and regular, otherwise wall mounted side lights with adjustable arms or heads can also be effective.

With the halo or surround of light on the edge or front of the mirror it can be more effective to have more low voltage lights than too many high voltage ones as they will create an intense unflattering light that will make you look pallid. The right level of good quality light will give an accurate colour rendition and colour temperature, which are important, especially if you are using the lit area to apply your makeup.

For close inspection there are magnifying mirrors that have integral surrounding lights, so that the illumination is directly positioned to shine onto the face, or section of the face that is being examined. These enlarging mirrors are wall mounted and the electric cables are enclosed in the casing of the arm or support.

Decorative lighting

Floor lights are becoming increasingly popular in contemporary bathrooms. These lights are contained in sealed casing and are used to uplight a shower cubicle from the outside, or in the side panels of the bath. They can also be used in the corners of the room to emphasize height and space.

Shelf lighting is sometimes used in the bathroom. A single, long glass shelf can be used to support decorative objects and by positioning a small light below or on either side of the shelf you can create an effect

where the shelf appears to glow. This can be eye-catching when the rest of the room is in a subdued light.

Lighting in a shower cabinet is best done with ceiling mounted spots or enclosed fittings, such as a nautical bulk head light. Spots or directional lights can be positioned directly above an enclosed cabinet, or angled to shine through the glass or side panel of a shower cubicle of a shower over a bath.

Above: *In this small bathroom, in a converted attic space, dormer windows have been set into the roof to provide good natural light.*

Left: *Here the lighting not only makes it easier to see, it also highlights and makes a special feature of the glass basin.*

Bathroom storage

A variety of items and products need to be stored in a bathroom – towels should be kept aired and dry, whereas bottles of shampoo and bath preparations are often slippery, soapy and damp, so need to be kept separate and contained so that any drips or leaks are not allowed to travel.

Storage units

Storage can be provided either by built-in or freestanding units. Built-in units can provide storage in places such as under the basin, in linen and boiler cupboards and even under window seats. They are particularly helpful in small bathrooms where furniture can be made to measure.

Large storage units can be subdivided into narrow shelves for smaller items and wider ones for bulkier things. Even within deep shelves you can section the space with baskets or boxes to keep smaller objects in order.

In some bathrooms there will be a boiler or water heater, which is a bulky, rather unattractive thing.

Above right: Traditional bath racks that hold soap and sponges are still widely used.

Right: In a shower, the shelves should also be constructed so that water will drain off them rather than sit in stagnant puddles.

Depending on the type of boiler it may be possible to disguise it with a built-in cupboard but check with a professional before doing so as some require ventilation.

If you don't have a boiler and would prefer freestanding options there are many available. These vary from modern designs with light wood or steel frames and glass panels to the more traditional armoire with short legs.

Baskets are useful but natural rattan or woven coconut fibre types should be used for dry things, rather than wet. Baskets can be used to hold waste as well as dirty linen.

Know your materials

Roller blind kits can be purchased from most large department stores. They are a good value option if you have large windows and they also allow you to use your own choice of fabric. The kits supply the winding mechanism, a wooden or metal roller, the brackets to attach the blind to the window and a string pull. Some kits also include the stiffening spray needed to make your chosen fabric more rigid. If possible, try and get one that also gives the fabric a degree of fire retardency.

to dry in between colours for the recommended time before reapplying strips of masking tape.

6 When all the stripes have been painted, iron on the reverse side making sure that the instructions on the fabric painting medium are followed. This is to ensure that the paint is colourfast.

Assembling the blind

7 Attach the fabric to the roller mechanism using the adhesive strip provided. Reinforce this with a staple gun if your blind is long and heavy.

8 Using a needle and a piece of co-ordinating thread, sew a channel for the rod at the bottom. Feed the rod through the channel and then slot it in place. Finally, attach the pull cord supplied with the roller blind kit.

Spray the material with fabric stiffening spray for blinds to make them fire retardant.

Use a pencil and a ruler to draw stripes of different widths onto the fabric.

With a medium paintbrush, paint the stripes and use masking tape to ensure clean lines.

Alternative

If you want a more permanent, formal way of dividing your room consider fitting a series of doors that can be folded back to create one large room when required. These doors can run on small wheels, which slot into tracks on the floor and ceiling. Alternatively they can be hung on sets of door hinges and anchored in place with simple bolts that slot into plates on the floor. Ready-made bi-fold doors and tracks can be bought from DIY stores, or you could search for reclaimed doors. Panelled doors can be customized by removing the top panels and replacing them with fretwork or glass. This allows plenty of light to filter through while still giving each side of the room a degree of privacy. Fretwork screen panels can be bought in a variety of designs and materials, including MDF, hardboard and pressed metals. Glass panels can be bought from a glazier who will cut them to fit. You can choose from plain, frosted or specialist coloured or stained glass panels; they should be fixed in place with glazing beads or putty.

When the stripes are dry, iron on the reverse side to ensure that the paint is colourfast.

Attach the fabric to the roller mechanism using the adhesive strip provided in the blind kit.

Sew a channel at the bottom of the blind, then feed the rod through and slot in place.

Storage and display

In work and play areas storage is important. In a work space you will need to have reference books and files to hand and in a play area different types of toys and games should all be kept in their own containers or drawers so that they don't get lost or form one hideous jumble.

Work space storage

In a work space the most important thing is to avoid too much clutter. Keep things that you need to hand and store items that are seldom used on upper shelves or more distant cupboards and filing cabinets. Avoid a build up of files, boxes and paperwork around you as it can make you feel hemmed in and overpowered by your surroundings. The best way to keep paper under control is to edit it regularly, don't let an 'In' tray build up to a state where it overflows into a second basket.

If your desktop is organized it also makes it easier to cope with things that pass over it. A good basic stationery kit such as paper clips, rubber, stapler and sellotape should be kept in a divided or sectioned drawer, as this will enable you to know exactly where each thing is and it will be easy to lay your hands on them when you need them.

Small items such as paper clips and notice board pins can be effectively stored in clear glass jam jars with screw on lids. The lids keep the contents firmly inside but the glass sides make it simple to identify what is where. Clear plastic containers can be useful but the lids tend not to stay as firmly in place as the old-fashioned screw type, and in time thin, shiny plastic may become brittle and crack.

But a working space doesn't need to be dull and regimented. In fact, stationery and office accessories is an area where colour, pattern and design have recently made a huge impact.

Right: A filing cabinet can be positioned underneath your desk, which will make it easy to reach paperwork and also makes good use of space.

Below: Box files are extremely useful and can be labelled so that you can locate items very quickly.

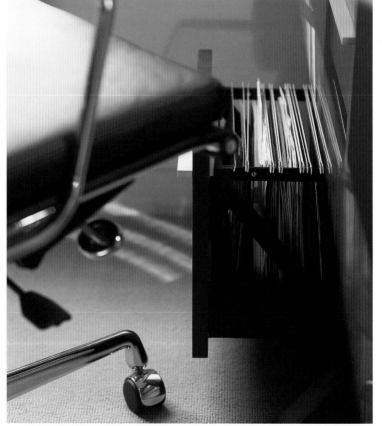

Files that were once covered in a standard grey or dull casing are now widely available in brightly coloured covers, which can make it easier to identify an individual file at a distance. Instead of buying a dozen files in the same uniform finish, have different coloured ones so that you will be able to memorize what colour relates to a particular topic. This will also give your work space a more lively appearance. Or, you can create your own (see box, page 280).

Another useful piece of apparatus can be a wall grid. This may be made of wood or metal and is a panel of bars onto which items can be hung. Wall grids are generally more robust than notice boards and with small butcher's hooks can be a good place for hanging tools such as scissors, hammers and spanners.

Larger sections of wall grid can support small shelves and may be used in the area of wall in front of a work station. The various hooks and attachments can then be used to display stationary elements such as sellotape, sticky labels, a clock, scalpel or cutting knife, rulers etc, putting everything on display and immediately to hand. This type of arrangement is better for a wall by a desk or secondary work station, rather than the primary one as the equipment hanging in front of a person trying to work may become distracting and make the space feel reduced and cluttered.

If a lot of storage and shelving is necessary in your work space

you can make it seem less dominant by painting it the same colour as the wall. This will make the shelves appear to be an integral part of the wall rather than a feature that is set against it.

Useful work space furniture

If your work requires you to gather information, swatches or reference material from elsewhere and bring it back to your desk then a trolley may be a useful addition to your furniture. The trolley can be used to move material from one area to another in one move rather than you staggering backwards and

Above left: Storage specifically designed to hold certain items, such as tapes and CDs not only contains them but it also makes them easier to view and select.

Above: This is another example of a specially designed cabinet. It neatly contains a CD player, CDs and videos.

Left: In a small study reinforced glass or perspex shelves are useful because they provide ample storage but don't appear too heavy or block out light.

Decorative labels for storage boxes

Labelling and identifying the contents of boxes and files is important so that they can be easily noted. For business files use clear white labels with bold black printed letters. If files or boxes are used in a damp or moist environment, or will be lifted with wet hands, then cover the labels with a strip of clear adhesive plastic. For young children of pre-reading age colour coding can be helpful, so that dolls' clothes are in a pink box, toy soldiers in a red one and books in green etc, or you can cut out appropriate pictures to make it easy for them to see what belongs where.

Right: *This storage system has a variety of sizes of shelves and forms an efficient office space along just one wall.*

Below: *Magazine holders come in a variety of materials, colours and finishes so they can co-ordinate with your decorative scheme.*

forwards several times with armfuls of files. The trolley can also be pulled right up to your desk where you can easily access the documents so using the upper levels of the trolley as an extension to your desk.

As well as modern office equipment, old or antique pieces can be useful as well as interesting and attractive. Old wooden shop display systems with glass-fronted drawers can make a pleasant change in a home office and will blend in more easily with traditional furnishings and fabrics. Plan chests with their rows of large flat drawers not only

provide ample storage but are usually of such a size and construction that the top can be used as an additional work surface, a partial room divider or even a place to put a kettle or coffee machine.

Just as the plan chest can be used to create a low or partial divider a small bookcase can be used in the same way. These low barriers help to divide work from home space but don't cut off the flow of light or line of vision. A three-shelf bookcase, up to 92cm (3ft) high can be secured to the floor and an adjacent wall to ensure that it is stable. The side

facing the work space will display the shelves and provide storage whereas the back will face into the other half of the room and may be concealed by the back of a sofa or painted to match the wall in that area. (See page 270 for further ideas on how to create a separate space for your work area.)

Display in work spaces

Although the primary function of your work space should be practical, there is no reason why you should not create a display of a few ornaments on top of a set of box files to create a comfortable, welcoming environment. If you have a pinboard beside your desk you will also be able to place things such as a calendar, family photos and useful phone numbers on it. This can be livened up with posters too. Be careful not to let your work space become too cluttered though.

Storage in play areas

If a child's bedroom doubles as a play area, by putting toys away in boxes out of sight at the end of the day you are removing the temptation for a small person to nip out of bed once the door is closed and continue playing. Good toy storage can help young children as they learn about discipline and tidiness too. It also helps to keep the floor area clear when games time is over, so that if there is a change from day to night time activity the space will quickly and easily adapt. Adults also need to be able to check on sleeping children without falling over rollerskates, toy trains or treading on a favourite doll or toy.

Plastic crates with lids that stack neatly one on top of another work well in a child's room. These can be arranged along a wall and labelled so that the contents are easily identified without having to open each and every box. Drawers on wheels or castors can be slotted under a bed or bunks and narrow shelves are ideal for books and small toys, such as soldiers, small cars or dolls.

If a small child learns that his or her toys are always returned to the same box or bag then they quickly learn the routine. This will also save the parent or helper the thankless task of searching endlessly for a specific item.

Having easily accessible storage should stop smaller items or play things getting separated or lost. For a slightly older child's bedroom, you could store smaller items such as paintbrushes and crayons or favourite soft toys in a wall or door hanging with pockets. This is simply made from a strong cotton such as calico or canvas, or even a more interesting material such as denim (see box, right). The panel can be fixed to the wall or the back of the door by hooks and eyelets or with a stout piece of cord attached to either end of the top piece of dowel and looped over a couple of sturdy hooks. The pockets can be made in contrasting colours to the back panel or decorated with felt letters, cut-outs of the things that are stored in them or decorated with buttons to add interest.

Display in play areas

In a child's room storage can also double as a display area. For example, a troop of cowboys can look fun if they trot across a shelf in a room where the theme revolves around cowboys and Indians. If Barbie is the dream doll of the moment and the bedroom is painted pink in her honour, then the doll herself should be on show to be a part of the overall scheme.

Display areas can also be informative. A pinboard for school certificates or good reports, as well as homework and activity timetables, will be useful. Pictures may also need to be pinned up – by using a cork notice board you can protect the wall surface from new pin holes when the current fad changes.

Making your own hanging storage

First you need to cut a long rectangle out of your chosen material. If you are thinking about hanging it behind a door then take the dimensions of the door and reduce it so that the back sheet is about 61cm (2ft) shorter than the door measurement from top to bottom and about 23cm (9in) narrower at either side. Hem the back panel and make a casing top and bottom to hold a length of dowel the same width as the material. Slide the dowel into the casing and sew over the ends of the fabric to keep it in place.

Measure the items you plan to put in the pockets and cut the material to the same size with an additional generous hem allowance. Hem the top edge, then turn in the sides and bottom of the pocket and sew onto the back panel.

Left: *This tall system of shelves in a child's bedroom not only stores toys and books efficiently but also displays them attractively.*

tongue and groove display panel

Lightweight slatted panels are ideal in a home office or a study with changing storage needs. We made the panels using tongue and groove floorboards, with the tongues removed. The ingenious part is that the grooves provide an anchor for shelves and pictures, which can be hung at varying heights. Simply unhook and rearrange to change the layout if required. The panels can be fixed directly to the wall or, for a less permanent version, fix them onto vertical battens, which are fixed to the wall. Use picture hooks made to fit over a picture rail to suspend pictures.

Materials

Timber battens

Softwood tongue and groove floorboards

Wood screws

Knotting solution

Acrylic primer

White acrylic satinwood paint

Wood glue

Tools

Handsaw

Workbench

Tape measure

Sharp plane or jigsaw

Abrasive paper

Electric drill

Countersink bit

Paintbrush

Hacksaw

Screwdriver

Measuring the area

1 Decide on the height and width of the screen. Using a handsaw, cut the timber battens and floorboards to the required dimensions.

2 Secure each floorboard in turn on a workbench and, with a sharp plane or a jigsaw, remove the tongue.

Securing the floorboards

3 Lay out the cut floorboard lengths, allowing 1cm (½in) spacing in between each one. Place the vertical battens in position at each end. If you are making a wall over 4m (13ft) wide you should add another central batten for stability.

4 Drill and screw through the back of the batten into each floorboard using a countersink bit, ensuring the screw head sits beneath the surface of the wood.

Using a handsaw, cut the battens and tongue and groove floorboards to the required size.

Secure each floorboard to the workbench and remove the tongue with a jigsaw.

Know your materials

We used tongue and groove floorboards here because they are sturdier than tongue and groove wall panelling and the deeper groove along their length was perfect for hanging picture hooks and shelves from. It is important to treat the knots (the rounded marks where branches were) with knotting solution. This is a shellac-based product that seals the knots and prevents resinous sap bleeding through the paint.

5 When all the floorboards are secured on the battens turn the panel the right way up and, with a piece of abrasive paper, sand thoroughly. Using an old paintbrush, apply knotting solution to any resinous knots (this will prevent resin bleeding through the paintwork and spoiling the finish).

Painting the floorboards

6 Apply a coat of acrylic primer followed by two coats of white acrylic satinwood paint and allow to dry.

Making the shelf

7 Use another floorboard (with the tongue removed) to make the shelf. Cut two pieces of the same length and butt together to form the back and base. Cut two identical squares with the corners cut off to form the sides. Glue and screw together. Treat with knotting solution, then prime and paint with white acrylic paint.

8 Use a hacksaw to cut a length of L shaped metal trim to fit the top of the shelf.

9 Drill, countersink then screw the longest edge of the metal trim in position on top of the shelf. This will slot neatly over the floorboard lengths and anchor itself in the groove.

Use a countersink bit to screw through the back of the batten into each floorboard.

With a paintbrush, apply knotting solution to any resinous knots to prevent resin bleeding.

Apply a coat of acrylic primer and then two coats of acrylic satinwood paint to the boards.

Alternative

One of the most attractive methods of storing CDs is to slip them horizontally into a grooved panel of wood. Hardwoods with an attractive grain look best, but if you want to make one you will need a router with a groove cutting bit. You can adapt this idea, making a simpler version by adding pieces of doweling to the front of a flat panel.

Sketch out the rough dimensions to plan the amount of materials you will need. Get a panel of wood or MDF cut to fit your space, and sufficient square section dowels cut to the same width. Make sure that the dowels are deep enough to hold the CDs firmly in place. Use a soft pencil and set square to lightly mark the position of the dowels on the back and front of the panel, making sure that each is a CD width apart. Spread a thin layer of wood glue over one side of each dowel and position them all. Tap a row of thin panel pins through from the back of the panel to hold the dowels in place. Finally, attach the panel to the wall with screws or fix mirror plates to each side.

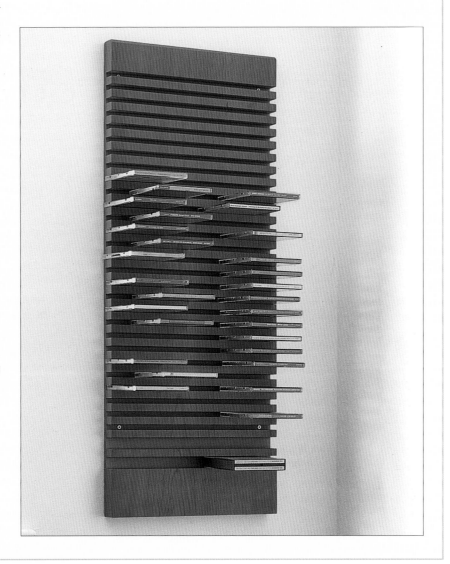

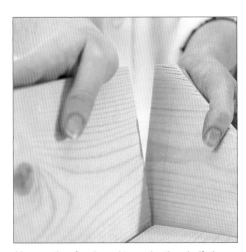

Use another floorboard to make the shelf, then treat with knotting solution, prime and paint.

Use a hacksaw to make an L shaped metal trim to fit the top of the shelf.

Drill, countersink and screw the longest edge of the metal trim in place on top of the shelf.

lighting for work and play

The type and arrangement of lighting that you choose for both work and play areas are important: work areas should be bright and airy, conducive to concentrating on the task in hand, while in children's rooms safety is a priority.

Below right: A moveable task light that will focus light directly on paperwork or a screen is a basic necessity in a working or study environment.

Work space lighting

The computer screen should, where possible, be sited near a window and natural light, but the screen must be angled to avoid glare that is hard on the eyes and may obliterate parts of the screen. Don't have the ambient light level in the room too low. The levels of light in the room and the screen should be comparable.

A specific adjustable work light is essential to supplement fading daylight. A standard domestic table lamp with shade or central room light is not good enough as they may cast shadows on the screen, making it difficult to see. Desktop or task lights, such as recessed and directional spotlights, will also be needed in order to light up the rest of the desk surface.

Playroom lighting

It is best to provide high level ambient light for a play area so that the lower levels of the room are as flex- and cable-free as possible. Fit childproof safety covers in the wall sockets to deter small fingers from investigating the holes and equip light fittings with safety plugs that have partly sheathed pins.

It is best to avoid small china base table lamps or anything that is easily broken – instead opt for robust light fittings. There are

many specially designed for children's rooms, available through large department stores.

Lights not only provide illumination but can also be a fun and interesting part of the scheme, particularly in a play area. For example, crescent moon and colourful umbrella style paper shades are all available.

If the children using the play room spend most of their time at floor level then you will need to have a good broad beam overhead light such as recessed spots in conjunction with wall

lights. The wall lights can be contained in an enclosed shade, so that there is no direct access to the bulb and so that the bulb is contained should it blow.

If the play area doubles up as a work room for an older child or adult, adjustable task lights could be attached to the wall so that they can be positioned over a desk or work area without being in the way of the play area. This type of work light should be angled so that the beam shines diagonally across the papers on the table, to focus on the work.

Customizing files

In your home office you can customize your files with decorative wrapping paper, such as silver, glossy pastel shades, or coloured sticky back plastic and choose colours that represent the topic contained within the file. For example, you could use blue for water-related matters and green for landscape gardeners or grass seed merchants.

Left: *A desk is best positioned near a source of natural light. Here mirrors are used to reflect and make the most of the light.*

Below left: *Task lights should provide a good even level of light but should not be too strong or create glare, which can be hard on the eyes.*

Using natural light

It is best to keep window dressings simple to make the most of natural light. In a work area an adjustable roller or Venetian blind is ideal because it can be used to shield bright, direct sunlight, yet can be rolled or pulled up out of the way on darker days.

In a play room, opt for simple curtains, blinds or something like a folded Roman blind that can be effective and attractive. The latter should be placed at a level out of the way of sticky fingers. If the play area is really more of an adult recreation room then you may need to tailor the window treatments to suit the hobby. For example, if photography or making family videos is an abiding hobby then black out blinds may be needed.

Creating your own decorative shade

Customize a lampshade for a child's playroom by painting the outer surface or sticking on cut-out shapes. You could try cutting out motifs from extra curtain or bedding material and applying these to the shade. If you are using a floral motif, leave a little of the edge of the petal hanging over the lower edge of the shade for a decorative finish. Always buy a kite-mark or safety approved shade and only decorate the outside of it.

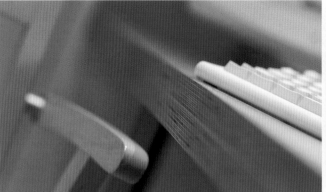

Workplace accessories

Work areas within the home should be softer and more comfortable than a commercial or business space, yet they do need to function efficiently. Storage and good planning are the keys to success, and a built-in desk can convert a wasted space under a staircase or at the end of a corridor into a useful additional room. Because these are domestic environments you can have fun with accessories such as files and pencil holders and can indulge in bright colours and fun schemes. However, they shouldn't be too wild as they might distract you. Once the desk and storage space have been allocated, the next most important items to target are ventilation, lighting and seating. Ventilation is important if you are using electrical machines as they generate heat and may make a room stuffy and dry. Target lighting, provided by an adjustable spot or desk lamp, will be vital for good viewing and also for the care of your eyesight. Finally, an ergonomically designed, adjustable chair is another must for good posture and back support.

CLOCKWISE FROM TOP LEFT:

An old pewter tankard doubles as a pencil holder – this is a practical yet quirky storage solution.

Smooth edges, such as those on the arm of this chair and the desk edge, make a more pleasant and safer working environment.

Good storage is essential to keep things in order and easily accessible, especially in small spaces.

The shelves of bookcases can be arranged so that they accommodate specific sizes and types of books.

Transparent shelves don't appear as heavy or dense as solid wood or MDF, and in a small room can make it appear more spacious. However, you should only use reinforced laminate glass or perspex for this type of shelf construction.

Small filing cabinets can be used as a desk base. This also means that frequently used files and papers can be kept close at hand.

Clear labelling will make it much more easy to identify the contents of your files and drawers.

Glare on a computer screen can make it difficult to focus on so have an adjustable side light and blinds at the window to allow you to achieve the right level and direction of light for your working environment.

Bright, light colours can be very invigorating when used in a study or workroom.

If you do a lot of paperwork ensure that you have plenty of tabletop or desk surface in order to lay the material out on.

Co-ordinating stationary can make a desk area visually pleasing and inviting.

This neat study area has been built in at the end of a corridor, but still provides adequate and dedicated working space.

Work lights need not be dull – this modern design has an adjustable head that slides up and down the main steel support.

Old cabinets can be used as storage for paperwork or toys. The solid front panels can be removed from the doors and replaced with fine wire mesh or even pleated fabric to give a more homely feel.

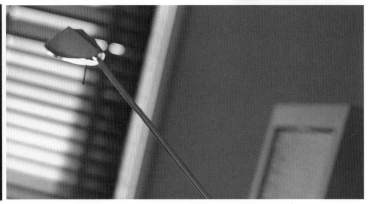

Connecting
areas

Planning connecting areas

Passage and hallways are an often overlooked part of the home, yet they are important not only because they link one room to another but also because, if they are decorated in an attractive clutter-free way, they can make the experience of passing through them more enjoyable.

Halls, landings, staircases and passageways link rooms and various levels in a home, but are often narrow, dark and difficult to make the most of. If you have a long corridor try to subdivide it into three parts, such as the entrance hall, the inner passageway or corridor and the end, so that in each section there is a focus.

Halls

The area immediately inside the front door is a busy place where people arrive and depart, where post is received and coats, boots, hats and gloves are usually kept. It is also an area that forms a barrier between the outside world, a place of transition between the reality of urban living and work and the cosy, domestic interior.

To accommodate the transition and these functions you should create a space that is tranquil and organized. To cope with the comings and goings in this area there should be a variety of storage and a place to sit while putting on and taking off shoes. It should also be decorated so that it appears bright and inviting.

Accessories

The first accessory in this entrance area is usually a roughly textured mat on the floor immediately inside or just outside

Right: Glass panels above the two main doors off this passageway allow natural light from the rooms on the other side to penetrate this windowless, internal area.

Below: Lighting is extremely important within a hallway. Here, low lighting that is situated just above the skirting boards illuminates the passageway.

the door. The inner floor in this area should be covered with a practical finish – something that can be easily cleaned. Stone, wood, flag stones or tiles are good but can be softened or brightened with a runner, which must be backed with a good, non-slip fixing.

The floor covering should be strong and resilient as there will be a lot of wear and tear. As nice as a pure wool carpet would be it may mark quickly. You can opt for a fitted carpet but put a rug or mat over the area immediately inside the door, or a runner that covers

the central track from the doorway, so protecting the carpet that is underneath.

Passageways

Corridors and passageways. are in the 'centre' of the home and will invariably have doorways that open into and out of this space but it is less frenetic and busy than the front door area.

The corridor or passageway is not often filled with people – if it is busy people are usually just passing through so it can be an area where some privacy can be had while making or receiving a call. To accommodate this

another table and chair would be useful. The table may be needed for telephone directories, a phone book, a jotter and a pen. A table lamp may also be helpful. If you do not have enough room for a table then a couple of shelves could be fixed to the wall instead.

Depending on the size of your passageways and corridors, you may find it useful to have pieces of furniture arranged as drop-off or staging points. For example, if you have a kitchen on one side of a passageway and a living/dining room on the other side, a low table or a small chest by the living/dining room door could be very useful for resting a tray of plates or a hot dish while you open the door.

In a long passageway a resting point outside a bedroom door may also be handy for putting things on while distributing clean linen, light bulbs, books or other items along the way.

Left: *Hallways need to be practical so a unit that can hold coats, shoes and other items is a great addition.*

Above: *Folding doors that concertina back on themselves are useful to divide areas where space is limited.*

A chest of drawers can also be a worthwhile addition in a corridor or passageway linking bedrooms. The linen for the various rooms can be stored here. After laundering all the sheets can be returned to the same central container. As a general rule, all the furniture in passageways should be light, narrow and well spaced so that the corridor is not an obstacle course.

The end point

The third zone is the end of the corridor or passageway – this should be made a focal point rather than dismissed as a dark or dreary place. If you come in through the main door and look down the corridor the eye should be greeted by an appealing sight

This area should be well lit so it is easy to see, and the length of distance can be assessed. Knowing where the corridor or passageway ends gives a psychologically comforting idea of where you are and what lies between you and the end wall.

Landings

If the hall or passageway passes through a landing area, around a corner or past a bay window there may be additional space or width at this point. In this case the area may be used to create a cameo setting. This can be a simple easy chair and occasional table with books and magazines, or a large piece of sculpture. If the area is big enough to accommodate a good sized table, wall mounted bookcases and a chair it could also be used as a study or casual working space.

Top: *A curving wall is an interesting architectural feature in this area.*

Above: *A wall mounted table forms a decorative feature in this landing.*

Right: *Shield-like lights and stencilled gilded wallpaper add interest to a long hallway.*

Opposite: *Staircases can be sculptural features, as this dramatic example is.*

Staircases

Staircases often lead to and from hallways and connect one level to another. Stairs need to be well lit and should have a handrail or structure that encloses the steps

providing a safe support should anyone accidentally trip or slip. In some homes a skylight or a few windows on an upper level may provide natural light for the stairs.

By setting light wells and dormer windows into the roof you can provide an invaluable source of daylight. The window need not open, it can be a fixed panel, and if it is not overlooked, does not need to be screened. In a period home these roof lights were known as lanterns and were often interesting shapes such as ovals divided into triangular segments,

like an orange. This type of skylight created a feature in an otherwise bland area.

The sides of the staircase can be filled in with reinforced glass panels, with fine spindles of metal or wood or traditional turned rails to let more light circulate.

Carpets, runners and floor coverings used on stairs must be firmly held in place. With runners, stair rods can be used to keep them secure.

A bookcase could also be tailor made to fit under a staircase. This is another awkward space that

needs to be used carefully. Another option, depending on the size, is to box in to provide a separate toilet or cloakroom, or even a general store for vacuum cleaners and cleaning products. Otherwise it can be left open and shelved or dressed with a table and chair or filled with a good sized wine rack.

Decoration and style

As corridors tend to be in the inner part of a home they are often windowless and dark, so you will have to rely on decorating tricks and techniques to make the place seem light and airy.

A traditional but practical form of decoration in hallways and stairwells is the use of the dado rail. This is a narrow, raised wooden batten or moulding, often with a rounded or simple decorative finish. Below the dado rail the wall can be papered with a thick protective finish and painted in a dark, even gloss paint that will withstand inadvertent kicks and scuffs. The upper level can be painted in a light bright colour, so giving the upper part of the hallway a lift and a feeling of spaciousness.

This type of scheme can be given an unusual Oriental twist by painting the lower level of the wall in black and the upper levels and skirting board in red. This Chinoiserie style reflects the lacquerware favoured in China and can be lit with ceiling recessed downlighters for a dramatic effect. Also any gilt or silver framed pictures or mirrors put on the walls will stand out and sparkle against the background.

The Print Room is another technique that can be used to decorate the hallway is an 18th century device that can be given a modern twist. To create a traditional Print Room the walls of a small room or vestibule were

painted in a mid-tone to strong colour and over the dry paint black and white prints of scenic views, portraits or landmarks were pasted. The prints were then framed with borders to look as though they were actual paintings. This technique can easily be adapted and photocopies or black and white photographs could be used in a similar way.

A mirror is also an attractive feature at the end of a passageway, but avoid a single full length mirror as it can be unnerving to watch yourself advancing. An oval mirror or a collection of different shapes and sizes of mirror can be arranged in an unusual and interesting way.

Linking spaces

As a corridor is a link between rooms it is advisable to keep its decoration simple. A fussy ornate or floral paper may make the space seem smaller and may also be overpowering. However, plain walls need not be dull – they can be easily decorated with pictures and mirrors or real or imitation wood panelling.

Long passageways or connecting areas are a great place to hang a co-ordinating series of pictures, prints or paintings. A set of black and white photographs, a series of prints or characters, or even a collection of plates or framed scarves can create interest as well as forming a link from one end of the space to the other. Even if the pictures aren't from the same series they can be linked by subject matter, for example flowers and butterflies.

Another way of linking a space is by using a frieze or by painting the skirting board in a bright or dominant colour so that your eye follows it around a corner or up to another level. A carpet, runner or floor covering of the same colour and pattern will also help to give an area unity, but in long passageways this can exaggerate the length and make it feel longer. In cases like this it is best to have a series of mats or rugs that create pools of interest in sections or areas along the hallway.

Opposite top: An oblong window has been set into the top of a long wall that covers two levels of stairs. The window is a feature on the otherwise blank wall and it gives a vista out onto the upper level.

Opposite bottom: Safety is an important factor on stairways. Here fine, high tension steel cables take the place of traditional rows of banisters and spindles, providing a secure barrier at the side of the stairs.

Left: Open tread stairs allow light to pass from one floor to another and also appear less solid and bulky than enclosed treads.

Below: The internal wall that once formed a corridor between the kitchen and the adjacent room has been knocked down to hip height, creating an open passageway.

Connecting areas
storage

Connecting areas, such as hallways and passageways, are usually busy places where much of the day-to-day activity of a household will take place. As such, storage here must be space efficient and flexible to the needs and requirements of all the family.

Right: For hall storage a narrow enclosure with a decorated opaque glass panel conceals coats and hats perfectly.

Storing books

Hallways and landings are ideal places for storing books as they require only a narrow shelf, which can be tailored to fit into confined or difficult spaces. Even larger books can be accommodated – if they are too tall for the shelf they can be laid down on their side or stacked horizontally.

Storing coats and shoes

You will need a variety of different storage options in your connecting areas. A coat rack is a common feature here. The traditional way to cope with this is to put a strong wooden batten on the wall and fix a row of hooks to it. This serves the purpose but is not very inspiring or attractive. To liven it up the batten could be painted and the hooks made of brass. For a more modern design the backing could be in steel or plastic and the hooks an unusual contemporary material, such as wood or chrome. The levels of hanging could also be varied so that short items can be hung halfway down the wall and longer ones above.

Two level hanging arrangements are good for families, so that the children's clothes can be kept at a height they can reach, while the adult clothes are at an upper level. This configuration also gives you double the hanging capacity in the same amount of space. The most effective arrangement is to stagger the hooks by placing the lower hooks halfway between the upper hooks. This also stops the garments from hanging directly over one another.

Smaller items such as gloves, hats and scarves are better kept in a drawer or on a shelf so that they don't become entangled in the larger pieces of clothing. For hats and bicycle or motorbike helmets a shelf above the coat hooks is a practical solution. Umbrellas are best in a stand. An old chimney pot or a tall cylindrical container is ideal.

Shoes and boots are more difficult to accommodate. They should be stacked in pairs and contained in a low box-style construction, subdivided into compartments. Each pair of shoes can fit into its own niche but boots may have to be rolled or folded. If the box is on the floor, firmly fixed to the wall, the top may be softened with long padded cushions and used as a seat.

If the shoe-box seat is not an option then a straight-backed chair or stool are ideal alternatives. Any seat in this

Left: *Mirrored insets in these cupboard doors reflect the light, making the room appear more spacious.*

area should be functional: it only needs to be comfortable enough as a temporary rest. If you have a porch or bay window you may also consider building in a window seat that is hinged so that the base could be used as a storage place for shoes.

An alternative is a low, two shelf system along which shoes can be arranged in lines. This can be made with planks of wood or rails. The rails at the back can be slightly raised so that the heels of the shoes rest over them.

Shelving

A table or shelf will also be practical and provide a place to put post. The table should be of a narrow console style that lies flat against the wall. Hall tables often become a focus for clutter, junk mail and debris so you need to be disciplined about keeping it tidy if you choose this option.

A shelf can be small, neat and fixed directly to the wall above a radiator in a hallway. Radiators are often positioned by the main door so that on arrival the reception area is heated and comforting.

The shelf may also help to guard people from direct contact with the heat of the radiator and it will also stop small objects from falling down behind it (see box, right).

Keys are another item you will need in this area. It is where you keep the car keys as well as those for the house and office. A small wall mounted key rack can keep everything in place and to hand.

A key rack can be simple, such as cork backing with rows of small cup hooks or more elaborate, such as a little cupboard with a door that closes to hide the keys.

Installing a radiator screen

The easiest way to make a screen is to use a box made out of MDF, chipboard or wood to fit around your radiator and fix to the wall – you could employ a carpenter to make this for you. Once the frame is in place you can fill the front panel to hide the main expanse of the radiator with a number of different materials. Expandable, wooden garden trellis is a cheap and easy option – this can be painted or stained any colour and then fixed within the surround. Metal grilles, especially those with a brass finish, often have attractive trefoil motifs. Fabric is another option: this can be used as a straight taut panel, or pleated so it has a curtain-like appearance. Avoid a solid front as this will restrict the flow of warm air and reduce the efficiency of the radiator.

leaf and

vine design

Inspired by the flowing shapes of plaster and wrought ironwork used throughout history, this design is perfect for adding interest to a dull hallway. We have used traditional stencilling techniques to repeat the motif, but both the size of the pattern and the muted colourway give a contemporary feel. Using subtle shading and highlighting techniques to mimic the way that light falls gives a three-dimensional illusion. The pattern is cut out of two A1 sized pieces of stencil card and designed so that the pattern repeats itself when the card is repositioned.

Materials

Masking tape

Base colour: green emulsion (acrylic) paint

Large sheets of stencil card

Darker green emulsion (acrylic) paint for the vine

White emulsion (acrylic)

Grey/green emulsion (acrylic)

Matt acrylic varnish

Tools

Roller and tray

Drawing pins

String

Pencil

Scalpel

Stencil brushes

Artist's brushes

Preparing the surface

1 Mask off the area above the effect, then apply the base coat and allow this to dry. Lay two sheets of stencil card on a flat surface and, with a drawing pin and string, make a compass positioned in between the two sheets of card.

2 Draw the first circle with a diameter half the width of the card. Reposition the drawing pin and draw two more circles either side of the first, just touching it.

Making your design

3 Join up the circles with a pencil to form an undulating pattern, which will form the stem of the vine. Use French curves to follow the pattern, giving the vine its width.

4 Use curve templates to form the curling ends of the vine and also to add in various random leaf shapes.

5 Use a scalpel to cut out the design, making sure that you leave 'bridges' where necessary.

Applying colour

6 With masking tape, position the stencil on the wall and apply the vine colour with a dry stencil brush using a stippling action. Position the second sheet of stencil card so that it joins up with the first pattern and stencil. Repeat this process until the whole wall is stencilled.

7 In order to paint the shadow, decide which direction the light is coming from and use a small artist's brush to apply a thin dark grey/green line along the areas of the vine that would naturally be in shadow.

8 To add the highlights use a small artist's brush to apply an off-white shade along the areas of the vine where the light would fall. (If you have a natural light source in your hallway or room, such as a window, work with it rather than against it. This will mean that the painted highlights and shadows on the stencilled vine will fall in the same way as they would naturally when the light falls on real three-dimensional objects.)

9 When the surface is dry, varnish it with several coats of matt acrylic varnish.

Using a drawing pin and a piece of string make a compass positioned in between the card.

Use a sharp scalpel to cut out the design making sure there are bridges where necessary.

Apply the vine colour carefully with a small dry stencil brush using a stippling action.

wall montage
of black and white photographs

Rather than leave treasured photographs languishing in a drawer or photo album why not use them to transform a wall? We used a computer, scanner and printer to enlarge and tint our black and white coastal images. If you do not have access to a computer, many photo shops can produce poster size prints from original negatives. Alternatively you could enlarge images and alter their tonal values on a photocopier. The paper images can be applied directly to a wall using wallpaper adhesive or you can stick them to a piece of primed hardboard that can be screwed onto the wall.

Materials

Sufficient paper images to cover your chosen area

PVA adhesive or artist's fixative spray

Wallpaper paste

Acrylic varnish

Tools

Guillotine or craft knife

Metal ruler

Paintbrush

Set square

Pencil

Adhesive brush

Bucket for mixing

Soft cloth

Cutting the images

1 Use the guillotine or craft knife and metal ruler to cut out the images. Make sure that all the squares are an identical size.

Fixing the ink

2 To fix the ink test an area of the image by brushing with PVA adhesive diluted with water (one part PVA to two parts water). If the ink starts to run while applying the PVA use an artist's fixative spray instead.

3 Using a set square and pencil, divide up the wall into square sections of around a metre square (10 sq ft) – this will vary according to the size of your images. This will allow you to work on one section at a time.

Fixing the images to the wall

4 Take the required number of images to fill one square on your wall, making sure that the

Use a guillotine to cut the images so that they are all square and the same size.

Brush the images with a little PVA adhesive to fix the ink or use an artist's fixative spray.

Know your materials

Artist's fixative spray is used to fix artist's chalky paste and charcoal drawings. However, it also works well on computer printouts and photocopies that could run if stuck with paste. The spray is available from art and craft shops and should be applied evenly in a well ventilated room. To avoid breathing in fumes, wear a mask. If you prefer, you could use two parts to one part solution of water and PVA glue.

images are varied in terms of colour, subject and tone. Paste the back of the images using standard wallpaper paste and a soft brush. Allow to soak for at least five minutes (this allows the paste to be absorbed into the fibres of the paper, which will then swell) before applying to the wall using the pencil lines as a guide.

5 Smooth any wrinkles or bubbles of paste by gently rubbing the image with a soft cloth, making sure that you work from the centre of the image outwards. Allow the montage to dry thoroughly overnight. If any of the edges have lifted during this time you can simply apply some extra paste with a small brush and

then smooth over the surface once again using a steam roller or cloth.

6 Protect the images by varnishing with a matt or satin acrylic spray adhesive (to avoid brush marks). Alternatively, apply a conventional varnish with a clean, good quality paintbrush.

With a set square and pencil, mark out the area on the wall where the images will be fixed.

Using an adhesive brush, paste the back of the images with standard wallpaper paste.

To remove any wrinkles or air bubbles rub the images gently with a soft cloth.

Alternative

If you do not want to stick images directly onto your wall it is still possible to create a striking graphic display by mounting and framing your photographs. This works most successfully if all the images are black and white and of a similar size. Simple black lacquer frames make a strong statement without detracting from the images themselves. Special non-reflective perspex can be used in rooms with strong natural light, as this stops glare on the images. Perspex is a safer option than glass, particularly in the bathroom, although it is more prone to surface scratching.

Arrange the images on the floor to decide on their positioning. To align the frames perfectly, use a tape measure and spirit level and lightly mark the position of the nails in pencil on the wall. Make sure you use the correct picture nails and hooks for the type of wall you are hanging on (different varieties are available for solid and partition walls). For accurate results check that the hanging wire is positioned at the same point on each frame.

Once finished, use a matt or satin acrylic spray adhesive to protect the images.

ighting
connecting areas

Connecting areas and hallways are best lit by wall or ceiling lights as this will reduce the amount of restrictions at floor level. Uplighters reflecting off a white ceiling will also double the impact of the light source. Decorative shades can also be used to bring interest and decoration to a long passageway.

Using wall lights as a decorative feature

Wall lights can be used decoratively by creating a frame to surround the light so that it looks like a picture. Taking the light fitment as the centre point, create a frame around it using beading or flat backed bevelled wood and paint the frame in a stronger shade of the wall colour, a contrasting tone or a metallic finish, such as bronze. Inside the frame put a mount or a panel of another colour, or if the rest of the wall is plain, a piece of decorative wallpaper. This will build up an eye-catching surround to the light and make it more than just a source of illumination.

Right: A band of decorative mirrors, close to the top of the walls, reflects the light given out by the ceiling fixture and amplifies it several times over.

Far right: Wall lights are practical in a hallway as they can be fixed above head height and, if the beam is focused on the ceiling, they will supply a soft, indirect light.

When entertaining or holding a party the vestibule or initial section of the hall is the first part of your home that guests and visitors see and experience so it should have a warm and welcoming appearance. To achieve this the lighting should be adequate, but not overly bright.

Ambient lighting

In the evenings, guests arriving for a dinner party could be greeted by a low ambient light augmented by a large church candle or an arrangement of candles. The smaller tea light candles can be set in glass votive holders, which will add extra interest. However,

candles should always be placed in safe, sturdy containers. At night you can place candles in front of mirrors in connecting areas so that the flames are reflected and create twice the impact.

Faux skylights

Lighting is important in a corridor because there is seldom much, if any, daylight. In a modern home you can use large panel lights on the ceiling that look like skylights.

When the light or lights are turned on they will provide a bright but diffuse light, which will illuminate an ample area beneath and create the impression of there being a window above. The light could be put on a dimmer so that during daylight hours the strength of light could be equivalent to natural light outside, but in the evening dimmed to a subtle glow.

Wall lights

Wall lights are another possibility for lighting linking areas. In a long corridor you will need a combination of wall lights to create an ambient atmosphere, and ceiling lights or lamps to ensure that the floor and lower levels of the passageway are lit.

There are also torch-like wall lights that resemble a handheld flare and simple semi-circular plaster bowls that can be painted to blend in with the main wall colour in the hallway.

In a rustic setting curved, terracotta roof tiles, like those seen on Italian villas, can be hung up on the wall with the underside facing forwards. In this curved area a small dish or candle holder can be attached and a taper, tea light or pillar candle set and lit. Alternatively, the tiles could be drilled and wired to take a small electric bulb. There are electric candle style bulbs that have a built-in flicker and are hard to distinguish from the real thing.

Recessed lighting

Another possibility for decorative lighting, which can be used in an older home, is to put a long but narrow tubular bulb behind the cornice or in a picture rail recess to direct light upwards and cast shadows of the decorative edge of the plaster work.

Spotlights

A line of recessed spotlights is an effective way of lighting a corridor. They can also be set on dimmer switches so that the level of light can be varied.

You may like to put them on separate circuits so that a pool of light can be directed onto an object or arrangement at the end of the hall, while the front and middle parts are in darkness or more subdued illumination. However, make sure the beam of a spotlight is not shining directly into the face of a visitor.

Picture lights

Picture lights add to the overall level of ambient light in a corridor as well as highlighting the pictures hung on the wall. Picture lights can be fine, linear, modern designs, no bigger than a fountain pen or traditional, larger brass versions. Both versions need to be wired from the skirting board up to behind the pictures. This will require channels to be cut into the plaster of the wall, which, after the wires have been placed, will then be replastered and smoothed. The overall effect can be used to create a miniature gallery.

Below left: Spotlights recessed along the edge of the floor by the skirting board are a way of introducing artificial light to a passageway.

Below: Recessed ceiling lights supplement the natural light source from the windows in the dining area.

Index

ndex